Word Identification Strategies

Building Phonics into a Classroom Reading Program

Fifth Edition

Barbara J. Fox
North Carolina State University

Boston Columbus Indianapolis New York San Francisco Upper Saddle River
Amsterdam Cape Town Dubai London Madrid Milan Munich Paris Montreal Toronto
Delhi Mexico City São Paulo Sydney Hong Kong Seoul Singapore Taipei Tokyo

Vice President, Editor-in-Chief: Aurora Martínez Ramos
Editorial Assistant: Meagan French
Executive Marketing Manager: Krista Clark
Associate Editor: Barbara Strickland
Production Editor: Gregory Erb
Editorial Production Service: S4Carlisle Publishing Services
Manufacturing Buyer: Megan Cochran
Electronic Composition: S4Carlisle Publishing Services
Cover Designer: Linda Knowles

Credits and acknowledgments borrowed from other sources and reproduced, with permission, in this textbook appear on appropriate page within text.

Library of Congress Cataloging-in-Publication Data
Fox, Barbara J.
   Word identification strategies: building phonics into a classroom reading program/Barbara J. Fox.—5th ed.
     p. cm.
  Includes bibliographical references and index.
   ISBN 978-0-13-261128-2 (alk. paper)
  1. Word recognition. 2. Reading—Phonetic method. 3. Reading (Elementary) I. Title.
LB1050.34.F69 2010
372.4′65—dc22

                                            2010044144

10 9 8 7 6 5 4 3   RRD-VA 15 14 13 12

www.pearsonhighered.com

ISBN-10:   0-13-261128-7
ISBN-13: 978-0-13-261128-2

Contents

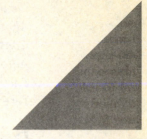

CHAPTER 2

Phonemic Awareness 21

CHAPTER 3

Early Word Identification in Preschool and Early Kindergarten   73

CHAPTER 4

Analogy-Based Phonics in Late Kindergarten and First Grade   99

CHAPTER 5

Letter-Sound Phonics in Late Kindergarten, First, and Second Grade   135

CHAPTER 6

Analyzing the Structure of Long Words in Third Grade and Above 195

APPENDIX

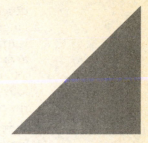

Preface

This Fifth Edition of *Word Identification Strategies: Building Phonics into a Classroom Reading Program* explains how children learn to read and spell new words, and how to be an effective teacher of word identification from preschool through the end of the elementary school. This book is intended for kindergarten through fifth-grade pre-service teachers, practicing classroom teachers, reading specialists, literacy coaches, and special educators. This book takes a theory-based, developmental approach to teaching word identification. It describes the stages of word learning and spelling from preschool through fifth grade, best practices for teaching word identification, and classroom teaching activities that are consistent with the theoretical perspective. Also included are sections in chapters on meeting the needs of English language learners and children at risk, and e-resources for teaching phonemic awareness, analogy-based phonics, letter-sound phonics, and the structure of long words.

What's New in This Edition

Since the last edition was published, our classrooms have become more diverse; new research has come forward to guide our teaching practices; the number of English language learners in our classrooms has increased; we have a better understanding of how to meet the needs of children at risk; and electronic resources are available in greater supply and offer more pedagogically sound resources for teaching phonics and other word identification strategies. My purpose for writing this revision is to specifically describe the sequence for teaching and learning different strategies so as to provide teachers with an understanding of what to teach and when to teach it, all within the context of new information, meeting the needs of changing student populations, and taking advantage of increasing electronic resources to support learning.

Each bulleted item describes one of the many new features of this revision:

• In order to make this book more relevant and useful for teachers, I have placed new sections on teaching English language learners in Chapters 2 through 6. By embedding a section on English language learners in each methods-oriented chapter, suggested teaching practices are directly tied to the needs of children as they pass through the developmental stages of word learning and spelling described in this book. New sections include suggestions for teaching English language learners and important considerations for successfully teaching English learners as well as classroom-ready recommendations for teaching phonemic awareness, letter names and a sound for each letter, analogy-based phonics, letter-sound phonics, and the structure of long words. New information, new ideas, and new references make these new sections more applicable to meeting the needs of the English learners in your classroom.

- In response to the suggestions of reviewers and in order to give teachers more strategy-specific teaching guidance, Chapters 2 through 6 now have a separate section on teaching children at risk. These new sections directly link the developmental needs of children to recommended teaching strategies and research-based guidance for effective teaching. Teachers learn how to meet the needs of children at risk from the perspective of the particular word identification strategy that is the focus of each chapter. Methods that are particularly successful with children who struggle are explained, issues for teaching children at risk are considered, and teaching activities in each chapter that are especially relevant for raising the achievement of children at risk are described.

- In light of the explosion of electronic resources, Chapters 2 through 6 include a list of e-resources that support teaching and learning. E-resources predominantly consist of websites that offer interactive lessons and games appropriate for interactive whiteboard (IWB) or classroom computers, paper-and-pencil or classroom activities, and printable materials. The e-resources in this revision are used by practicing teachers. Most have been in existence for some time, and many are supported by well-known groups or organizations. Most e-resources cited in this book are free to classroom teachers or offer some free materials along with access to other materials with a paid subscription. Some of the resources are supported by advertisements. The e-resources in Chapters 2 through 6 are a representative sample of resources available when this revision was written. No doubt, new e-resources will become available and some of the cited resources will change. With the information in this text, you will be able to select additional resources that follow the best practice advice in this book and are appropriate for children's development as readers and spellers.

- Forty-four new references have been added to bring the information in this new revision in line with the current thinking in the field. Some citations have been deleted so as to streamline this revision, and highlight more recent and critical research findings.

- This revision sharpens the focus on the grades when certain word identification strategies and skills are taught in the elementary school reading program as well as when children typically move into different word identification and spelling stages. The grade-specific timeline throughout the entire text develops an understanding of the overall scope and sequence of the word identification program in the elementary school. This understanding makes it possible for preservice and practicing teachers to develop goals and expectations for their own teaching and for the learning of their students.

- The section on assessment tools for measuring phonemic awareness (Chapter 2) was reorganized so as to divide tools into those that are informal and allow for some teacher judgment in scoring, and formal, norm-referenced tools with specific testing protocols. Two online informal tools have been added, new editions of assessment tools are cited, and more detailed descriptions of some tools are included.

- Also new to this edition are additional tables in Chapters 4, 5, and 6. Three of the four appendices in the previous edition have been reshaped and placed in tables to make it easier for teachers to access information. A new table explaining the different syllable patterns was added to Chapter 6 as well as a table explaining rules for adding suffixes to words, and a table listing common Greek and Latin word parts. A new table in Chapter 4 lists frequently occurring rimes; the table of letter-sound patterns in Chapter 5 has been revised and simplified. The appendix providing further explanations of letter-sound patterns in the previous edition has been streamlined for simplicity and to make information more easily accessible.

What Readers of This Book Will Learn About Teaching Word Identification

Readers of this book will learn the different word identification strategies children use to read and spell new words, the sequence in which word learning and spelling develop from preschool to the end of elementary school, and how to effectively teach these strategies from a developmental perspective. The reader also will learn how reading and spelling new words unfolds in a predictable development sequence that begins long before children pay attention to the specific words in books, and ends when children leave fifth grade with the ability to use many different word identification strategies.

Chapter 1 explains the proper place of phonics in classroom reading programs; how to keep phonics meaning-based through teaching self-monitoring, self-correcting, and cross-checking; the importance of metacognition; and the stages of word learning. In Chapters 2 through 6, the reader will learn how to teach English language learners and children at risk who are at different developmental stages of word learning and spelling, and become aware of e-resources that support teaching and learning. Chapter 2 explains the sequence in which phonemic awareness develops, the contribution of phonemic awareness to learning to read, best practices for teaching phonemic awareness, informal and formal assessment tools, and classroom activities for developing rhyme awareness, awareness of the individual sounds in words, and the ability to blend separate sounds into words.

Chapter 3 explains the early word identification strategies typically used by children in preschool and early kindergarten, and best practices for teaching letter names and a sound for each letter. Chapter 4 explores teaching analogy-based phonics; how children in late kindergarten and early first grade begin to use the onsets and rimes in familiar words (the *s* and *at* in *sat*) to learn word family words, such as *cat*, *mat*, *fat*; best teaching practices; why analogy-based phonics is easier for beginning readers compared with letter-sound phonics; and classroom teaching activities. Chapter 5 describes the letter-sound patterns of phonics, how to teach letter-sound phonics, a sequence for teaching letter-sound patterns, best teaching practices, and classroom teaching activities. Chapter 6 focuses on how children in third grade and above use large multi-letter groups or chunks in the structure of long words to read and spell multi-syllable words; how some long words consist of prefixes, suffixes, or Greek and Latin roots that give readers insight into word meaning; how long words are constructed of syllables that give readers cues to pronunciation; best practices for teaching the structure of long words; and classroom activities for developing the ability to use word structure to read and spell long words.

While phonics is necessary for learning to read, teaching word identification should not be the most prominent component of classroom reading programs. We cannot afford not to teach phonics, but we cannot afford to overdo it either. Phonics is a means to an end, not an end in and of itself. Children learn phonics and develop word identification strategies so they can read, spell, and learn new words and, in so doing, build a large vocabulary of words they instantly recognize. Instant word recognition, in turn, is necessary for fluent reading. In taking a developmental approach to word identification, this book gives teachers the information they need to match what is taught to what children need to learn. I hope that this cross-grade developmental approach combined with the new additions to this revision will support effective teaching in every grade.

ACKNOWLEDGMENTS

I am indebted to the many teachers who welcomed me into their classrooms, to the children who were willing readers and eager participants in the activities their teachers shared, and to the principals who encouraged and supported their teachers. Without them, this book could not have been written. I would also like to thank the reviewers of this text for their insightful comments and welcomed recommendations: Carianne Bernadowski, Robert Morris University; Anitra E. Butler, Prince George's Community College; Theresa Deckebach, Cabrini College; Laura C. S. Jones, Nazareth College; and Colleen Lelli, Cabrini College.

CHAPTER 1

Word Identification in Your Classroom Reading Program

This chapter explains the proper place of word identification in your classroom reading program. You will learn about methods we use to teach word identification, how children read words, and how to determine the most appropriate balance between word identification and other components of the reading program. You will come to understand metacognition and learn how to encourage readers to keep word identification meaning-focused by monitoring their own comprehension, correcting their own word identification mistakes, and cross-checking to make sure that the words they identify fit the reading context. You will also learn how children use a combination of language and letter and sound cues to read words, the stages of word learning, and why understanding these stages is important for teaching children to read and learn new words.

KEY IDEAS

- Emphasis on word identification should be in proportion to children's individual needs.
- Phonics helps children develop rich reading vocabularies, contributes to reading fluency, and supports reading independence.
- Readers may use a combination of letter and sound, sentence structure (syntactic), and meaning (semantic) cues to read new words.
- Metacognitive awareness—reflecting on and being aware of personal knowledge, strategies, and skills—is important for using phonics to read and learn new words.
- Cross-checking helps readers make sure that the words they identify fit the reading context.
- Readers monitor their own reading to detect word identification mistakes or miscues.
- When readers realize that a word does not fit the reading context, they self-correct to fix their word identification miscue.
- Children read words by analogy, letter-sound decoding, analyzing word structure, predicting, or instantly on sight.
- Word learning develops in predictable stages. With an understanding of how word learning develops, you will teach exactly what children need to know to add new words to their reading vocabularies.

KEY VOCABULARY

Alphabetic principle

Analogy-based phonics

Analytic phonics

Cross-checking

Embedded phonics

Letter-sound phonics

Meaning (semantic) cues

Metacognitive awareness

Self-correcting

Self-monitoring

Sentence structure (syntactic) cues

Spelling-based phonics

Synthetic phonics

As a proficient reader, you instantly recognize the words you commonly encounter when reading. Instead of figuring out words, you focus on comprehension. This is exactly as it should be. However, consider what it is like for young readers who come across many unfamiliar words. Meeting a large number of new words is a major impediment to comprehension, and so it is not surprising that these children concentrate on developing their reading vocabularies.

Consider the note in Figure 1-1 written by Maria. If you speak and read Spanish, Maria's message is crystal clear. The words are easy to recognize, the sentences are well formed, and you know why the picture and the message are a perfect match. Suppose instead that you speak Spanish but cannot read it. Now the format of the note and Maria's drawing are the only reliable clues to meaning. You might make an educated guess based on information gleaned from the picture and your own background knowledge. From the heart-shaped drawing, you might logically infer that this is either a valentine or a love letter. But unless you recognize the words Maria wrote, your grasp of meaning is limited, and your comprehension is at best an approximation of Maria's message.

To go beyond supposition, you must learn the same things beginning readers learn—how to use phonics and the multiletter groups, or chunks, in word structure (the -er in *sharper*) to read new words. Just recognizing words is not

Figure 1-1   Maria's note: Can you get the message?

enough; you must also know the meaning of the words Maria wrote, understand the sentence structure, and appreciate the social context in which notes such as this are written and read. (See the translation of Maria's note at the end of this chapter.)

WHY DO WE TEACH PHONICS?

Written English uses the **alphabetic principle.** This is the principle of using letters to represent sounds. An alphabetic writing system makes it possible for any reader who knows the code to pronounce words the reader has never seen in print before. *Phonics* is the relationship between the letters and sounds and approaches for teaching these relationships. Letter-sound relationships are a set of visual directions—a map, if you will—telling readers how to pronounce new words they have never seen before. You teach phonics when you demonstrate that the letter *b* represents the sound heard at the beginning of /banana/[1], /boat/, and /bubble/. In helping children compare and contrast the sounds represented by the letters in *hid* and *hide*, you are teaching phonics. When you challenge readers to think about a word that begins with *c*, ends with *t*, and makes sense in the sentence *Mark's _____ eats tuna fish*, you are a teacher of phonics. And when you encourage writers to spell a word "the way it sounds," you help children think about and analyze our alphabetic writing system, which is what you do when you teach phonics.

Phonics makes it easier to read and learn new words. Good decoders know more words (Eldredge, 2005) and read faster than poor decoders. If you teach first grade, you can expect the good decoders in your classroom to read twice as fast as their classmates with poor phonics skills. By the end of first grade, good decoders will read twice as much as poor readers in the same amount of time. This affords twice as many opportunities for better readers to read known and new words, and to develop larger reading vocabularies. One advantage of phonics is it takes a relatively small amount of letter and sound information to identify and learn a large number of words. For instance, the children in your class who know the sounds that *t* and *ur* represent can figure out the pronunciation of words that share these letters, such as *turn*, *hurt*, and *turtle*. Phonics is a bridge between the spoken words children already know and the written words they do not recognize. In using phonics, readers identify unfamiliar words by associating sounds with letters. Remembering how the letters in written words represent sounds in spoken words helps children remember words. The more children read and write the same words, the stronger their memory becomes and the faster they recognize the words (Ehri, 2006). Eventually the sounds, spellings, and meanings of words are joined together in memory. Children then recognize words instantly, at a glance, without conscious effort or attention. Instant word recognition includes information on the word's spelling, sound, and meaning.

---

[1] In this book, for simplicity, instead of using a standard system of phonetic symbols, letters that typically stand for sounds are used and placed between slashes (/ /). Single vowels represent short-vowel sounds, while long-vowel sounds are either described as such, identified by spelling pattern (*ou*, *ee*), or indicated by the use of a macron (¯).

Phonics makes an important contribution to fluent reading. Good decoders are more fluent readers than poor decoders (Schwanenflugel, Hamilton, Kuhn, Wisenbaker, & Stahl, 2004). Accurate, expressive, fluent reading is possible only when readers instantly and accurately recognize the words in text (Eldredge, 2005). Let us consider why instant word recognition is so important for fluent reading. Effortless word recognition frees the mind to think about reading expressively. Freeing the mind from attention to individual words is important because attention is limited. Readers can pay attention to meaning or they can pay attention to figuring out words, but they cannot do both things at once. Because readers do not have to focus on identifying the words, they can concentrate on reading fluently and comprehending text. In fact, fluent reading is not possible without instant word recognition. You may encounter a few good decoders who cannot read fluently, but you will never encounter a fluent reader who does not instantly recognize the words in text. Readers who do not immediately recognize words have several choices, none of them conducive to fluent reading. Readers might skip words, stop to decode them, or guess. In so doing, readers change the focus from reading in meaningful phrases with expression to decoding or guessing. This, of course, disrupts expressive, fluent reading and interferes with comprehension.

Phonics affects fluency as early as the first grade. Developing expressive, accurate, fluent reading in first grade is important. Once the trajectory toward fluency is established, children seem to stay on the same course unless the classroom reading program is adjusted to provide more reading instruction. High-fluency readers at the end of first grade are high-fluency readers at the end of the second grade; low-fluency readers at the end of first grade are likely to be low-fluency readers at the end of second grade.

Phonics is also important for developing fluency and supporting comprehension, but phonics does not make children fluent readers or good comprehenders, as we see in Figure 1-2. Like all complex tasks, fluent reading is based on several more basic skills. The basic skills must be in place or developing appropriately in order for readers to carry out complex tasks. Phonics is one of the basic skills. Phonemic awareness is another basic skill, as discussed in Chapter 2. Although knowing phonics does not automatically result in fluent reading, it is a critical basic skill. Phonics is a tool for learning words. Knowing words, in turn, makes it possible to read fluently. So, we see that phonics contributes directly to developing a large vocabulary of instantly recognized words. A large vocabulary of instantly recognized words, in turn, supports comprehension and makes it possible to read fluently (Eldredge, 2005).

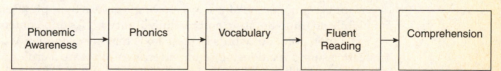

Figure 1-2   The relationship of phonics to vocabulary and fluency.
Figure constructed from the findings of Eldredge (2005) and Schwanenflugel, Hamilton, Kuhn, Wisenbaker, & Stahl (2004).

CHARACTERISTICS OF EFFECTIVE PHONICS INSTRUCTION IN YOUR CLASSROOM READING PROGRAM

Your classroom reading program will be successful when you teach phonics directly, systematically, early, and meaningfully, and when children have many opportunities to use their letter-sound knowledge in reading and writing. Let us consider these five characteristics of phonics in a successful classroom reading program.

1. *Teach phonics directly* Effective classroom teachers teach phonics directly. In direct instruction you, the teacher, explain, model, and demonstrate how to use phonics when reading and spelling. Children then practice under your guidance. Should children encounter difficulty, you are there ready to help them use phonics and correctly apply information. If children need more instruction, this is the time to provide further explanation and additional demonstration of how to use phonics. Last, as children become more skilled, you gradually withdraw your support, until finally children are successful on their own, without your assistance.

2. *Teach phonics systematically* Systematic phonics instruction follows a scope and sequence. It leaves nothing to chance. It is important to have an overall plan for teaching all the important letter-sound relationships of phonics, to teach in a logical sequence, to make sure the plan is implemented, and to ensure that all children have the opportunities they need to be successful in learning useful letter-sound relationships. In teaching systematically, you, the teacher, know what to teach and when to teach it. Following a carefully crafted scope and sequence ensures that children learn what they need to know to use phonics to help them build a large reading vocabulary that underpins comprehension and fluency. Systematic, sequential instruction also gives you a basis for forming flexible skill groups if some children are behind or ahead of their classmates in learning and for teaching precisely what children need to learn to become efficient, effective readers.

3. *Teach phonics early* By early, we mean beginning in kindergarten or first grade, well before children are independent readers (National Reading Panel, 2000).

4. *Keep phonics instruction meaningful* It is important to teach phonics within the context of words that illustrate certain phonics letter-sound relationships and patterns (see Chapter 5). But it is also important to select words for phonics lessons that are important for everyday reading and spelling. Capitalize on the naturally occurring opportunities for children to learn and use phonics by weaving phonics into the ongoing activities in your classroom. Look for ways children can use their phonics knowledge while sharing literature and reading library books and content area books, and then point out words in these texts that are examples of the phonics letter-sound relationships and patterns children are learning.

5. *Support children as they use phonics while reading and spelling* Reading a variety of genres and writing for a variety of purposes gives children rich experiences in applying their phonics knowledge. Reading and spelling

experiences bind together what you teach about letters and sounds, and what children apply when they use phonics while reading and spelling. And, of course, the more children use phonics while reading and spelling, the more words they learn and the better their ability to read more challenging text and to spell more challenging words.

KEEPING PHONICS IN BALANCE IN YOUR CLASSROOM READING PROGRAM

When something is balanced, it is in proportion. Phonics is in balance with the other components in your classroom reading program when you select just the right approach, just the right materials, and just the right emphasis to develop the reading potential of every child. A balanced program includes many teaching methods, all in proportion to children's individual needs. What children know about reading connected text and the skills they bring to reading changes as their reading ability develops. It is no wonder then that the role of word identification in first grade is quite different from its proper place in a fourth-grade classroom. Yet the goal is the same: We want children to use word identification strategies we teach them to learn new words on their own and to use phonics to help them develop a large vocabulary of instantly recognized words.

In a balanced program, kindergarten, first-, and second-grade children learn to identify words by letter-sound patterns, which is the traditional grist of **letter-sound phonics** (Chapter 5). However, in this book we also include in a balanced reading program the teaching of analogy-based phonics (Chapter 4), which teaches children to identify new words by noticing shared letter groups, such as the *at* in *hat* and *fat*, and the teaching of large multiletter groups, or chunks, in the structure of words (Chapter 6), such as prefixes (the *re-* in *rerun*) and suffixes (the *-ed* in *jumped*). And, of course, balanced programs ensure that children have many and varied opportunities to use their knowledge of phonics, analogous letter groups, and multi-letter chunks in word structure when they read and spell.

The International Reading Association's (1997) position is that teachers should ask *when, how, how much,* and *under what circumstances* to teach phonics. We can see from this statement that phonics is not an all-or-nothing curriculum component. Rather, it is a portion of the curriculum that complements other reading and writing activities, and enables children to read and spell independently.

When Should You Teach Phonics?

The answer to *when* is the right time to teach phonics depends on children's development as readers. For children to develop a large vocabulary of instantly recognized words, classroom reading programs must dedicate a significant amount of time to phonics in the early grades. Because children in third grade and above already know how to use phonics, a balanced program for these children focuses on the multi-letter chunks in word structure (prefixes, suffixes, base words, contractions, syllables, and root words, including Greek and Latin roots, as explained in Chapter 6). Thus, letter sounds should be taught in the first few grades (National Reading Panel, 2000), and the structure of long and complex words should be taught in grades three through five. This brings us to the next point—*how* to teach phonics.

How Will You Teach Phonics?

Although there is a plethora of phonics teaching materials available, teaching the letter sounds of phonics can be distilled into five teaching methods: (1) synthetic, (2) analytic, (3) embedded, (4) analogy based, and (5) spelling. If you teach reading or language arts in an elementary school, you will use one or more of these methods.

1. **Synthetic (explicit) phonics** is part-to-whole instruction. Synthetic phonics starts with teaching letter sounds (part). Children then use these associations to read and spell words (whole). For example, children first learn that the letter *s* represents /s/, *i* represents /i/, and *t* represents /t/. Children then blend these three sounds together to pronounce /sit/. On hearing themselves pronounce /sit/, children realize that *sit* represents the spoken word /sit/.

2. **Analytic (implicit) phonics** is whole-to-part instruction. Children learn whole words first. Then later children are taught, or encouraged to discover, which sounds go with which letters (part). For example, children learn to read words with a short /a/ letter sound, as we hear in *bat*. Then the teacher writes a known word, *bat*, on a chart, and asks children to pay special attention to the short /a/ sound. Next, the teacher asks children to suggest other short *a* words they already know to add to the list, such as *fan*, *mad*, *Sam*, *bad*, *ham*, and *map*. Everyone then studies the list and concludes that a single *a* in a short word stands for /a/.

3. **Embedded phonics** is taught "as needed"—that is, teachers teach only those letter-sound associations that children need to decode words in the books they are reading. Because children's needs depend on the words in the books they are reading, embedded phonics does not teach letter-sound relationships in a prescribed order. Bear in mind that the National Reading Panel (2000) concluded that teaching phonics in a prescribed sequence is more effective than teaching phonics on an as-needed basis.

4. In **analogy-based phonics** with word families, children learn to use the parts of words they know to identify new words that share the same patterns. Analogy-based phonics groups words with the same patterns into word families (the *it* family, for example, consists of *sit*, *fit*, and *lit*), teaches children how to pronounce and spell families, and emphasizes wide-range reading and writing. You will learn more about this approach in Chapter 4.

5. In **spelling-based phonics** children study words that are spelled with letter-sound combinations that are consistent with their ability to understand these relationships. Phonics is taught through spelling, sorting, comparing words spelled with the same and different patterns of letter sounds, and comparing words children do not know with words they already know how to read and spell.

How Much Time Should You Spend Teaching Phonics?

How much time and energy you spend on phonics depends on children's knowledge of the alphabetic principle and their ability to use phonics when reading and spelling. Unfortunately, there are no hard and fast rules for how much time to spend teaching phonics. Generally speaking, we spend proportionally more time teaching phonics in kindergarten through second grade when children do not know letter-sound relationships. In grades three through five, teachers teach children how to use word structure to read long words. (Chapter 6 has more information on teaching the structure of long words.)

The precise amount of the school day to spend on phonics varies, depending on the teaching materials and methods available to you in your classroom and on children's development as readers. To strike the right balance in your classroom reading program, consider children's needs and then select the intensity (how much) that is the best match for the individuals and groups you teach. Greg (Figure 1-3) knows only a few words, relies almost entirely on pictures to guess

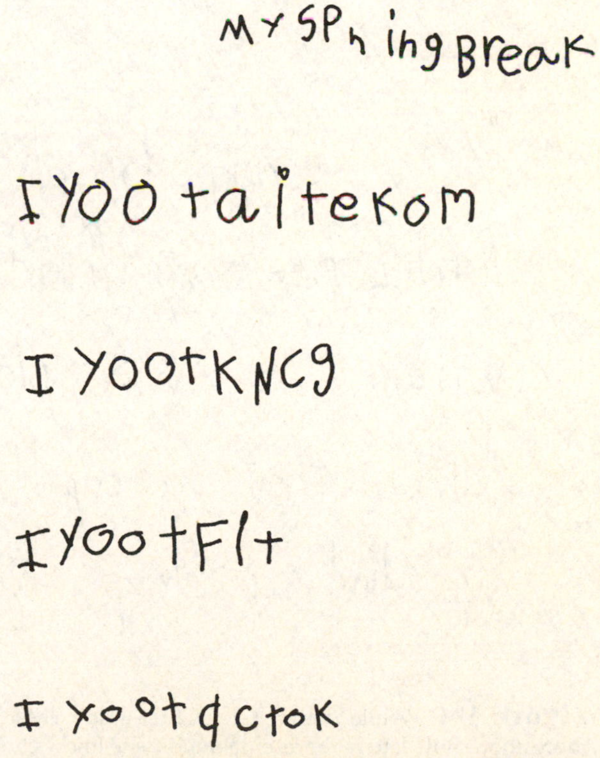

MY SPh ing Break

IYOO taiteKom

I YOOtKNCg

IYOOtF/t

I YoºtdctoK

Figure 1-3 At the end of the first grade, Greg knows only a handful of words. He will benefit from explicit instruction in all aspects of reading, including phonics, and from opportunities to use letter and sound relationships when reading and spelling.

the meaning of text, inconsistently uses beginning and ending letter sounds to identify words, and forgets words from one day to the next. He does not always separate words with white spaces when he writes and does not consistently use letters to represent sounds.

Sharon, whose work can be seen in Figure 1-4, understands what she reads, uses phonics and context clues to read new words, and uses letter-sound relationships when spelling. Her reading vocabulary is growing rapidly, and she is developing reading independence. We can see from her writing that Sharon correctly spells many words, understands the sounds most consonants represent, and is learning how vowels represent sounds. (Look in Chapter 5 and Appendix A for explanations of consonants and vowels.) While both Greg and Sharon will benefit from more phonics knowledge, Greg has far more to learn than Sharon. For this reason, an appropriate classroom balance would include more phonics instruction for Greg than it would for Sharon. So, we see that the answer to how much phonics to teach in the early grades depends on children's understanding of letter-sound relationships and on their ability to use these relationships in everyday reading and writing.

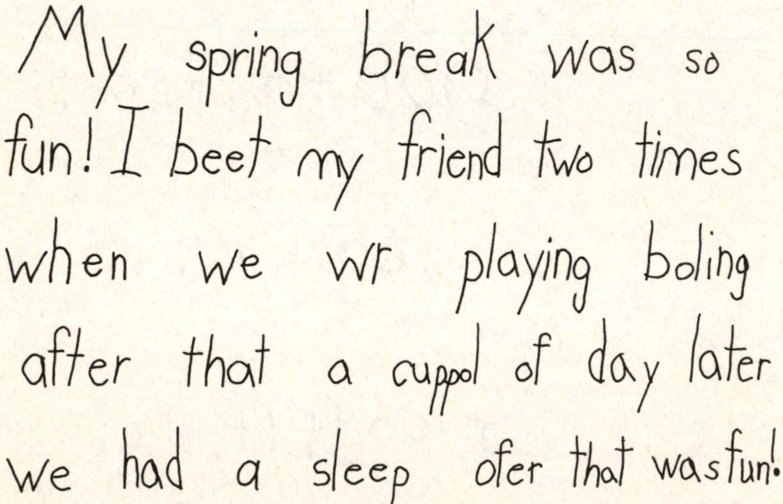

My spring break was so fun! I beet my friend two times when we wr playing boling after that a cuppol of day later we had a sleep ofer that was fun!

Figure 1-4   While Sharon, Greg's first-grade classmate, will benefit from learning more about how letters represent sounds, she knows and uses many more letter-sound associations when she reads and writes than Greg. An appropriate classroom balance would include less concentration on phonics for Sharon than it would for Greg.

Under What Circumstances Should You Teach Phonics?

The answer to *under what circumstances* depends on how teachers differentiate instruction. Children may learn (a) all together in a large group, (b) in small groups, (c) in flexible skill groups, or (d) individually. Large groups typically include everyone, or nearly everyone, in the class, whereas small groups include a handful of children who are reading on or near the same level. Another kind of group, a flexible skills group, consists of children reading at vastly different levels who need to know more about specific letter-sound associations, specific reading strategies, or specific reading skills. These groups are disbanded once children know and apply the information and strategies when reading. Children also may be taught individually. According to the National Reading Panel (2000), all types of groups are effective, provided that instruction is systematic.

Many factors go into finding the right balance among phonics and other components of your classroom reading program—the grade you teach, children's ability to use letter-sound relationships when reading and writing, and the size and growth of children's reading vocabulary, to name a few. A classroom phonics program for a child like Greg, who brings less phonics knowledge to reading and writing, looks quite different from a program for a child like Sharon, who has more phonics knowledge. Even though the individual teachers in your school may not agree on the answers to when, how, how much, and under what circumstances to teach phonics in a balanced program, they all teach children how to read new words in text, which is the topic of the next section.

How Children Read Words

Children may read unknown words by analogy, letter-sound decoding, analyzing word structure, or predicting the word's identity. Children read known words automatically or instantly from memory. The elementary reading program is designed so that all children are able to use analogy, letter-sound decoding, word structure, and predicting to read new words by the time they leave the elementary school. The goal is for all children to leave the elementary school with a large vocabulary of instantly recognized words learned through applying analogy, letter-sound decoding, word structure, predicting, spelling, and writing. By the time children move to middle school, they should instantly recognize nearly all the words they see in print, and they should be proficient at using analogy, letter-sound decoding, word structure, and predicting to read and learn new words.

Analogy

In using analogy, readers look for familiar letter groups in new words and then use this information to identify new words. For instance, on seeing a new word, *pig*, readers realize that *ig* is also in a known word, *big*. Readers then use this information (*ig*) to read *pig*. When spelling, children realize that the /ig/ in /big/ also is in /pig/, a word they already know how to spell. Spellers then use this analogous information in combination with the beginning letter sound (/p/ = *p*) to spell *pig*.

Letter-Sound Decoding

Readers associate sounds with letters, say the sounds, and blend all the sounds together to pronounce a familiar spoken word. For example, on seeing *dark* for the first time, readers associate the /d/ with the letter *d*, the /ar/ with *ar*, and the /k/ with *k*. Having pronounced each sound individually, readers then blend these sounds together to pronounce the whole word (/d/ + /ar/ + /k/ = /dark/). On hearing /dark/, children recognize it as a word in their speaking vocabulary and, therefore, associate both meaning and sound with *dark*.

Analyzing the Structure of Long Words

Readers analyze the structure of long and complex words (structural analysis) into large multi-letter groups or chunks, including compound words, contractions, prefixes, suffixes, syllables, and Greek and Latin roots. You will learn about these multi-letter chunks in Chapter 6.

Prediction

Readers may use pictures, context cues, or a combination of context and beginning and/or ending letters to predict a word's identity.

1. *Picture cues*   Readers use the information in pictures to guess or predict unfamiliar words.
2. *Context cues*   When readers use context cues to predict the identity of an unfamiliar word, they rely on a combination of meaning (semantic) cues and sentence structure (syntactic) cues. **Meaning cues** are the sensible relationships among words in phrases, sentences, and paragraphs. Readers use meaning cues to narrow down word choices and to verify that an identified word makes sense within the larger scope of the sentence or passage. When readers use meaning-based cues, they ask themselves, "Does this make sense?" **Sentence structure cues** are the basis on which readers decide whether an author's word order is consistent with English grammar. In using these cues they ask themselves, "Does this seem like language?"
3. *Context cues plus beginning and/or ending letters*   Readers predict words that match the context and are spelled with the letters readers notice at the beginning and/or end of words. Brian's note, seen in Figure 1-5, illustrates how meaning, sentence structure, and beginning and/or ending letter cues work

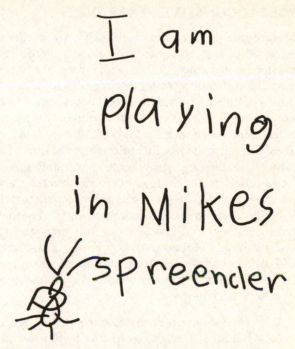

Figure 1-5   Brian's note: How do you figure out the meaning?

together. You, the reader, instantly recognize all the words as belonging to your reading vocabulary except one: *spreencler*. From sentence structure (syntactic) cues, you infer that *spreencler* is a noun, not a verb, adverb, or adjective. From meaning (semantic) cues, you surmise that this unknown object is something children enjoy during play. You can combine meaning, sentence structure, and letter-sound cues by asking yourself, "What word begins with *spr*, ends in *er*, and makes sense in the reading context?" Although Brian's spelling of *spreencler* is unconventional, the beginning and ending letter cues, as well as the meaning and sentence structure cues, are enough to figure out that Brian meant to say that he is playing in Mike's *sprinkler*.

Instant Recognition

Children instantly recognize known words. They recognize words in their reading vocabulary quickly, accurately, and effortlessly from memory. Known words are on the "tip of the tongue," always ready and immediately available any time children see them. Children instantly know the pronunciation and meaning of these words. This type of word reading does not require conscious attention or effort, which frees the reader's mind to focus on understanding text.

METACOGNITIVE AWARENESS

Metacognitive awareness is the self-conscious understanding of our own knowledge, skills, and strategies. From a word identification perspective, metacognitive awareness is a conscious understanding of how, when, and why to use different word identification strategies. It includes the self-awareness, or personal insight, into what an individual reader knows about letters and sounds, and why this knowledge is important. Metacognitively aware readers can explain to you, their teacher, the letter-sound relationships of phonics and the structure of long words. They can tell you why this information is important and explain how, when, and why to use different word identification strategies. Asking readers questions about letter-sound relationships and word structure, and asking them to explain why they select particular strategies helps readers to develop metacognitive awareness. When readers explain in their own words what they know about letter sounds and word structure and give reasons for using the strategies they do, they develop a self-awareness of their own knowledge and an appreciation of why and when to use different strategies. To help children become aware of what they know about letters and sounds, and how and when to use word identification strategies, ask questions such as these:

1. When would you use this same way to figure out another word?
2. What other kinds of words can be figured out just the way you figured out this one?
3. What do you do when you come to a word you do not know?
4. If the first try doesn't make a real word, what sound(s) could you try next? (This question helps children develop flexibility in decoding.)
5. What did you learn today that will help you be a better reader?

Encourage children to reflect on their knowledge of letter and sounds by pointing to a word and asking the following:

1. How did you know that is _____? Is there another way to tell?
2. How did you know that _____ (pointing to a letter sound or letter-sound group) makes the _____ sound in _____ (the word the child read correctly)?
3. When you see a _____ (describing a particular letter-sound group), what sound should you try first?
4. How would you write _____ (a word with a letter-sound association children are learning in your classroom)? Then follow up with the question: Why did you write it this way?

As children answer questions like these, they organize observations, form generalizations, change or alter information and ideas, and perhaps most important, become more confident in their own knowledge, better decoders, and more sensitive to how using word identification strategies supports the reading of text.

KEEPING WORD IDENTIFICATION MEANING-FOCUSED THROUGH TEACHING CHILDREN TO SELF-MONITOR, SELF-CORRECT, AND CROSS-CHECK

Good readers monitor their own comprehension, decide when to self-correct a misidentified word, and, should readers correct a misidentified word, cross-check to ensure that the word they corrected makes sense in the reading context. Self-monitoring, self-correcting, and cross-checking, when used together, are powerful tools for ensuring that the words children read are consistent with the reading context. Readers use self-monitoring to decide when comprehension is adequate, when comprehension has broken down, and when it is necessary to fix a word identification miscue. If readers determine that an identified word does not fit the context, they self-correct their own miscue. Readers then cross-check to see if the word they self-corrected makes sense.

Self-Monitoring

Self-monitoring is self-regulating one's own reading. Readers use self-monitoring to determine when the text makes sense and when it does not. Readers who self-monitor are aware of their own comprehension. So long as readers understand text, they direct their attention to meaning. When, through self-monitoring, readers realize that the text no longer makes sense, they may (1) try different comprehension strategies, (2) reread or look back in the text to pick up the strand of meaning, or (3) pause to correctly identify a troublesome word. Good readers are so accomplished at self-monitoring that they do this automatically. Beginning readers or struggling readers need to learn to monitor their own reading. Self-monitoring will come easily to some children, others will need extra help from you to consistently monitor their own reading. Use the following prompts to encourage children to self-monitor.

1. Take another look at _____.
2. You read _____. Are you right?
3. You made a mistake in this sentence (paragraph or page). Can you find it?
4. What's wrong with _____?
5. Could it be _____ (pointing to a misidentified word)?

Self-Correcting

Self-correcting is the process of fixing a miscue. When readers detect a miscue through self-monitoring, they correct a misidentified word. Sometimes correcting a misidentified word takes several attempts, especially for inexperienced readers. If readers' first attempt to correct a misidentified word (or miscue) is unsuccessful, they try again. All good readers self-correct. They do this because they realize that the goal of reading is to understand text, and they realize that misidentified words can affect meaning. Use the following prompts to support readers as they self-correct.

1. What's the tricky part in this word?
2. What is another word that begins with _____ (ends with _____ or has _____ in the middle) and makes sense?
3. You were almost right. See if you can figure out what you need to fix.
4. Call attention to vowel letters by saying, Take another look at _____ (point the vowel pattern). What sound does the vowel make in this pattern?

Encourage children to look at the letters, think of the context, and reread to confirm meaning. Reinforce self-correcting, saying, "I like the way you went back to fix that word," or "You did a good job going back to figure out a word that makes sense."

Cross-Checking

Cross-Checking gives readers valuable feedback on their own decoding. In cross-checking, readers ask themselves whether a word they identify makes sense in the reading context. Thus, one consequence of cross-checking is a metacognitive or conscious awareness of successful word identification. Readers know when an identified word is consistent with the context and when an identified word does not make sense. If, through cross-checking, readers realize that the identified word does not make sense, they try again to correct their miscue. If readers realize that the identified word makes sense, they return to textual reading. Use the following prompts to help children develop and use cross-checking.

1. Reread it and think about what would make sense.
2. You read _____. Does _____ look right and sound right?
3. Does what you just read sound like a real word?
4. You read _____. Can we say it that way?
5. Does _____ make sense?

Cross-checking may involve rereading a phrase or sentence to accept or reject the identified word. Once satisfied that the newly identified word makes sense in the reading context, children immediately refocus their attention on reading connected text.

STAGES OF LEARNING TO READ NEW WORDS

Word identification strategies and information change over time as children become more accomplished readers. Learning to read new words can be divided into stages or phases. When we know which stage children are in we have the information we need to provide instruction that meets each individual reader's needs. Children move through four word-learning stages—prealphabetic, partial alphabetic, alphabetic, and consolidated—on their way to the fifth stage, the automatic stage, where they instantly recognize all the words in text (Ehri, 2005).

As children enter each new stage, they use new information and new word identification strategies. Strategies develop in a reasonably predictable sequence that begins long before children read storybooks or go to school. Though the exact order in which strategies develop is not completely understood, we do know that readers use some strategies before others. The earliest strategies are used when children are in the prealphabetic stage.

Prealphabetic Word Learners in Preschool and Early Kindergarten

The prealphabetic stage begins in preschool and usually ends some time during kindergarten (Ehri, 2005; Ehri & McCormick, 1998). Children in this stage are usually three to five years old. Prealphabetic word learners do not understand the principle of alphabetic writing. Children know few, if any, letter names. They cannot separate or segment words into sounds (see Chapter 2 for an explanation of segmenting words into sounds). During the prealphabetic stage, children learn that words are separated by white spaces, one written word matches one spoken word, and print goes from left-to-right and top-to-bottom on pages. As we would expect, the word recognition strategies these children use do not call for paying attention to the letters and sounds in words. Children associate meaning with pictures in familiar books, recognize words by their familiar everyday surroundings, such as the word *stop* on a stop sign or recognize words because of their unique shapes, as explained in Chapter 3. Children at this stage pretend to read by turning pages and reading the pictures or reciting text from memory. When writing, children scribble or draw wavy lines to represent cursive writing. Eventually children replace scribbling with letterlike forms (mock letters) and pictures. As children become more sensitive to letters, they randomly mix real letters, mock letters, and numbers. Even though children use some real letters, we cannot read what they write because their letters do not represent sounds.

Partial Alphabetic Word Learners in Kindergarten and Early First Grade

Children enter the partial alphabetic stage sometime in kindergarten or at the beginning of first grade, as described in Chapter 3 (Ehri, 2005; Ehri & McCormick, 1998). Partial alphabetic word learners are usually five or six years of age. These children are beginning to understand the alphabetic principle. They use upper- and lowercase letters when writing, though they have a decided preference for uppercase letters. As children move through the partial alphabetic stage, they learn letter names and the sounds of most consonants. Children also learn short-vowel letter sounds, as heard in *bat*, *bet*, *bit*, *hot*, and *hut*, provided that the short-vowel sounds are part of the kindergarten classroom reading program. Children read a few words from memory, and recognize new words by associating one or two letter sounds with them. Partial alphabetic word learners use letter names to read words, provided that the letter names contain a portion of the letter sounds. For example, children might use the name of the letter *s* to read *stop* because the letter name—/esss/—contains part of the letter sound, /s/. In spelling, children use one or more letters, usually consonants, to write whole words (*k* for *cat*; *dg* for *dog*). During the partial alphabetic stage, children become aware of rhyming words and the beginning and ending sounds in spoken words. Consequently, children use their knowledge of consonant letter sounds to read words by associating sounds with beginning and ending letters. Children's reading vocabulary is growing, but only slowly and with a great deal of repetition in reading and writing.

Alphabetic Word Learners in Late Kindergarten Through Second Grade

Children usually enter the alphabetic stage in late kindergarten or early first grade. Most stay in the alphabetic stage through second grade, though some may linger in this stage a bit longer. The alphabetic stage begins when children identify words by associating a sound with each letter. Most notably, alphabetic word learners pay attention to vowel letters when reading and spelling. Children sound out new words (discussed in Chapter 5) or read new words by analogy (discussed in Chapter 4). When children spell, they include a letter for every sound heard, although not always in a conventional way (*truk* for *truck*). They learn to separate spoken words into sounds and blend sounds into spoken words (Chapter 2). Children's reading vocabulary grows rapidly, and they learn words on their own through reading and writing. By the end of this stage, children have all the phonics tools they need to sound out and read many unfamiliar words on their own.

Early in this stage decoding and textual reading is somewhat labored. Children spend so much of their attention on figuring out the identity of new words that they plod through text. Reading is slow and, because readers may often stop to decode words, reading tends to be somewhat disfluent. This situation is only temporary, however. Associating sounds with letters helps children remember the words they read and spell. The more skilled alphabetic word learners become at using phonics to read and spell words, the more words children add to their reading vocabulary. As a consequence, children's reading vocabulary grows by leaps and bounds. During this stage, children learn all the basic reading skills they need to be independent readers. By the end of the alphabetic stage, readers have a large enough reading vocabulary and good enough word identification skills to focus their attention on comprehension, not word identification, and to use reading as a tool to learn from content area textbooks.

Consolidated Word Learners in Third Grade and Above

Toward the end of second grade, and most certainly by fourth grade, children enter the consolidated stage (Ehri, 2005; Ehri & McCormick, 1998). Consolidated word learners learn to associate sounds with multiletter groups in long and complex words. These children learn to identify prefixes and suffixes, syllables, and word parts borrowed from Greek and Latin, as described in Chapter 6. Children understand how prefixes, suffixes, and words parts borrowed from Greek and Latin affect word meaning. They understand how various syllable patterns represent sound and become accomplished at reading unfamiliar long words by dividing them into pronounceable syllables. Recognizing the multiletter groups or chunks in long words is a streamlined approach to reading and spelling new words. And, not surprisingly, children's reading vocabulary continues to grow rapidly. At this point in their development as readers, children learn the majority of new words on their own through reading and writing. They read a wide variety of texts for different purposes. In reading content area texts they focus on comprehension to learn new information and develop new concepts.

Automatic Readers

Automatic readers are proficient, accomplished readers. These readers instantly recognize all, or nearly all, the words they see in text. Words are read rapidly, accurately, and effortlessly. Word identification, self-monitoring, self-correcting, and cross-checking are automatically carried out without conscious attention or effort. When readers meet complex words they do not know, they have many strategies for reading and learning them. Readers pay full attention to comprehension because they no longer need the energy for word identification. At this point in their development as readers, children recognize more words in print than they use in conversation. Now, at last, the size of the reading vocabulary surpasses the size of the speaking vocabulary. Because text consists of words in readers' sight vocabulary, reading is pleasurable, rapid, and fluent.

Movement toward the instant recognition of a large number of words is gradual. Children transition from one stage to another as they learn and use more complex information and strategies. When children first begin to use a new strategy, their ability to apply the strategy and their understanding of the print and speech relationships needed to use the strategy is immature. With instruction, and ample reading and writing experiences, children's knowledge gradually matures and their ability to use the new word identification strategy improves. When children are relatively comfortable using a certain strategy and have a good understanding of the print and speech relationships that support it, they gradually move into the next higher stage, which calls for applying a more efficient strategy that is based on a more elaborate understanding of print and speech relationships. As is to be expected with any complex learning process, sometimes children use strategies to read and spell words that are characteristic of more than one stage. Gradually, however, the strategies from earlier stages fade away so that, whenever possible, readers use their most streamlined strategy to read and spell words.

Further Thoughts

When you, the teacher, are familiar with the stages and understand the knowledge and abilities that underpin the use of strategies in the different stages, you will make decisions that will help children move from one stage to the next. When you understand the stages of word learning and the strategies that children in various stages use to read and spell new words, you have the information you need to relate what you teach to what children need to know to move to the next word learning stage. You will select just the right material to match the skills and abilities of children, and challenge children to develop new and more effective strategies. You will be a more effective teacher because you are teaching exactly what children need to know to become better at reading and spelling the new words that may stand in the way of understanding text.

Our goals are to develop readers who have such large fluent reading vocabularies that they seldom see words they do not already know how to read and to produce writers who correctly spell nearly all of the words in their fluent reading vocabularies. When all is said and done, word identification is not *the* goal of reading instruction. Rather, it is a means to an end, a way to help children learn new words on their own so as to support fluent reading, and, in the process, become confident readers who focus their attention on understanding text, on learning from text, and on enjoying reading as a leisure activity for a lifetime.

Translation of Figure 1-1, Maria's Valentine
Dear Mrs. Saracho,

You are a great teacher. I am learning new things every day. I hope that you will be able to teach here next year. You are the nicest teacher in fifth grade.
Love,
Maria

REFERENCES

Ehri, L. C., & McCormick, S. (1998). Phases of word learning: Implications for instruction with delayed and disabled readers. *Reading and Writing Quarterly: Overcoming Learning Difficulties, 14*(2), 135–164.

Ehri, L. C. (2005). Learning to read words: Theory, findings, and issues. *Scientific Studies of Reading, 9*(2), 167–188.

Ehri, L. C. (2006). More about phonics: Findings and reflections. In K. A. D. Stahl & M. C. McKenna (Eds.), *Reading research at work: Foundations of effective practice* (pp. 155–165). New York: Guilford Press.

Eldredge, J. L. (2005). Foundations of fluency: An exploration. *Reading Psychology, 26*(2), 161–181.

International Reading Association. (1997). *The role of phonics in reading instruction: A position statement of the International Reading Association* [Brochure]. Newark, DE: Author.

National Reading Panel. (2000). *Teaching children to read: An evidence-based assessment of the scientific research literature on reading and its implications for reading instruction: Reports of the subgroups* (NIH Publication No. 00-4754). Washington, DC: U.S. Government Printing Office.

Schwanenflugel, P. J., Hamilton, A. M., Kuhn, M. R., Wisenbaker, J. M., & Stahl, S. A. (2004). Becoming a fluent reader: Reading skill and prosodic features in the oral reading of young readers. *Journal of Educational Psychology, 96*(1), 119–129.

CHAPTER 2

Phonemic Awareness

Becoming Aware of the
Sounds of Language

This chapter describes how children develop insight into the sounds of language. You will learn about the importance of language awareness for learning to read, different types of language awareness children bring to your classroom, and informal and formal assessment tools to determine children's insight into the sounds in words. In this chapter you will find best practices for teaching phonemic awareness, classroom-tested activities to develop rhyme awareness and phonemic awareness, a list of e-resources, and suggestions and considerations for teaching English language learners and children at risk.

KEY IDEAS

- Phonemic awareness is the understanding that words consist of sounds, and the ability to separate words into sounds and blend sounds into words.

- Phonological awareness refers to awareness of the words, syllables, rhymes, and sounds in language. Phonemic awareness is a subset of phonological awareness.

- Awareness of the words, rhymes, and sounds of language develops in a relatively predictable sequence that begins with awareness of the words in language and ends with awareness of the sounds in words.

- The ability to separate words into sounds and the ability to blend sounds together are the key components of phonemic awareness.

- Phonemic awareness is important for learning to read. Children with good phonemic awareness are better word learners, better readers, and better spellers than children with poor phonemic awareness.

KEY VOCABULARY

Adding sounds

Blending

Deleting sounds

Manipulating sounds

Phoneme

Phonemic awareness

Phonological awareness

Rhyme awareness

Segmenting sounds

Sound boxes

Sound stretching

Substituting sounds

The language children bring to school serves many purposes. Language gives children a way to interact with others, express their feelings, and learn about their environment. When children carry on everyday conversations, they concentrate on communication, not on the individual sounds from which the words are created. All this changes when children begin to learn to read. As they move toward literacy, children begin to think about spoken language in a totally different way: They stand back from the meaning of language in order to analyze speech. As they do this, children discover that the words they use in everyday conversation consist of individual sounds.

Nadia is discovering the individual sounds in spoken words and learning how letters go with sounds. When Nadia writes, as in the note in Figure 2-1, she thinks about the sounds in the words she wishes to spell and then associates letters with them. When Nadia reads, she looks for familiar letter patterns in unfamiliar words, considers the reading context, and then reads a word that fits both the reading context and the sounds that the letters represent.

Unlike Nadia, Marty is not aware of the sounds in words, and he does not know how letters represent sounds. Yet Marty does know that writing is important and that writing goes from left to right (see Figure 2-2). Marty experiments as he writes a few recognizable letters, uses some mock letters, and simulates cursive writing with the long wavy line traversing the page. As Marty

Figure 2-1   Nadia uses her emerging awareness of the sounds in words and her developing knowledge of letter-sound patterns to write: I went to Sue's and ate pizza.

becomes aware of the sounds in words and as he learns how letters go with sounds, he will begin to use letters to represent the sounds in the words he wishes to spell and, consequently, his teacher will be able to read his writing.

WHAT IS PHONEMIC AWARENESS?

Phonemic awareness is the ability to analyze language, and the ability to act on this analysis to separate words into sounds and to blend sounds into words. A **phoneme** is the smallest sound that differentiates one word from another. For example, the phonemes /s/ and /r/ differentiate /sat/ from /rat/. Children with well-developed phonemic awareness can separate words into sounds, and blend sounds into words. For example, these children will tell you, their teacher, that /man/ consists of /m/-/a/-/n/; that /a/ is the middle sound in /man/; that taking the /m/ away leaves /an/; and that the sounds /m/ + /a/ + /n/ blend together to say /man/. Phonemic awareness refers *only* to awareness of the sounds in words. Phonological awareness is a broader term that includes awareness of the sounds in words and awareness of larger language units.

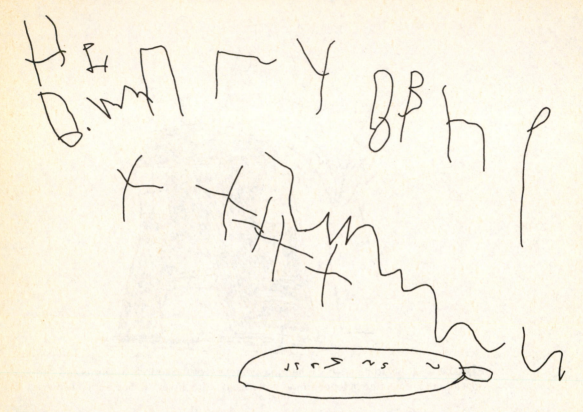

Figure 2-2   Marty, a kindergartner, is not yet aware of the individual sounds in words and how letters represent sounds. He uses a few real letters, mock letters, and scribbles as he experiments with writing.

What is Phonological Awareness?

Phonological awareness refers to awareness of the words, syllables, rhymes, and sounds in language. We might think of phonological awareness as a large umbrella, as illustrated in Figure 2-3, that covers awareness of all the different units in speech. Children with good phonological awareness know that (a) sentences consist of words, (b) words consist of syllables, (c) some words rhyme while others do not, (d) words consist of individual sounds, and (e) blending individual sounds together produces meaningful spoken words. Children who are aware of words will tell you that /my dog/ consists of /my/ and /dog/. Children who say that /mad/ and /dad/ rhyme are aware of rhyming words, another phonological awareness skill. Later in this chapter we will explore rhyme awareness, a phonological awareness skill taught in many preschool and kindergarten classrooms.

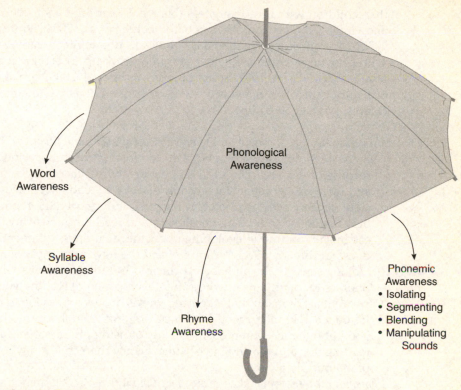

Figure 2-3 Phonological awareness and phonemic awareness.

PHONEMIC AWARENESS IS IMPORTANT FOR LEARNING TO READ

Phonemic awareness, unlike any other spoken language skill, does not help children communicate with you, their classmates, or their parents. Though phonemic awareness is not necessary for carrying on everyday conversations, it is necessary for children to understand the principle of alphabetic writing—the use of letters to represent sounds. To grasp the principle of alphabetic writing, children must realize that the sounds they hear in spoken words are represented by the letters they see in written words. Without the understanding that words consist of sounds, the letter-sound relationships of phonics makes no sense at all. Phonemic awareness, in combination with phonics, makes it possible for beginning readers to decode, read, and spell words by associating sounds with letters. Phonemic awareness is a good predictor of reading success in the early grades (Frost et al., 2009; Schatschneider, Fletcher, Francis, Carlson, & Foorman, 2004). The children in your classroom who begin school with good phonemic awareness will make faster reading progress than children with low awareness (National Reading Panel, 2000; Muter, Hulme, Snowling, & Stevenson, 2004; Schatschneider et al., 2004; Strattman & Hodson, 2005). The positive relationship between phonemic awareness and reading achievement is evident whether children grow up in economically advantaged families (Nicholson, 1997; Spira, Bracken, & Fischel, 2005), are at risk for reading difficulty (Carroll & Snowling, 2004), or speak English as their second language (Manis, Lindsey, & Bailey, 2004).

Phonemic awareness contributes to phonics, vocabulary, and fluency.   Phonemic awareness plays an indirect role in developing vocabulary and fluent reading (as we see in Figure 1-2 in the preceding chapter). Kindergartners and early first graders who are just learning to read have few words in their sight vocabularies. However, as early as kindergarten the foundations for developing a rich reading vocabulary and reading fluency are being established through developing phonemic awareness. Phonemic awareness does not directly affect vocabulary and fluency, but it is essential for making sense of the alphabetic principle and using phonics. Children need phonics to identify new words and develop a large reading vocabulary. A vocabulary of instantly recognized words makes it possible to read fluently. If you teach kindergarten, first, or second grade, look for the children with good phonemic awareness to be better at using phonics, have a larger reading vocabulary, and have better fluency than children who are less phonemically aware.

Phonemic awareness and phonics are related but different.   Phonemic awareness is the realization that words consist of individual sounds; phonics is the relationship between letters and sounds. Phonemic awareness pertains to *spoken language*; phonics pertains to the letter and sound connections between *written and spoken language*. We can *hear* the sounds in words (phonemic awareness); we can *see* the letters that represent the sounds (phonics). When you explain that /m/ is the beginning sound in /map/, you are teaching phonemic awareness. When you explain that the letter *m* represents /m/, you are teaching phonics. Although phonemic awareness and phonics are different, they develop in a complementary way as children learn to read and write. A complementary relationship means that getting better in one thing results in improvement in the other. In one direction, when children learn the letter-sound relationships of phonics, their awareness of the sounds in words increases. In the other direction, when children develop increased awareness of the sounds in words, they become better able to use the letter-sound patterns of phonics to read and spell. From a practical standpoint, you can expect teaching phonemic awareness to help children make use of phonics. You also can expect phonics instruction to result in greater phonemic awareness. Therefore, teaching *both* phonemic awareness and phonics to beginning readers is the best way to maximize the possibilities for learning and, not coincidentally, the possibility for increasing children's reading vocabulary and eventually their reading fluency.

PHONEMIC AWARENESS DEVELOPS SEQUENTIALLY

Phonemic awareness develops in a relatively predictable sequence in which children first become aware of large language segments and then become aware of increasingly smaller ones (Lonigan, 2006). Awareness of the words in everyday conversations develops first. While some children may discover words as early as age three, many become aware of words at about age four. Most children begin kindergarten with word awareness. Syllable awareness—the ability to identify syllables in long words and to divide long words into groups of sound—develops after word awareness. Look for syllable awareness to develop in children with word awareness as early as age four, and most certainly by early kindergarten for most children. Rhyme and beginning sound awareness develop after word and syllable awareness and before sound awareness. Rhyme awareness and beginning sound awareness are thought to be a single level or category of language awareness, because the two skills develop at approximately the same time (Anthony & Lonigan, 2004). Some four-year-olds in preschool and five-year-olds in kindergarten identify rhyming words and beginning sounds (Justice, Invernizzi, Geller, Sullivan, & Welsch, 2005). Developing awareness of *all* the individual sounds in words is more difficult (Pufpaff, 2009). Children usually become aware of all the sounds in words sometime in kindergarten or early first grade as they learn to read and write. Children increase their phonemic awareness through direct instruction in phonemic awareness, through instruction in the letter sounds of phonics, and with opportunities to use letter-sound knowledge when reading and spelling.

Let us take a closer look at the types of language awareness children develop. For the purpose of organizing our thinking, we will divide language awareness into word awareness, syllable awareness, rhyme and beginning sound awareness, and sound awareness.

Word Awareness in Preschool

Children separate sentences into individual words. These children will say that /John ate dinner/ consists of /John/, /ate/, and /dinner/. To develop word awareness, instruct children to (1) tell you the individual words (or parts) in sentences, (2) tap once for each word, (3) clap once for each word, (4) move a chip for each word, or (5) count the words in sentences or phrases.

Syllable Awareness in Preschool and Early Kindergarten

Children pronounce one "word" in a compound word or delete a syllable in multisyllable words. Children will tell you that /snowball/ without /snow/ leaves /ball/, and that /window/ without /win/ leaves /dow/. Encourage children to develop syllable awareness by asking them to delete syllables: "Say /pencil/. Now say it again without the /pen/." Tapping and clapping for each syllable are also effective methods. Tapping and clapping give children practice hearing, saying, and feeling (clapping or tapping) syllables.

Rhyme and Beginning Sound Awareness in Preschool and Kindergarten

We will consider rhyme and beginning sound awareness together because these two abilities develop at about the same time. In order to identify rhyming words, children must separate the rhyme from the beginning sounds. For example, to tell you that /bat/ and /hat/ rhyme, children must realize /at/ is common to both words. This understanding depends on awareness of the rhyming sound, in our example /at/, and on realizing that /b/ and /h/ are separate portions of the words. Consequently, children who are aware of rhyme are either aware of the sounds that precede it or will quickly develop beginning sound awareness as they participate in rhyming activities.

Rhyme Awareness: Children who have **rhyme awareness** identify words that do and do not rhyme, and think of rhyming words on their own. Children will tell you that /pig/ rhymes with /dig/ and that /cat/ does not. When asked to think of words that rhyme with /hot/, children might say words like /not/ and /pot/. Identifying rhyme is easier than thinking of rhyming words. To help children learn to identify rhyme, ask questions like "Does /man/ rhyme with /can/?" "Does /man/ rhyme with /rat/?" "Which words rhyme? /box/-/car/-/fox/" "Do these belong together? /mad/-/sad/-/bad/" "Which one doesn't belong? /mad/-/dad/ -/boy/" Encourage children to think of rhyme by asking them to "Say a word that rhymes with /cat/. With /man/. With /dog/." You might also ask children to "Say a word that sounds like bat." Another alternative is to ask, "If I say mouse, you would say . . ." Children then answer with /house/ or another rhyming word.

Beginning Sound Awareness: Children identify and separate or segment beginning sounds. For instance, children will say that /mop/ and /moon/ begin alike, and that /pill/ does not begin the same. Children will also tell you, their teacher, that /mop/ begins with /m/ and /pill/ begins with /p/. Help children pay attention to beginning sounds by asking, "Say the first sound in /mop/." "Does /mop/ begin with /m/ or /n/?" "Think of another word that begins with the same sound as /mop/." Help children split a word into its beginning sound and rhyme by asking them to "Say /mop/. Say the first sound in mop." "Now say the rhyming sound in mop and hop." (Chapter 4 has ideas for teaching activities to encourage and support children as they apply this skill to reading and writing words.)

Sound Awareness and Blending in Kindergarten Through Second Grade

Phonemic awareness, or the awareness of the sounds in language, consists of a cluster of skills and abilities. To be technically correct, we should consider beginning sound awareness as a phonemic awareness skill because children are aware of an individual phoneme—the beginning sound—in words. Beginning sound awareness, which as we have learned develops concomitantly with rhyme awareness, is the easiest type of sound awareness.

Ending Sound Awareness: Children identify words that do and do not end with the same sound, and pronounce the last sound in words. For example, children will say that /mad/ and /lid/ end with the same sound, that /mad/ and /ham/ do not, and that /mop/ ends in /p/ and /can/ with /n/.

Middle Sound Awareness: Children identify words that do and do not have the same middle sound, and say the middle sound in words. Children will tell you, for instance, that /boat/ and /soap/ have the same middle sound; that /boat/ and /beet/ have different middle sounds; and that /ō/ is the middle sound in /boat/.

Segmenting (Separating Words into Sounds):   Children who **segment sounds** will say each sound in the order in which it occurs in a word. For example, children will tell you that /ship/ consists of /sh/, /i/, and /p/. These same children can count the sounds in /ship/ (/ship/ has three sounds), tap for each sound (/sh/ one tap, /i/ one tap, /p/ one tap) or move a chip to represent each sound.

Blending: Children who **blend** fold individual sounds together to pronounce words. Good blenders can tell you that /s/ + /o/ makes /so/ and that /f/ + /i/ + /n/ makes /fin/. Blending is not "saying it fast." Saying it fast is pronouncing one isolated sound after another in close succession (/f/-/i/-/n/). The trick to blending is to fold sounds together so that the sounds themselves melt into each other.

Manipulating Sounds in First and Second Grade

Manipulating sounds include (1) adding sounds, (2) deleting sounds, or (3) substituting sounds. Adding sounds and deleting sounds are easier than substituting sounds. Some trickier types of sound manipulation can develop well beyond the second grade. However, the types of sound manipulation that support the use of phonics to read and spell develops in most children well before the end of second grade.

Adding Sounds: Children **add sounds** to the beginning or end of a word. For example, children add /b/ to /oat/ to make /boat/ or add /s/ to /dog/ to make /dogs/. This simple type of manipulation *may* develop in late kindergarten for some children, in first grade for others.

Deleting Sounds: Children **delete sounds** from the beginning or end of a word and say what is left. For instance, children delete /p/ from /pin/ to pronounce /in/, or /s/ from /cats/ to say /cat/. Some children *may* develop the ability to delete beginning (/sat/ - /s/ = /at/) sounds in late kindergarten. Others will not develop this skill until the first grade.

Substituting Sounds: In **substituting sounds,** children replace a beginning, ending, or middle sound with a different sound. Beginning and ending sound substitution usually develops in first grade. For example, if you ask children to, "Say /man/. Now say it again but say /p/ instead of /m/," children will say /pan/. Beginning sound substitution is often called initial consonant substitution. This is an important skill for using phonics. For example, a child who knows beginning letter sounds might substitute the /b/ represented by the *b* in the written word *bat* for a /c/ represented by *c* to read *cat*. Initial consonant substitution illustrates how phonemic awareness and phonics work together. Phonemic awareness makes it possible for children to substitute the /b/ sound for the /c/ sound to change /bat/ into /cat/. Phonics knowledge, on the other hand, is necessary to realize that the *b* in *bat* represents /b/ and the *c* represents /c/, thereby giving children the information they need to read both *bat* and *cat*. In substituting ending sounds children replace the /n/ in /man/ with a /p/ to pronounce /map/. Substituting middle sounds is the more difficult. Here children replace the /a/ in /map/ with /o/ to say /mop/. The ability to substitute sounds develops through the second grade.

From a classroom teaching perspective, the most important skills to develop are the abilities to (1) segment words into each and every sound and (2) blend individual sounds into words. These two abilities are directly applicable to using phonics letter sounds to read and spell new words.

RHYME AND BEGINNING SOUND AWARENESS

Some children as young as age three may be sensitive to rhyme. Kindergartners who have experience with poetry and rhyming language games are generally quite good at identifying rhyming words. These children tend to be better readers later in school than kindergartners who are not sensitive to rhyme. Justin, who was aware of rhyming language as a kindergartner, demonstrates rhyme awareness in a poem he wrote after his first-grade class had shared the book *Ten Apples Up on Top!* (LeSieg, 1961). This book, which tells the rhyming story of animals balancing apples and being chased by an angry bear with a mop, clearly influenced Justin's thinking as he composed. Notice in Figure 2-4 how Justin uses two of the rhyming words from the storybook—*top* and *mop*—to create his own special poetic mood, message, and expression.

Rhyme awareness, coupled with awareness of beginning sounds, makes it possible for beginning readers to learn short words that rhyme. There are two ways rhyme awareness may help Justin as he learns to read: First, rhyme awareness may act as a scaffold to help Justin identify the sounds in words. Second, rhyme awareness may prime Justin to look for the letters in written words (*mop* and *top*) that represent the rhyme /op/ in spoken words. Children like Justin who are aware of rhyme (/mop/ and /top/) may think of the rhyme (/op/) as one type of sound, and the beginning sounds (/m/ and /t/, in this example) as another. In so doing, children separate the beginning sound (/m/ or /t/) from

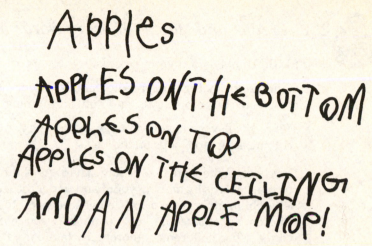

Figure 2-4 Justin's rhyming poem, "Apples," shows that he has developed an awareness of rhyming sounds in language.

the rhyming sound (/op/). Later children learn to substitute one beginning sound for another. For instance, Justin might begin by saying the word /mop/ and then substitute /h/ for the /m/ to pronounce /hop/. *Substituting* one sound for another is important for reading new words by analogy, as explained in Chapter 4.

Classroom Activities for Developing Rhyme and Beginning Sound Awareness

Although children are naturally drawn to rhyming language, they may not develop rhyme awareness by simply participating in normal classroom activities (Layton, Deeny, Tall, & Upton, 1996). It is important, therefore, to support those children in your classroom who are not yet aware of rhyming language. Activities that ask children to produce their own rhyming words have been shown to improve children's rhyme awareness, even when those activities are brief, lasting only a few minutes. Therefore, even relatively short activities, when consistently and repeatedly used with children like Nadia (see Figure 2-1) and Marty (see Figure 2-2), help children develop rhyme awareness and beginning sound awareness. Along with these activities, read ABC books, rhyming books, and poems; make a wall of words that begin with the same letter and sound; recite nursery rhymes; and call children's attention to the jump rope rhymes they hear older children recite on the playground.

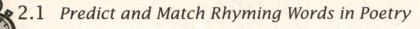

2.1   *Predict and Match Rhyming Words in Poetry*

Skill: Thinking of rhyming words.

Children in small groups predict familiar rhyming words in often-read poems, match rhyming words, and think of rhyming words.

Things You'll Need: Poems on large charts; sticky notes; rhyming word cards with masking tape loops on the backs.

Directions: Write a poem on a large chart. As children read the poem in chorus, track words by moving your hand under the words as they are read. This helps children focus on print, demonstrates left-to-right direction, and helps children appreciate the connection between written words and spoken words. When children are thoroughly familiar with the poem, cover up one or more rhyming words with sticky notes. Read the poem together with the children, and ask them to supply the hidden rhyming words. Then remove the sticky notes to reveal the rhyming words. Ask children to think of other rhyming words.

On another day, give children the rhyming word cards with masking tape loops on the back. Have children put the rhyming word cards on, next to, or under the rhyming words in the poem. Follow up by making a chart of rhyming words to display in your classroom. You may also wish to add a few rhyming words to the word wall in your classroom.

2.2   *Rhyming Word Bookmark*

Skill: Identifying rhyming words or the beginning sounds in words.

Children make a handy bookmark with this small group or center activity.

Things You'll Need: A bookmark pattern on sturdy paper with room for a picture in the top square, as shown in Figure 2-5; pictures that do and do not rhyme with the top picture or pictures that do and do not begin with the same sound as the top picture; scissors; glue. See e-resources for a site where you can create and print personalized rhyming bookmarks.

Directions: Children cut out pictures that either rhyme with the picture on the top of the bookmark or begin with the same sound as the top picture. Then children glue the pictures in the bookmark squares. Talk about words that rhyme or begin with the same sound. Extend this activity to written language by having children watch as you write the words under the pictures on their bookmarks. Or, you might ask children to join you in spelling for sounds (see activity 5.2). Laminate bookmarks to finalize the activity.

Figure 2-5 Making bookmarks is fun, gives children extra practice recognizing rhyming sounds or beginning sounds, and results in a handy place marker for the books children enjoy at school or at home.

2.3 *Sound-Picture Sort*

Skills: Identifying rhyming words or the beginning sounds in words.

Children work with partners, individually, or in learning centers (or literacy stations) to sort rhyming pictures or pictures that begin with the same sound.

Things You'll Need: Rhyming pictures or pictures that begin with the same sound on 3 × 5 inch cards. If used as a center or literacy station activity, it is helpful to have paper lunch sacks with pictures of rhyming words or pictures of words that begin with the sounds used for sorting taped to the sacks.

Directions: Discuss rhyming words or words that begin with the same sound. Show children the picture cards. Have children name each picture. It is important to have children name the pictures because sometimes they use a picture name you do not anticipate. When this happens, the sort does not work. Ask children to sort the picture cards that rhyme or have the same beginning sound. If used as a center or literacy station activity, ask children to put pictures into sacks with rhyming pictures, as shown in Figure 2-6, or pictures that begin alike. Also ask children to write their names on the sacks so you can check the sorts later.

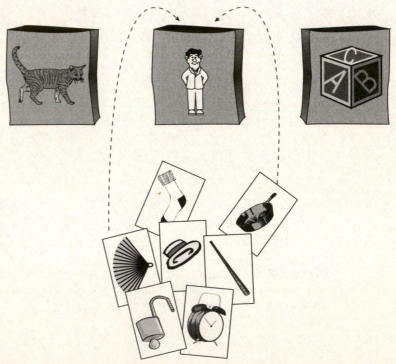

Figure 2-6 Sorting rhyming pictures into paper lunch sacks gives children an opportunity to analyze the rhyme in words and to differentiate one set of rhyming sounds from another.

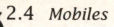

2.4 *Mobiles*

Skills: Identifying rhyming words or the beginning sounds in words; matching written words with pictures.

Children in small groups make mobiles that feature pictures and words that either rhyme or begin with the same sound.

Things You'll Need: Old magazines and catalogs; scissors; colorful construction paper cut into geometric shapes; glue; colorful yarn cut into different lengths; coat hangers to hang the mobiles; hole punch.

Directions: Have the children cut out pictures with names that either rhyme or begin with the same sound, and then paste the pictures onto one side of the colored pieces of construction paper. Write the word for the picture on the opposite side. Punch a hole in the top of each geometric shape, thread a colorful strand of yarn through the hole, and then tie the yarn to a coat hanger (see Figure 2-7).

Integrate this activity with mathematics by discussing the circles, triangles, squares, and rectangles that adorn the mobiles.

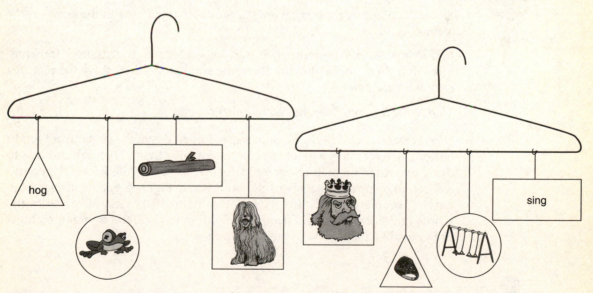

Figure 2-7 In making rhyming mobiles, children think about and read rhyming words and, if construction paper is cut into circles, triangles, squares, and rectangles, you have an opportunity to integrate language arts and mathematics.

2.5 *Collages*

Skill: Identifying rhyming words or the beginning sounds in words.

Small groups make collages of rhyming pictures or pictures that begin with the same sound.

Things You'll Need: Lots of pictures; oak tag; tape or glue.

Directions: Give children a few pictures, some that rhyme and some that do not—or, if focusing on beginning sounds, some that begin alike and some that do not. Children then select rhyming pictures or pictures with the same beginning sound, and glue or tape pictures onto a large sheet of paper. When the collage is finished, have the children say the picture names in chorus.

Extend this activity to written language by writing words on cards, reading the words, and matching the words with the pictures on the collage.

2.6 *Draw Pictures that Rhyme or Begin Alike*

Skill: Thinking of rhyming words or words that begin with the same sound.

In this small group, individual, or learning center activity, children draw pictures that rhyme or begin with the same sound, and then share the pictures with their classmates.

Things You'll Need: Paper folded in half; crayons.

Directions: Give children a piece of paper folded down the center from top to bottom, or ask children to fold the paper you give them. Then ask children to draw two rhyming pictures, one picture on one side of the folded paper and a different picture on the other side, as shown in Figure 2-8. If focusing on beginning sounds, have children draw two items that begin alike. Write the words under the pictures. Encourage children to share the rhyming pictures or begin-alike pictures with their classmates.

2.7 *Memory Game*

Skill: Identifying rhyming words or the beginning sounds in words.

This is a rhyming or beginning sound version of the ever-popular Concentration® and is a good game for children to play with a partner or while pairs of children visit the centers or literacy stations in your classroom.

Figure 2-8   After Gerald drew this pair of rhyming pictures, his kindergarten teacher shared them with the class. The rhyming pictures are bat-cat; goose-moose; mouse-house.

Things You'll Need: A deck of cards with pairs of rhyming picture-word cards, as shown in Figure 2-9, or pictures of words that begin alike.

Directions: Pairs of players put the rhyming or beginning sound pictures face down on a table and take turns flipping up two picture-word cards. Players keep pairs of pictures that rhyme or begin-alike cards. Cards that do not rhyme or begin alike are turned face down again. The player with the most cards wins.

2.8   *Grab Bag*

Skill: Thinking of rhyming words or words with the same beginning sounds.

Small groups or individuals say words that rhyme with or begin with the same sound as pictures or objects hidden in a bag.

Things You'll Need: An opaque bag; an assortment of small objects or pictures.

Directions: Place objects or pictures in the bag; do not let the children watch as you do this. Put your hand in the bag and grab an object or picture. Show it to the children. Ask the children to think of a word that rhymes with the name of the object or picture, or to think of a word that begins with the same sound. Set that object aside and take another from the bag. You might also want to write the words that children suggest, thereby connecting spoken words with written words.

Figure 2-9   A rhyming picture-word memory game. Recognizing pairs of rhyming picture-word cards reinforces sensitivity to, and awareness of, rhyme in spoken and written language.

2.9 *Shower Curtain Toss*

Skill: Thinking of rhyming words or words with the same beginning sounds.

In this large muscle activity, small groups toss a beanbag onto a shower curtain with pictures taped on it and then say a word that rhymes or begins with the same sound as the picture name.

Things You'll Need: Plastic shower curtain; beanbag; pictures; tape.

Directions: Tape pictures to a shower curtain and put the shower curtain on the floor. Children stand around the curtain and take turns tossing a beanbag onto (or near) a picture. Children say the picture name and then say a word that rhymes with it or that begins with the same sound.

Spare Minute Activities for Developing Rhyme Awareness

2.10 *Rhyming Word Lists*

Skills: Thinking of rhyming words; reading rhyming words.

Directions: Make lists of rhyming words. For example, if *swing* is a rhyming word that has come to children's attention, ask them to suggest other words, such as *king, ring, sing*. Make different charts with lists of rhyming words. Post the charts in your room; refer to them when talking about rhyme or use them as resources for writing.

2.11 *Rhyme Frames*

Skill: Identifying rhyming words.

Directions: Read rhyming poems. Call attention to rhyming words by framing them (cupping your hands around words). Also use a word window—a piece of oak tag with a "window" or hole in the middle—to frame words. Ask the children to use their hands or the word window to frame rhyming words. In a few spare minutes, you might ask children to frame rhyming words written on the board, word wall, or bulletin board.

2.12 *Thumbs-Up Puppet*

Skill: Identifying rhyming words or words that begin with the same sounds.

Directions: A colorful puppet is a good way to encourage children to partici- pate in rhyme and beginning sound awareness activities. The puppet says two (or more) words, and children decide if the words rhyme or begin alike. Children put their thumbs up for rhyming or begin-alike words, down for nonrhyming words or words that begin differently.

PHONEMIC AWARENESS

At age six, Melanie already knows how letters represent sounds. Figure 2-10 shows the clever way she writes *sn-snow balls*, *ch-chillier*, *ch-ch-ch-chilly*, and *ah ah ah ahchoooooo*! She literally separates language into sounds before her readers' eyes. Melanie can separate or segment words into sounds, and she can blend individual sounds into meaningful words. Melanie is making good progress learning to read. She uses phonics to help her decode words she does not instantly recognize; she understands what she reads; she self-monitors, self-corrects, and cross-checks to

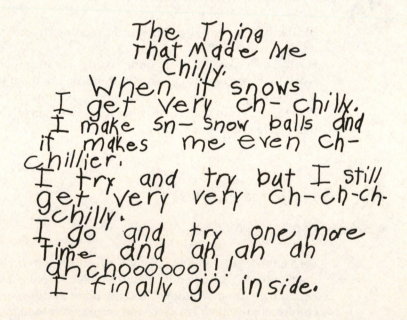

The Thing
That Made Me
Chilly.
When it snows
I get very ch-chilly.
I make sn-snow balls and
it makes me even ch-
chillier.
I try and try but I still
get very very ch-ch-ch-
chilly.
I go and try one more
time and ah, ah ah
ahchoooooo!!!
I finally go inside.

Figure 2-10 Melanie demonstrates sound awareness when she separates the beginning sounds from words in her story to help her readers experience the sensation of being cold.

make sure the words she identifies make sense in the reading context. Melanie's phonemic awareness will continue to improve through classroom reading instruction and through her experiences with reading and spelling words. Because Melanie knows a great deal about the sounds of words, her teacher blends phonemic awareness instruction in with other types of instruction, particularly phonics instruction. But not all the children in Melanie's class are so successful. Some struggle to identify sounds in words and to blend. These children have limited reading vocabularies and cannot successfully use phonics to read and spell new words. Melanie's teacher spends more time using direct instruction to develop the phonemic awareness of these children. The teacher also combines instruction in phonemic awareness and phonics, and shows children how to use phonemic awareness while reading and spelling. All things considered, if some of the children whom you teach have not discovered the sounds in language, they will benefit from activities that increase phonemic awareness, becoming better readers and better spellers as a consequence.

Phonemic awareness is important for using phonics, but it is also important for spelling. Children with good phonemic awareness are better spellers than children with poor awareness (Caravolas, Hulme, & Snowling, 2001). When children do not know how to spell a word, they use their phonemic awareness and knowledge of letter sounds to spell by matching letters with sounds. Children begin by saying the word to themselves, listen for individual phonemes, and then write the letters that represent the sounds they hear. In following these steps, children separate the words they wish to spell into individual sounds—a crucial phonemic awareness skill. This might explain why phonemic awareness increases when kindergartners are prompted to "spell words like they sound" (Martins & Silva, 2006). We would expect the effect of phonemic awareness to be most evident in the early grades before children have memorized the spellings of many different words. It makes sense, then, that the words that first and second graders correctly separate into sounds are spelled with greater accuracy than the words children incorrectly separate into sounds (Foorman, Jenkins, & Francis, 1993).

BEST PRACTICES FOR DEVELOPING PHONEMIC AWARENESS

You can expect the children whom you teach to develop greater sensitivity to the sounds in words when you include phonemic awareness in your balanced classroom reading program. In following these best practices, you ensure that phonemic awareness instruction is effective and in proportion to children's needs.

1. *Teach awareness of beginning sounds, followed by awareness of ending sounds, and then awareness of middle sounds* (Cassady & Smith, 2004).   This is the sequence in which phonemic awareness develops in most children.
2. *Teach phonemic awareness, letter names, and letter sounds together* (Christensen & Bowey, 2005).   Teaching phonemic awareness along with letter names and

letter sounds is more effective than teaching phonemic awareness alone. Teaching phonemic awareness in isolation is only marginally beneficial (Castles, Coltheart, Wilson, Valpied, & Wedgewood, 2009). If your classroom program weaves an emphasis on phonemic awareness into the fabric of phonics instruction, you may not need to provide the average reader with additional phonemic awareness instruction beyond that included in your well-planned, sequenced, and explicit program (Ukrainetz, Ross, & Harm, 2009). For the child who needs more phonemic awareness instruction, combine some of the activities in Chapters 3 and 5 with activities in this chapter.

3. *Teach just one or two phonemic awareness skills at a time.* Teaching one or two phonemic awareness skills is twice as effective as teaching many skills at once (National Reading Panel, 2000).

4. *Teach phonemic awareness early, in kindergarten and first grade.* Becoming aware of the sounds in language is important for understanding the alphabetic principle in kindergarten (Ehri, Nunes, Willows, Schuster, Yaghoub-Zadeh, & Shanahan, 2001), and necessary for using phonics to read and spell in first grade.

5. *Teach in small groups.* Teaching small groups of children is more effective than teaching large groups (National Reading Panel, 2000). Children in small groups have more opportunities to personally respond to you, their teacher. And you have more opportunities to observe the effects of instruction when you teach small groups of children.

6. *Pace instruction to the needs of the child.* Children differ in the level of phonemic awareness they bring to your classroom. Spend more time teaching phonemic awareness to children with low awareness and move high-awareness children like Melanie on to other reading and writing activities.

7. *Show children how to use phonemic awareness when reading and spelling new words.* We cannot assume that children will automatically infer how to use their developing phonemic awareness skills when they read and spell. Therefore, you will be a more effective teacher when you model how to use phonemic awareness to read and spell words, and when you give children opportunities to practice using, under your guidance, the phonemic awareness skills they are learning.

8. *Begin with short, two-sound words.* It is easier to separate short, two-sound words into phonemes (/at/ + /a/ = /t/) than to segment three- and four-sound words. Move on to longer words when children are comfortable segmenting and blending short words.

CLASSROOM ACTIVITIES FOR DEVELOPING PHONEMIC AWARENESS

The activities in this section develop awareness of the sounds in words and the ability to blend. By and large, you will want to use these activities with younger children, say kindergartners or first graders, or older children who lack phonemic awareness and, therefore, have difficulty using phonics to read new words. In addition to these activities, you may wish to modify some of the rhyme awareness activities to use them to develop phonemic awareness. Modify these activities to suit your own teaching style and use them along with the letter and sound activities in Chapters 4 and 5.

Sound Awareness

2.13 *Stretching Sounds*

Skill: Segmenting.

In **sound stretching**, the teacher says a word slowly while children in a small group listen for sounds. Sound stretching helps children identify the individual sounds in words.

Things You'll Need: Nothing special.

Directions: Call attention to sounds by saying a word slowly, keeping the sounds connected while at the same time stretching them out. Bring your hand to your mouth and "pull" the sounds as you stretch them. For instance, in stretching /man/, you would stretch the word to pronounce something like "/mmmaaannn/." Children listen to the stretched word and tell you the beginning, middle, and ending sounds. Then ask the children to bring their hand to their mouth and stretch along with you.

2.14 *Guessing Stretchy Picture Names*

Skill: Awareness of beginning, middle, or ending sounds.

The teacher stretches portions of picture names, and children in a small group identify the picture names the teacher pronounces.

Things You'll Need: Pictures; a table or pocket chart.

Directions: Place two pictures on the table or in a pocket chart. Point to one picture. Say the picture name with the first sound stretched; then stretch the first sound and pronounce the name of the second picture. Children tell you the proper picture name. For example, you might show children a picture of a fan and one of a fish, point to the fish and ask, "Is this /fffish/ or /fffan/?" Children say the correct word. Call attention to ending sounds by stretching the last sound. For instance, you might point to the fan and ask, "Is this a /fishshsh/ or a /fannn/?" Stretch middle sounds saying "Is this a /fiiish/ or a /faaan/?" Look in the section on teaching phonemic awareness to children at risk for advice on pronouncing sounds.

2.15 *Segmenting Colorful Sounds*

Skills: Segmenting.

Children in a small group line up a colored square for each sound in a word.

Things You'll Need: One-inch colored construction paper squares.

Directions: Give each child three or four colored squares. Say a word slowly, stretching it to clearly pronounce all the sounds. Children move one colored square for each sound heard. Then have children point to individual squares that represent specific sounds in the word. For the purposes of illustration, let's assume that children pushed three squares for /fan/. You might have children, "Point to the square for the first sound in /fan/." Another option is to ask children to "Point to the /f/." Similar questions might be asked for middle and ending sounds.

 2.16 *Manipulating Colorful Sounds*

Skills: Manipulating sounds; associating sounds with letters.

Children in a small group move colored squares to add, delete, or substitute sounds in words you, the teacher, pronounce.

Things You'll Need: One-inch colored construction paper squares.

Directions: After children line up squares for the sounds in a word, as described in the previous activity, have children add an extra square to represent a new sound. Let us suppose children have lined up a red square for /f/, a green square for /a/, and a blue square for /n/—to represent /fan/. Ask children to line up another colored square to represent /fans/. For example, children might add a black square for /s/, resulting in a row of red, green, blue and black squares. Continuing with our example, you might have children delete a sound from fan by pointing to the red, green, and blue squares and asking, "If this says fan, make it an." Or you might ask, "What do we need to do to make this an?" The result is a row of two green and blue squares. Children substitute sounds by exchanging one colored square for another. In our example, children might substitute the red square (/f/) for a yellow square (/m/) to represent /man/. Now the squares consist of yellow, green, and blue to represent /man/. Substituting middle sounds is the most difficult task, so ask children to do this after they are able to substitute beginning and ending sounds. Ask children to pronounce each new word they make. Show children how to sweep their fingers under the new words as they say them aloud.

Extend this activity to written language by writing letters on the squares after children have moved them into a line. This increases awareness of the connections between the sounds in spoken words and the letters in written words and helps introduce letter-sound relationships.

2.17 *Sound Boxes*

Skill: Awareness of beginning, middle and ending sounds.

Sound boxes are connected boxes where each box represents a sound in a word. This activity may be used with small groups or when working with individual children.

Things You'll Need: Sound boxes, as shown in Figure 2-11a; tokens; pictures with two-, three-, or four-sound names (optional).

Directions: Give each child a piece of paper with several groups of sound boxes. You may also wish to give children pictures to help them remember the words they are segmenting. As you stretch a word, children push a token into a box for each sound heard. When children do not have much experience with sound boxes, pronounce words with beginning and ending sounds that you can say without interrupting airflow, such as the /mmm/ and /nnn/ in /man/. It is easier to demonstrate sounds when we can stretch them—/sss/ and /aaa/ (short a as in *fan*). Later, introduce sounds in which the airflow is

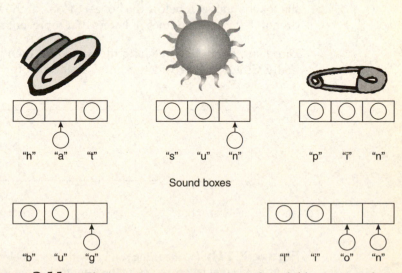

Sound boxes

Figure 2-11a Phonemic awareness increases when children move tokens into boxes for the sounds they hear in words and point to the tokens that represent beginning, middle, and ending sounds.

interrupted, as the /t/ and /b/ in /tub/. Sounds in which the airflow is interrupted cannot be effectively stretched and, therefore, are somewhat more difficult for you to demonstrate in the sound boxes activity. Once children have moved a token for each sound heard, ask them to point to the box that represents a single sound and to tell the sound's position—beginning, middle, end—in the word. Then have children blend sounds to pronounce the whole word, tracking (sweeping) their fingers under boxes as they say the sounds.

2.18 *Sound Boxes with Letters*

Skills: Awareness of beginning, middle and ending sounds; blending; associating sounds with letters.

This sound box activity introduces children to the letters that represent sounds. In so doing, we combine phonemic awareness with rudimentary phonics. The letters help children remember the sounds and, additionally, provide a good platform for talking about sounds and calling attention to word wall words that contain the letters and sounds.

Things You'll Need: Sound boxes, plastic letters or other letters, perhaps letters on cards, as shown in Figure 2-11b. If you use boxes with the letters printed in them, bear in mind that when children move tokens into boxes that already have letters in them, the tokens cover up the letters. Therefore, you will want to take extra care to make sure that children peek under the tokens (or move the tokens above or below the boxes) to look at the letters when you ask children to tell you the names of letters that represent sounds.

Directions: Begin by stretching the word and then pronounce the word normally. Children move a letter into a sound box for each sound in a word. (If

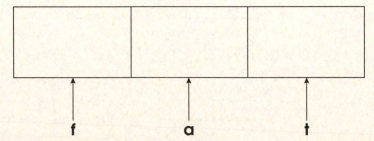

Figure 2-11b Connecting sounds with letters helps children gain insight into the principle that letters represent the sounds children hear in words.

letters are written in the boxes, move a token into each box for each sound heard.) Ask children to say the name of each letter as they (or you) identify the letters that go with the sounds (see Figure 2-11b.). Have children blend the sounds together while sweeping their hands under each sound as it is blended.

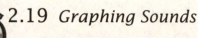

2.19 *Graphing Sounds*

Skill: Segmenting.

Children working in small groups under your guidance make a graph showing words with two, three, or four sounds.

Things You'll Need: Pictures; tape; a large piece of newsprint. Beforehand, draw two, three, and four connected boxes at the top of the newsprint, distributing groups of connected boxes fairly far apart. Fasten the newsprint to a bulletin board.

Directions: Children count the sounds in picture names. Children then tape the pictures below the connected boxes that match the number of sounds in the names. When finished, children have made a graph similar to the graph in Figure 2-12.

Integrate this activity with mathematics by adding up the words under each group of connected boxes, as well as the total number of words found.

2.20 *Picture-Sound-Letter Sort*

Skills: Awareness of beginning or ending; associating sounds with letters.

In this activity children sort pictures according to shared sounds and then identify the letters that represent the shared sounds.

Things You'll Need: A large piece of chart paper divided into two or three columns with a letter and a picture at the top of each column.

Directions: Prop up pictures on the chalk tray. Hold up one picture. Ask children to say the beginning or ending sound. Talk about the letter that represents that sound. Find the letter in the alphabet display in your classroom. Look for the letter in the words on the word wall. Ask a volunteer to glue the

Figure 2-12 Graphing sounds gives children practice identifying the number of sounds in words, and the finished graph is a wonderful resource for integrating language arts with mathematics.

picture in a column under the letter that represents the beginning sound or ending. Figure 2-13 shows a paper for a beginning sound sort. Leave the chart on display on a chart rack or thumbtack it to a bulletin board. Write the letter beside each picture on the chart. Have children follow this example when sorting for ending or middle sounds.

Figure 2-13 Associating letters with sounds (picture-sound-letter sort) and sorting by beginning, ending, or middle letter-sounds gives children practice listening for sounds and associating letters with sounds.

2.21 *Presto-Chango*

Skills: Substituting sounds; associating sounds with letters.

Children working individually or with a partner change one word into another by substituting sounds. This activity is appropriate for children who know a sound for each letter but need practice substituting sounds.

Things You'll Need: Letter tiles or letter cards.

Directions: Give children letter tiles or letter cards. Have children use the letter cards to spell a word, for example, *mat*. You say a new word, such as /sat/. As soon as you say "Presto-chango," children find a letter that changes *mat* to *sat*, and substitute one letter for another. Award one point to the first child to make the change or to every child who makes the correct word on the first try. Talk about the sounds in words, the letters that represents the sounds, and how substituting letters and sounds changes one word into another.

Blending

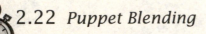 **2.22** *Puppet Blending*

Skill: Blending.

Children in a small group listen to a finger puppet say words sound by sound and then blend sounds together to pronounce the word.

Things You'll Need: A finger puppet.

Directions: Using a special finger puppet, explain that this special puppet talks only in sounds. For example, the puppet might say /m/-/a/-/n/. Ask the children to identify the word the puppet said, /man/. Continue pronouncing words sound by sound and asking the children to say the whole words.

2.23 *Arm Blending*

Skill: Blending.

Arm blending is a tactile, kinesthetic approach to blending that children can use on their own when reading all sorts of materials in all sorts of places.

Things You'll Need: Nothing special.

Directions: Have children imagine that they place sounds on their arms. For example, to blend /f/, /a/, /n/, children put their right hand on their left shoulder (reverse for left-handed children) and say /f/, their hand in the crook of their arm and say /a/, and their hand on their wrist and say /n/. Children blend by saying sounds as they slide their hands from shoulder to wrist. When finished, the children again pronounce the whole blended word.

Mentally "placing" sounds on their arms helps children remember the right sounds in the right order. The motion of the sweeping hand sliding down the arm is a kind of tactile analog for what the voice does when sliding sounds together during blending.

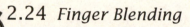

2.24 *Finger Blending*

Skill: Blending.

Children use their fingers to anchor sounds in memory and to guide blending. Finger blending requires more dexterity than arm blending and is appropriate for children who easily can touch together the fingers on one hand.

Things You'll Need: Nothing special.

Directions: For the purposes of illustration, let's suppose that children are blending /b/, /e/, /l/, /t/ into /belt/. Children touch their forefinger to their thumb while saying /b/, their middle finger to the thumb saying /e/, their ring finger to the thumb while saying /l/, and their little finger to the thumb saying /t/. To blend, children place each finger on their thumb as they pronounce sounds, thereby blending sounds into /belt/.

2.25 *Moving Sounds*

Skills: Blending; associating sounds with letters.

This is a kinesthetic, whole-body approach to blending. Standing at arm's length, children wearing letters move together while the teacher blends the sounds together.

Things You'll Need: Letters written on cards for each sound in a word.

Directions: Select words in which each letter represents a sound. Give each child a letter and ask the children to line up so that the word is spelled from left to right. Have children stand about an arm's length from one another. For purposes of illustration, let's suppose the children are going to blend /sun/. The child holding the first letter (the letter *s*) slowly moves toward the child holding the second letter (the letter *u*) as you stretch /sss/. When the child holding the *s* is shoulder to shoulder with the child holding the letter *u*, you stretch /uuu/, and the two children hold hands. When you stretch the /nnn/, the two holding hands move next to the child holding the *n* and all three hold hands. Have the whole group pronounce /sun/. Repeat a couple of times to give children practice. To get everyone in the small group involved, ask onlookers to arm blend /sun/ while others are demonstrating sounds on the move.

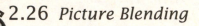

2.26 *Picture Blending*

Skill: Blending.

This activity uses pictures to develop the concept of blending.

Things You'll Need: Large pictures of familiar objects; scissors.

Directions: Show children a picture and say the picture name. Cut the picture into as many parts as you wish to use for blending. For example, you might cut a picture of a boat into three equal parts, one for /b/, one for /oa/ (long /o/), and one for /t/. Make blending easier by cutting the picture into two parts, one for /b/ and one for /oat/, so as to reduce the number of sounds (or sound groups) children blend. Point to each picture piece and say the sound it represents. For example, point to the first part of the boat picture while saying /b/, to the second part saying /oa/ (long /o/), and to the third when saying /t/. Explain that sounds go together to make a word just like pieces of a puzzle go together to make a picture. Demonstrate by moving the picture pieces together while you blend the sounds to pronounce /boat/. Then ask the children to push the picture pieces together while you blend. Give the children practice by asking them to blend the sounds along with you and by blending sounds on their own. Figure 2-14 is an example of picture blending for the word /boat/. Extend this activity to written language by writing the letters under each picture piece. After children blend, talk about the sounds in words and the letters the sounds represent.

2.27 *Sliding Sounds Together*

Skills: Blending; associating sounds with letters.

A picture of a slide depicts the blending process.

Things You'll Need: A picture of a slide sketched on the board, as illustrated in Figure 2-15.

Directions: Draw a large slide on the board. Write a word on the slide, distributing letters from the top to near the bottom. Demonstrate blending by pronouncing each sound as you slide your hand under each letter, adding sounds one after the other until you reach the bottom. Ask children to say the

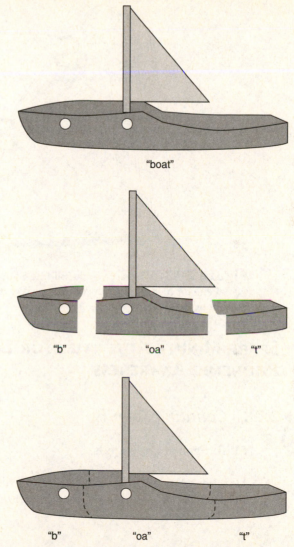

Figure 2-14   Picture blending gives children a concrete visual reference to illustrate the idea of blending sounds into words.

whole word and then write it at the bottom of the slide. Give children more responsibility by inviting a child to be the slider—the person who moves his or her hand down the slide. Ask the whole group to blend the sounds as the "slider" slides toward the bottom. The slider pronounces the whole word when the slider's hand reaches the bottom.

Figure 2-15 The slide in the Sliding Sounds Together activity gives learners a visual cue for blending. After sounds are blended, the whole word is written at the bottom of the slide.

SPARE MINUTE ACTIVITIES FOR DEVELOPING PHONEMIC AWARENESS

2.28 *Counting Sounds*

Skill: Segmenting sounds.

Directions: Say a word, such as /me/. Children count the number of sounds they hear. Children may say the number or hold up cards with the number of sounds they hear.

2.29 *Tapping Sounds*

Skill: Segmenting sounds.

Directions: Say a word and have children tap a pencil once for each sound heard. Begin with two-sound words (/ape/). After children can tap the phonemes in two-sound words, introduce three- (/cap/) and then four-sound (/soda/) words.

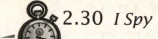

2.30 *I Spy*

Skills: Blending.

Directions: Spot something in your classroom. Pronounce the name, sound by sound. For example, you might say, "I spy a /b/-/oo/-/k/. What is it?" Children say the name.

2.31 *Lining Up*

Skills: Beginning, middle or ending sound awareness

Directions: Use this activity, or your own personal adaptation of it, as children line up for lunch, for recess, or to go home at the end of the school day. For example, you might say something like, "Line up if your name begins (or ends) with /m/." Ask children what letter their name begins (or ends) with. Or, "Line up if your name has an /s/ sound." Another version of this activity is to ask children to change their own names by substituting one beginning sound for another. In this case, /Anna/ might be /Danna/, /Dave/ might become /Mave/. Still another idea is to tell children that everyone is going on an imaginary trip to the grocery store. You will say the name of something to put in the cart but you will change the first sound. Children are to guess what you put in the cart. /Banana/, for instance, could be /manana/; /milk/ could be /tilk/. Once children understand how to play, have them take turns putting an imaginary item in the cart by saying its name with a different beginning sound.

2.32 *Thumbs Up*

Skill: Awareness of beginning, middle, or ending sounds.

Directions: Say a sound followed by a word. Children hold their thumb up if the sound comes at the beginning, they move their thumb sideways if the sound is in the middle, and they turn their thumb down if the sound comes at the end. For instance, if you say /boat/-/oa/ (long /o/), children move their thumb sideways to show that /o/ (long /o/) is the middle sound.

PHONEMIC AWARENESS ASSESSMENT TOOLS

You now have many rhyme and phonemic awareness activities from which to choose. Before using these activities, however, you need to know which children in your class would benefit from increasing their phonemic awareness. One way to find out about children's phonemic awareness is to observe children as they read and write every day in your classroom. If you wish to go beyond classroom observation, you will want to use an assessment tool designed specifically to determine phonemic awareness. In addition to the information below, you will find a searchable assessment database on the Southwest Educational Development Laboratory website (Wren & Litke, 2006).

Informal Assessment Tools

Informal assessment tools are user friendly. They take relatively little time to administer and score, and they allow some leeway for teacher judgment. The tools do not require special training to administer.

The Yopp-Singer Test of Phoneme Segmentation (Yopp, 1995) is intended for kindergartners and beginning first graders. The Yopp-Singer has 22 items that measure children's ability to segment two- and three-sound words into phonemes. Use this informal tool to identify children who need extra instruction above and beyond the instruction you typically include in your classroom reading program. Plan on spending about five to ten minutes assessing each child.

A recommended book for teaching phonemic awareness is *Phonemic Awareness in Young Children: A Classroom Curriculum* (Adams, Foorman, Lundberg, & Beeler, 1997). This spiral-bound book includes informal assessments for rhyme awareness, syllable counting, matching beginning sounds, and phoneme counting.

For preteaching and postteaching measures for rhyme awareness, blending, sound segmenting, and invented spelling, try the *Phonological Awareness Handbook for Kindergarten and Primary Teachers* (Ericson & Juliebo, 1998).

An initiative of the Public Broadcasting System (PBS), Reading Rockets (*http://www.readingrockets.org*) provides a printable tool that measures rhyme awareness, beginning sound awareness, blending, segmentation, and sound substitution, as well as information, activities, and guidance for teaching phonemic awareness in preschool and kindergarten.

Sponsored by the Los Angeles County Office of Education, Patti's Electronic Classroom (*http://teams.lacoe.edu/DOCUMENTATION/classrooms/patti/k-1/teacher/assessment/tools/tools.html*) offers user-friendly tools for assessing rhyme, beginning and ending sound awareness, and blending, as well as the Yopp-Singer Test of Phonemic Segmentation (described previously). This site includes teaching activities for rhyming words, syllable segmentation, beginning sound substitution, sound isolation, and phoneme segmentation.

Formal, Norm-referenced Assessment Tools

There are a number of formal assessment tools from which to choose. With a single exception, all require that you assess children individually.

The seventh edition of Dynamic Indicators of Basic Early Literacy Skills (DIBELS®) Next (*https://www.dibels.org/index.html*) is a recommended web-based tool. DIBELS® Next (Good & Kaminski, 2010) consists of short, individually administered reading tests to (a) assess children's performance in relation to expectations beginning, middle and end of the year (benchmarking), or (b) monitor the progress of children from kindergarten through sixth grade. DIBELS® Next is free and downloadable after you register on the website. Booklet copies of DIBELS® Next may be purchased from Sopris(*http://store.cambiumlearning.com/Program Page.aspx?parentId5074004444&functionID5009000008&site5sw*). School districts can also subscribe to receive downloadable printouts and reports. Extensive inservice training is available. A Spanish language version of the seventh edition is available for assessing early literacy skills, called IDEL® (Indicadores Dinámicos del Éxito en la Lectura). The Spanish version is not a translation of the English DIBELS® Next. IDAPEL® is an experimental version to measure developing literacy skills in the French language. IDEL® may be used for benchmarking and monitoring the progress of children learning to read in Spanish or who are in programs where Spanish and English literacy are both taught. Raw scores are expressed as the number of correct responses in one minute. DIBELS® Next consists of six measures, but not all are given at each grade: (1) First Sound Fluency (FSF) measures beginning sound awareness. The examiner pronounces words and the child says the first sound. The child receives two points for the number of beginning sounds identified in one minute, and one point for saying the beginning sound along with another vowel or consonant. FSF is given at the beginning and middle of kindergarten. (2) Letter Naming Fluency (LNF) consists of showing the child rows of letters and asking the child to say the name of each one in one minute. LNF is given at the beginning, middle and end of kindergarten, and in the beginning of first grade. (3) Phoneme Segmentation Fluency (PSF) assesses awareness of all the sounds in words. The examiner says a word and the child says each sound separately. The score is the total number of sounds segmented in one minute. PSF is given from the middle of kindergarten to the beginning of first grade. (4) Nonsense Word Fluency (NWF) asks the child to read nonsense short words that begin with a vowel and end with a consonant (CV) or begin with a consonant, followed by a vowel and finally a consonant (CVC). The child is given credit for the number of whole words the child reads and for letter-sounds the child identifies in one minute. NWF is administered from the middle of kindergarten to the beginning of second grade. (5) DIBELS® Oral Reading Fluency (DORF) is a series of passages the child reads for one minute followed by retelling. DORF is given from the middle of first grade to the end of sixth grade. Scores are computed for the number of words read correctly in one minute. Retelling is scored by giving credit for words in the retelling that are related to the passage. (6) Daze is a series of passages in which some words are replaced by boxes of three word choices. All passages are read silently for three minutes. The child selects the word that best matches the meaning. Daze is given to third- through sixth-graders.

The Lindamood Auditory Conceptualization Test (LAC-3) (Lindamood & Lindamood, 2004) has been used for nearly 30 years. The LAC-3, now in its third edition, is appropriate for kindergartners through adults, and requires that participants arrange colored squares to show the sequence of sounds in nonsense words. The results are reported in minimum levels of performance for success reading and spelling at or above grade level.

The Phonological Awareness Test 2 (Robertson & Salter, 2007) is intended for five- through nine-year-olds and includes rhyme awareness, sound segmentation, sound deletion, sound isolation, sound substitution, blending, phonics, decoding nonsense words, and invented spelling.

If you prefer a group paper-and-pencil test, consider the Test of Phonological Awareness–Second Edition: Plus (TOPA-2+) (Torgesen & Bryant, 2004). The kindergarten version assesses awareness of beginning sounds, while the first- and second-grade version assesses awareness of ending sounds. Percentile ranks and standard scores are reported. The authors suggest that the TOPA-2+ is most sensitive to kindergarten children's ability during the second half of the year.

The Test of Phonological Awareness in Spanish (TPAS) (Ricco, Imhoff, Hasbrouck, & Davis, 2004) assesses awareness of beginning and ending sounds, rhyme, and sound manipulation. In manipulating sounds, the child is asked to repeat a word, leaving out a syllable or sound.

The Test of Phonological Awareness Skills (TOPAS) (Newcomer & Barenbaum, 2003) is an individually administered test for children from five to ten years of age. The TOPAS measures rhyme awareness, segmenting, and blending. It takes up to 30 minutes to administer and is intended for assessing children who have trouble developing phonemic awareness.

The Comprehensive Test of Phonological Processes (CTOPP) (Wagner, Torgesen, & Rashotte, 1999) assesses phoneme awareness, blending, memory, and rapid naming. Scores include percentile ranks; age and grade equivalents; and quotients for phoneme awareness, memory, and rapid naming. With its dual focus on phonemic awareness and rapid naming, this instrument is appropriate for assessing readers who are learning disabled or struggling, and it may be part of test batteries used by the school psychologists in your school or district.

You will need to spend more time learning to administer and score formal tests because they have established protocols for administering, scoring, and interpreting test data. For these reasons, you may wish to begin with informal tools and then, if several children whom you teach are struggling and you need to know how these children compare to others of the same age or in the same grade, you may wish to use the formal, norm-referenced tests.

TEACHING PHONEMIC AWARENESS IN YOUR CLASSROOM READING PROGRAM

We teach phonemic awareness in kindergarten and first grade. By and large, phonemic awareness receives the most emphasis in kindergarten, somewhat less emphasis in first grade, and in every grade thereafter it is not directly taught to children making average progress. Although phonemic awareness is not directly taught after first grade, teachers in second grade and above do remind children to listen for sounds while spelling and blend sounds when decoding.

Kindergarten

Kindergarten classroom reading programs usually set aside about 30 minutes for teaching word work (also called word study), although some programs may devote more or less time to word work. Word work in kindergarten may include instruction in phonemic awareness, letter names, a sound for each letter, word families (explained in Chapter 4), phonics (discussed in Chapter 5), and high-frequency words. Kindergarten teachers integrate phonemic awareness and phonics throughout the day and across subjects and experiences, so kindergartners may well receive much more than 30 minutes of formal instruction.

The kindergarten classroom reading program develops phonological and phonemic awareness. In developing phonological awareness, teachers may focus on syllable and rhyme awareness. Teachers call children's attention to syllables by asking them to clap for the syllables in words, provided that children are not already aware of syllables. If children are not aware of rhyming sounds, teachers develop the children's ability to identify rhyming and nonrhyming words, identify the rhyming sounds in words, and think of rhyming words. Although kindergarten teachers develop phonological awareness, phonemic awareness is the heart of the program.

If you are a kindergarten teacher, you will teach phonemic awareness every day. You will teach phonemic awareness directly and explicitly, and in combination with phonics. You will teach kindergartners to identify and think of rhyming words, and to identify beginning and ending sounds. Depending on children's development as readers, you may also teach kindergartners to identify middle sounds, to blend, to add a sound to short words, and to delete a sound from short words. You will pair phonemic awareness with instruction in letter names or letter sounds. In either case, you will purposefully link a sound, such as /s/, with letters—a letter name (/ess/) or a letter sound (/sss/). After kindergartners know a few letter sounds, you will show children how to blend the sounds associated with them into words. Connecting phonemic awareness instruction with phonics helps to develop the ability to separate words into sounds and blend sounds into words, and gives the kindergartners whom you teach valuable practice using phonemic awareness while using letter-sound phonics.

First Grade

First-grade classroom reading programs typically set aside a little over 30 minutes for teaching word work, which consists of phonemic awareness, phonics, spelling, and high-frequency words. Generally speaking, first-grade teachers begin the year by teaching phonemic awareness every day in connection with phonics. After a few weeks, teachers might teach phonemic awareness three or four times a week, depending on children's development as readers. Toward the middle or slightly after mid-year, phonemic awareness is taught only twice a week to average readers, usually at the beginning of the week when letter-sound associations are introduced or reviewed. Phonemic awareness is always paired with phonics and frequently paired with spelling as well. However, you may decide to give certain children more intense, supplementary phonemic awareness instruction separate from, as well as along with, phonics and spelling. By the end of the first grade, the average readers in your classroom will be skilled at manipulating sounds and blending, and children will use these skills to read and spell new words. Direct, explicit phonemic awareness instruction is not necessary for average readers in the second grade.

Second Grade

Phonemic awareness is not directly taught to second graders making average or better progress because these children are already proficient at segmenting and blending. Phonemic awareness continues to develop, but is no longer a separate consideration for teaching, Phonemic awareness continues to improve as a consequence of phonics and spelling instruction, not direct instruction in phonemic awareness. Some teachers or some curriculum guides may suggest that phonemic awareness be directly taught in second grade and beyond, but this is not necessary for children who are sufficiently skilled to use phonics to sound out new words on their own, to learn new words through decoding, and to spell words they wish to write.

And so we see that phonemic awareness takes center stage in kindergarten and, perhaps, beginning in first grade, depending on the classroom reading program and children's development as readers. Emphasis on developing phonemic awareness begins to diminish by the middle of first grade. By the end of first grade, phonemic awareness is taught within phonics and spelling lessons. For average progress or better readers, direct, explicit phonemic awareness has disappeared from the classroom reading program no later than the beginning of second grade, not to resurface for the rest of the elementary school years.

TEACHING PHONEMIC AWARENESS TO ENGLISH LANGUAGE LEARNERS

English language learners and English-only children develop phonemic awareness in the same way (Chiappe, Siegel, & Wade-Woolley, 2002). Therefore, you will not need special materials to develop the phonemic awareness of the English language learners in your classroom. While you do not need special activities or materials, you may need to spend more time developing phonemic awareness. You may also need to devote extra time developing children's ability to speak English (MacDonald & Figueredo, 2010). Interestingly, phonemic awareness, once developed in one language, transfers to a second language when English learners have an average level of vocabulary knowledge in their first language (Atwill,

Blanchard, Christie, Gorin, & Garcia, 2010; Helman, 2009; Roberts, 2009). Consequently, you can develop phonemic awareness in either children's first language or second language, provided that you pay special attention to children's level of word knowledge. If possible, develop phonemic awareness in children's home language before English. English learners who have phonemic awareness in their home language develop phonemic awareness in English at a faster pace and with less instruction than children who do not have phonemic awareness in their home language. If, however, you have children in your classroom with less than average word knowledge in their home language, you will need to devote special attention and special effort to building their word knowledge along with developing phonemic awareness.

In general, children with better English pronunciation develop phonemic awareness with less effort than their English learner classmates whose English pronunciation is less well developed (Roberts, 2005). This said, you do not need to delay teaching phonemic awareness until English learners accurately pronounce English sounds. As it turns out, phonemic awareness activities are beneficial for helping English learners become sensitive to the sounds in English. Phonemic awareness activities help English learners pay attention to English sounds, and give children practice pronouncing English sounds. In paying attention to sounds, children learn which sounds belong to the English language. Practice pronouncing English sounds helps children pronounce the sounds. For instance, when you ask, "What sound do you hear at the beginning of /mouse/?" you help children notice /m/ and give children practice pronouncing /m/. When you ask, "Which words begin alike: /soap/-/sun/-/dog/?" you help children figure out which sounds belong in English (Lems, Miller, & Soro, 2010) and help children identify beginning sounds. Give children plenty of practice hearing and saying sounds, and accept approximations in pronunciation that are clear enough for you be certain as to the phonemes children are saying.

Some of the English language learners whom you teach may have difficulty developing phonemic awareness because certain sounds in their native languages are different from the sounds in English (Brice & Brice, 2009). In developing phonemic awareness, start with English sounds that are common to children's home languages and to English. When children are aware of sounds common to both languages, develop awareness of English sounds that are not common to the two languages. Select words for teaching phonemic awareness that are already in children's English speaking vocabulary. When selecting activities, take into account the word knowledge needed to be successful and children's knowledge of English words. Some activities call for more extensive word knowledge than others. For instance, in teaching rhyme and beginning sound awareness, children are likely to know more English words that begin with the same sound than English words that share the same rhyming sound. For example, while English learners may be able to think of words that begin with /t/, such as /toy/, /tall/, and /train/, they may have trouble thinking of many words that rhyme with /got/. To do this, children must draw on a large vocabulary of English words, such as *hot*, *dot*, *lot*, and *not*. Even with the support of easy-to-identify pictures, English learners may still need support from you to think of rhyming words (Roberts, 2009). Also consider children's English vocabulary when you ask them to sort. In order for beginning readers to successfully sort pictures based on a sound in the picture names, children need to recognize the pictures and know the English words for the pictures. If you are not sure whether English learners know picture names, show children the pictures beforehand and have children say the names. Then ask English learners to sort the pictures they can name; set pictures children cannot name aside until the names become part of their English speaking vocabulary.

The sounds in any language last a very short time. This short-lived quality can be especially challenging for English language learners. These children are learning English sounds and developing phonemic awareness at the same time. You will want to use letters—plastic letters, letter tiles, letter cards—to make the sounds more noticeable and to help children remember the sounds. Another way to help children focus on and remember sounds is to teach children a sound for each letter. To do this, combine the phonemic awareness activities in this chapter with some of the activities in Chapter 3. Also use pictures and manipulatives—objects children touch and move—to support learning. For instance, you might show children a picture of a boat and say, "This is a boat. What sound do you hear at the beginning of boat?" Or you might give children a plastic dog and a plastic man. Make sure children know the names of the items. Then use these manipulatives to help children develop phonemic awareness. For example, you might engage children in the following steps.

1. Hold up (or point to) the one that begins with /m/.
2. What is the first sound in /mmman/ (stretching the /mmm/)?
3. Hold up (or point to) the dog. Does dog begin with /d/ or /m/?
4. Find the man. Does man begin with /d/ or /m/?
5. What do you see in our room that begins with /d/? Point to (or go get) it.

Choose activities that include more than one modality—sight, sound, touch, taste, and movement. Drawing rhyming pictures (2.6), making collages (2.5) and mobiles (2.4), sorting (2.3), playing shower curtain toss (2.9), and putting thumbs up for puppet rhymes (2.12) are examples of activities that use more than one sense to develop rhyme and beginning sound awareness. Examples of multimodal activities to develop phonemic awareness include colorful sounds (2.15, 2.16), presto-chango (2.21), arm (2.23) and finger blending (2.24), sounds on the move (2.25), sliding sounds together (2.27), and tapping sounds (2.29). As you use these and other activities, carefully observe English learners, note when they are successful and when they struggle, and be ready to provide extra instruction and support. Give children many and varied opportunities to talk in your classroom. Plan classroom activities that help children develop their ability to speak and understand English (Herrera, Perez, & Escamilla, 2010; Pollard-Durodola & Simmons, 2009; Solari & Gerber, 2008). Have children work with an English-only partner and in small groups to give English learners more opportunities to use English. Model and explain phonemic awareness, create an accepting, positive atmosphere in your classroom, and bring children's cultures and home languages into your literacy program whenever you have the opportunity.

TEACHING PHONEMIC AWARENESS TO CHILDREN AT RISK

Children in kindergarten and first grade with low phonemic awareness are at risk of becoming struggling readers. Older children with low phonemic awareness or who were slow to develop phonemic awareness in the first few years of schooling typically know fewer words by sight and are poorer readers than children who developed phonemic awareness early and well. Your classroom reading program will be successful when you devote extra resources to developing the phonemic awareness of beginning readers who struggle with segmenting and blending. Low phonemic awareness and difficulty using phonics go hand in glove. Both are major sources of reading disabilities nationwide. Phonemic awareness helps children realize that the sounds they hear in spoken words are represented by the letters in written words. It stands to reason, then, that children with low phonemic awareness are also ineffective at using phonics to read and spell words. Poor phonics means that children learn fewer words than average or better readers, thereby resulting in a lower-than-expected reading vocabulary. However, when phonemic awareness improves, children are better at using phonics to read and learn new words (Elbro & Peterson, 2004; Hindson, Bryne, Fielding-Barnsley, Newman, Hine, & Shankweiler, 2005). This makes it possible for children to build the type of large reading vocabulary that supports fluency and comprehension.

Sandra (Figure 2-16), a first-grader, has difficulty segmenting and blending. She recognizes few words by sight, guesses new words, and relies on pictures to comprehend. Sandra's first-grade classmates already know how to segment short words into sounds and how to blend short words. These classmates understand the alphabetic principle, know how to read some words by sight, and are combining their phonemic awareness and growing phonics knowledge when reading and spelling. Like most first-graders, Sandra's classmates who are making average progress will benefit from more instruction in phonemic awareness. Unlike her classmates, Sandra brings to first grade the phonemic awareness we would expect of an early kindergartner. If Sandra is to be a good first-grade reader, she needs to develop better phonemic awareness, as well as learn about word families (Chapter 4) and phonics (Chapter 5). When we teach at-risk readers like Sandra, we follow best practice by asking children to segment and blend two-sound words first. When children are successful with two-sound words, we move on to three-sound and then four-or-more-sound words. We find that the following three segmenting teaching practices and three blending teaching practices help at-risk children whom we teach to develop phonemic awareness.

Segmenting

Develop awareness of beginning sounds first, followed by awareness of ending sounds and finally awareness of middle sounds. This is the order in which awareness of sounds typically develops in children. Make segmenting as easy as possible when teaching children at risk who struggle with phonemic awareness. There

Figure 2-16 Children who have low phonemic awareness do not understand the principle of alphabetic writing. They do not understand that letters represent the sound in spoken words.

is reason to believe it may be easier for some children to segment vowel-consonant (VC) combinations, such as /in/ = /i/-/n/, than to segment consonant-vowel (CV) combinations like /so/ = /s/-/o/ (Geudens, Dominiek, & Van den Broeck, 2004). Begin by teaching children to segment VC combinations that consist of two sounds (/an/, /up/, /if/). Activities like sound boxes (2.17, 2.18), colorful sounds (2.15, 12.16) and presto-chango (2.21) are good choices because these activities are multimodal and use tokens, tiles, or colored squares as visual reminders of the sounds. When children are successful segmenting VC words (/am/), teach them to segment two-sound CV words (/me/) followed by three-sound (/fin/) and four-sound (/desk/) words. (Review Chapter 5, Table 5-1, and Appendix A for explanations of vowels, consonants, and phonics letter-sound patterns.)

Blending

Begin with easy-to-blend consonant sounds. Some consonants are stretchy, others are not. The stretchy consonants are far easier to blend. All the vowels are stretchy. When we pronounce the stretchy sounds we continue our voices for

some time, as in /sss/. The nonstretchy consonants are another matter all together. In pronouncing these sounds our voices abruptly stop; we pronounce these sounds with a quick puff of air, as in /b/ and /j/. The nonstretchy consonants are problematic when they begin a word. Nonstretching consonants at the end of a word do not affect blending, so you need only consider the beginning consonant sounds. The stretchy, easy-to-blend consonant sounds are /f/, /l/, /m/, /n/, /r/, /s/, /y/, and /v/. In pronouncing the /r/, be sure to say /rrrr/, not /ruh/. The nonstretchy, difficult-to-blend consonants are /b/, /c/, /d/, /g/, /j/, /k/, /p/, /q(u)/, /t/, /w/, and /x/. (The c represents /s/ as in /city/ or /k/ as in /cute/.)

When we abruptly stop the airflow, we tend to add an extra vowel-like sound, an /uh/, as in /buh/ or /puh/. The extra /uh/ complicates blending because children have to drop the /uh/. It is easier to blend /m/ + /e/ into /me/ than to blend /buh/ + /e/ into /be/. Therefore, it is easier to blend a consonant with a vowel (/be/ + /t/ = /bet/) than to blend the beginning consonant with the onset rime (/buh/ + /et/ = /bet/) (Cassady & Smith, 2004). When children blend the combination of a nonstretchy consonant and a vowel (/be/) with a final consonant (/t/), they can stretch the middle vowel sound long enough to add in the final consonant sound (/be/ + /t/ = /bet/). When children are learning to blend, it is easier to teach them to blend the beginning consonant with the vowel (CV) and then the final consonant (/CV/ + /C/ = /CVC/). This sidesteps the problem of trying to blend a nonstretchy consonant and avoids the problematic extra /uh/ we add to the nonstretchy sounds.

We have success with arm blending (2.23) to help struggling blenders. We find that "placing" sounds on the arm gives children a physical referent that helps them remember sounds in the order in which they are to be blended, and guides children's voices as they blend. Finger blending (2.24), sliding sounds together (2.27), and sounds on the move (2.25) are also good choices. Show children how we can pronounce /h/ without the /uh/ if we are careful to say this breathy sound a bit louder than normal. Model and demonstrate saying the easy-to-blend consonant sounds to show children how to pronounce these sounds, and have children be mindful of pronouncing these sounds without the unnecessary /uh/ when sounding out and blending.

Teach phonemic awareness along with phonics, and use small group instruction (Koutsoftas, Harmon, & Gray, 2009). Use the activities in this chapter together with activities in Chapter 4 (word families) and Chapter 5 (phonics). Set aside time in the school day to teach phonemic awareness directly and spend more time teaching phonemic awareness to children at risk. Model phonemic awareness; have children practice under your guidance; and ask children to segment and blend in chorus. Introduce the easier tasks before the harder tasks. Create many opportunities for children to use phonemic awareness when reading and spelling new words. When children use phonemic awareness in reading and spelling, they become better decoders and spellers and, in the process, hone their segmenting and blending skills.

e-Resources for Teaching Phonemic Awareness

Software

Earobics® (*http://www.earobics.com*):

Earobics® is software to give children practice identifying rhyme and sounds in words, and blending. Earobics® is multileveled. It adjusts instruction to children's needs, and is available in languages other than English. Earobics® Foundation is for preschoolers, kindergartners, and first-graders. Earobics® Connections is aimed at readers who struggle in the second and third grades and above. What Works Clearinghouse (WWC), an initiative of the U.S. Department of Education's Institute of Education Sciences, found that Earobics® had positive effects on learning. Look for the WWC reviews at *http://ies.ed.gov/ncee/wwc/reports/beginning_reading/earobics/* for a review of this software.

Early Learning® (*http://www.lexialearning.com/*):

Early Learning® is software to reinforce and develop rhyme awareness, sound awareness, and blending. Macaruso and Walker (2008) found this program to be effective when implemented as part of a classroom literacy program. These researchers caution that consistent implementation and use, approximately 64 sessions per child, were important for obtaining the significant gains.

Websites with Games or Lessons for Computers and Interactive Whiteboards (IWB)

Internet4Classrooms (*http://www.internet4classrooms.com/skill_builders/rhyming_words_language_arts_kindergarten_k_grade.htm*):

This website, created by two teachers who wanted to provide access to free internet-based resources, offers a searchable collection of links to activities ranging from PreK–12. The link above lists sites that focus on developing rhyme awareness.

SMART Exchange™ (*http://exchange.smarttech.com/#tab=0 and http://exchange.smarttech.com/details.html?id=x5a357595a45145a2ab6638b2b24dd55d*):

This site has IWB phonemic awareness activities. The second address links directly to Sound Boxes, an activity where children move tokens into a sound box square for each sound heard in short a words that are from three to four sounds long. The last three pages ask children to complete sentences by filling in a missing word. Consider pairing this activity with the sound box activities (2.17, 2.18). Because this IWB sound box activity also focuses on printed words, consider using this activity with children who already have some knowledge of the sounds letters represent. There are a number of IWB lessons for developing rhyme awareness. For example, in Nursery Rhyme Endings, children sing along with nursery rhymes and fill in blanks for matching words. Consider pairing this activity with activities 2.1 (Predict and Match Rhyming Words in Poetry) and 2.11 (Rhyme Frames). Other rhyming lessons include those involving nursery rhymes, rhyming words, and picture rhymes.

Literactive (*http://www.literactive.com/Home/index.asp*):

There is a variety of interactive games on this website. Look in Level 1 for games like Washing Line Rhyme which calls for selecting a picture that rhymes with a word. Other examples of games that call for identifying beginning sounds include (1) Picture Plates, (2) Easel, and (3) Nine Squares. Examples of games in Level 2 are (1) Swings, (2) Slide, and (3) See-saw Speller. Swings calls for identifying ending sounds. Slides and See-saw Speller give children practice associating letters with ending sounds. In Hungry Hippos, a Level 3 game, children identify beginning sounds. Drum Machine, found in Level 4, asks children to count syllables by beating a drum for each syllable words of one to three syllables. You will need to register to access games and other resources.

Professor Garfield (*http://www.professorgarfield.com/pgf_home.html*):

Click on Transport to Reading and then click on Orson's Farm. Orson's Farm includes six games to practice and reinforce phonemic awareness skills: (1) Meet the Gang Rhyming Words, (2) Pumpkin Patch Phoneme Manipulation, (3) Lanolin's Greenhouse Phoneme Manipulation, (4) The Hay Loft Phoneme Blending, (5) Orson's Waller Blending, and (6) The Chicken Coop Oddity Task.

PBS Kids™: (*http://pbskids.org/lions/games/blending.html and http://pbskids.org/games/index.html*):

This website features Sesame Street: Elmo Rhymes, an IWB-ready game for identifying rhyming words, that is suitable for preschoolers and beginning kindergartners. Between the Lions games include Blending Bowl demonstrates blending beginning sounds and rimes into words (the vowel and any letter/sounds thereafter); (2) Lionel's Talking Gizmo, which calls for listening for words in sentences; and (3) Word Morph How to Be a Good Dog. which calls for substituting onsets and rimes. Sesame Street: The Nick of Rhyme gives children practice identifying rhyming words.

ReadWriteThink (*http://www.readwritethink.org*):

Sponsored by the International Reading Association and the National Council of Teachers of English, this site offers a variety of lesson plans for developing phonemic awareness. Some lesson plans feature printable downloads; others provide interactive games.

Scholastic® (*http://teacher.scholastic.com*):

This site includes lesson plans for phonemic awareness and tips for using IWBs. Look for Reggie the Rhyming Rhino: Help Reggie Find a Rhyme, an interactive picture-matching rhyming game, under Building Language for Literacy. Follow the link to the lesson plan for this game. The player can choose from 12 different locations for rhyming words, such as rhyming words found on a farm or in a firehouse. While most words sound alike (jam-ham), some word pairs sound alike but look different, as pear-chair, bowl-roll. All picture names are pronounced for the player. However, you might want to point out that the child is to listen for picture names that *sound* alike, and that not all words that sound alike also look alike. The Clifford the Big Red Dog© page has a Concentration game that asks children to identify words that have the same middle sound and Sound Match where children identify pictures with the same beginning sounds.

Starfall™ (*www.starfall.com*):

The tongue twisters activity is a good introduction to alliteration. Click on option 3—Its Fun to Read—on the main index to bring up a menu with the tongue twister activity. The tongue twisters and other activities are free. Some resources are available for purchase through the Starfall online store.

Classroom Activities

The Reading Treehouse (*www.aability.com*):

Activities are grouped into Games to Go, which can be played anywhere, and Block Challenges for more advanced children that require colored tiles and a flat surface and need to be played at a table or on the floor.

Reading Rockets® (*http://www.readingrockets.org*):

Look for a list of free blending and segmenting games, onset/rimes games, rhyming games, and syllable games under Classroom Strategies. Games include rationale, research in support of the games, books to coordinate with the games, and advice for differentiating instruction. Resources are also available for purchase through the online store.

Printable Materials

DLTK Growing Together (*http://www.dltk-teach.com/*) and (*http://www.dltk-kids .com/type/printable_bookmarks.htm*):

This site has a variety of printables, such as printables for bulletin boards, mini-books, and nursery rhymes to name a few. Create customized, printable bookmarks by selecting art and then typing your own bookmark title. Add words under the title by inserting breaks between words (explained in the pull-down Tips for formatting your title).

Patti's Electronic Classroom; Teams Educational Resources (*http://teams.lacoe.edu/ documentation/classrooms/patti/k-1/activities/phonemic.html*):

Sponsored by the Los Angeles County Office of Education as part of their Teams Educational Resources, this site provides rhyme awareness, syllable segmentation, beginning sound substitution, sound isolation, and segmentation activities.

Reading A-Z (*http://www.readinga-z.com/book/phonological-awareness-lessons.php*):

This web page provides links to numerous lessons to teach rhyme awareness, sound awareness, and blending. A paid membership is required to access the resources on this site.

Carl's Corner (*http://www.carlscorner.us.com/Syllables.htm*):

This page has several printable worksheets for counting syllables. Most printables call clapping for syllables in picture names and writing the number of syllables.

REFERENCES

Adams, M. J., Foorman, B. R., Lundberg, I., & Beeler, T. (1997). *Phonemic awareness in young children: A classroom curriculum.* Baltimore: Brooks Publishing.

Anthony, J. L., & Lonigan, C. J. (2004). The nature of phonological awareness: Converging evidence from four studies of preschool and early grade school children. *Journal of Educational Psychology, 96*, 43–55.

Atwill, K., Blanchard, J., Christie, J., Gorin, J. S., & Garcia, H. S. (2010). English language learners: Implications for limited vocabulary for cross-language transfer of phonemic awareness with kindergartners. *Journal of Hispanic Higher Education, 9*(2), 104–129.

Brice, R. G., & Brice, A. E. (2009). Investigation of phonemic awareness and phonics skills in Spanish-English bilingual and English-speaking kindergarten students. *Communication Disorders Quarterly, 30*(4), 208–225.

Caravolas, M., Hulme, C., & Snowling, M. J. (2001). The foundations of spelling ability: Evidence from a 3-year longitudinal study. *Journal of Memory and Language, 45*, 751–774.

Carroll, J. M., & Snowling, M. J. (2004). Language and phonological skills in children at risk of reading difficulties. *Journal of Child Psychology and Psychiatry, 45*, 631–640.

Cassady, J. C., & Smith, L. L. (2004). Acquisition of blending skills: Comparisons among body-coda, onset-rime, and phoneme blending tasks. *Reading Psychology, 25*(4), 261–272.

Castles, A., Coltheart, M., Wilson, K., Valpied, J., & Wedgewood, J. (2009). The genesis of reading ability: What helps children learn letter-sound correspondences? *Journal of Exceptional Child Psychology, 104*(1),68–88.

Chiappe, P., Siegel, L.S., & Wade-Woolley, L. (2002). Linguistic diversity and the development of reading skills: A longitudinal study. *Scientific Studies of Reading, 6*, 369–400.

Christensen, C. A., & Bowey, J. A. (2005). The efficacy of orthographic rime, grapheme-phoneme correspondence, and implicit phonics approaches to teaching decoding skills. *Scientific Studies of Reading, 9*, 327–340.

Earobics: Step 1—Sound Foundations for Reading & Spelling. (2000). Orlando, FL: Houghton Mifflin Harcourt Learning Technologies. Retrieved from http://www.earobics.com

Earobics: Step 2—Earobics Connections. (1995). Orlando, FL: Houghton Mifflin Harcourt Learning Technologies. Retrieved from http://www.earobics.com

Ehri, L. C., Nunes, S. R., Willows, D. M., Schuster, B. V., Yaghoub-Zadeh, Z., & Shanahan, T. (2001). Phonemic awareness instruction helps children learn to read: Evidence from the National Reading Panel's meta-analysis. *Reading Research Quarterly, 36*, 250–287.

Elbro, C., & Petersen, D. K. (2004). Long-term effects of phoneme awareness and letter sound training: An intervention study with children at risk for dyslexia. *Journal of Educational Psychology, 96*(4), 660–670.

Ericson, L., & Juliebo, M. F. (1998). *The phonological awareness handbook for kindergarten and primary teachers.* Newark, DE: International Reading Association.

Foorman, B. R., Jenkins, L., & Francis, D. J. (1993). Links among segmenting, spelling, and reading words in first and second grades. *Reading and Writing: An Interdisciplinary Journal, 5*, 1–15.

Frost, S. J., Landi, N., Menci, W. E., Sandak, R., Fulbright, R. K., Tejada, E. T., Jacobsen, L., Grigorenko, E. L., Constable, R. T., & Pugh, K. R. (2009). Phonological awareness predicts activation patterns for print and speech. *Annuals of Dyslexia, 59*, 78–97.

Geudens, A., Dominiek, S., & Van den Broeck, W. (2004). Segmenting two-phoneme syllables: Developmental differences in relation with early reading skills. *Brain and Language, 90*, 338–352.

Good, R. H., & Kaminski, R. A., (2010). DIBELS® Next. Retrieved from https://www.dibels.org/index.html

Helman, L. (2009). Emergent literacy: Planting the seeds for accomplished reading and writing. In L. Helman (Ed.), *Literacy development with English learners: Research-based instruction in grades K–6* (pp. 117–137). New York: Guilford Press.

Herrera, S. G., Perez, D. R., & Escamilla, K. (2010). *Teaching reading to English language learners: Differentiated literacies.* Boston: Allyn Bacon.

Hindson, B., Bryne, B., Fielding-Barnsley, R., Newman, C., Hine, D. W., & Shankweiler, D. (2005). Assessment and early instruction of preschool children at risk for reading disability. *Journal of Educational Psychology, 97*, 687–704.

Justice, L. M., Invernizzi, M., Geller, K., Sullivan, A. K., & Welsch, J. (2005). Descriptive-developmental performance of at-risk preschoolers on early literacy tasks. *Reading Psychology, 26*, 1–25.

Koutsoftas, A. D., Harmon, M. T., & Gray, S. (2009). The effect of tier 2 intervention for phonemic awareness in a response-to-intervention model in low-income preschool classrooms. *Language, Speech, and Hearing Services in Schools, 40*(2), 116–130.

Layton, L., Deeny, K., Tall, G., & Upton, G. (1996). Researching and promoting phonological awareness in the nursery class. *Journal of Research in Reading, 19*, 1–13.

Lems, K., Miller, L. D., & Soro, T. M. (2010). *Teaching reading to English language learners: Insights from linguistics.* New York: Guilford Press.

LeSieg, T. (1961). *Ten apples up on top.* New York: Random House.

Lindamood, C. H., & Lindamood, P. C. (2004). *Lindamood auditory conceptualization test* (Rev. ed.). Austin, TX: Pro-Ed.

Lonigan, C. J. (2006). Conceptualizing phonological processing skills in prereaders. In D. K. Dickinson & S. B. Neuman (Eds.), *Handbook of early literacy research, volume 2* (pp. 77–89). New York: Guilford Press.

Macaruso, P., & Walker, A. (2008). The efficacy of computer-assisted instruction for advancing literacy skills in kindergarten children. *Reading Psychology, 29*, 266–287.

MacDonald, C., & Figueredo, L. (2010). Closing the gap early: Implementing a literacy intervention for at-risk kindergartners in urban schools. *The Reading Teacher, 63*(5), 404–419.

Manis, F. R., Lindsey, K. A., & Bailey, C. E. (2004). Development of reading in grades K–2 Spanish-speaking English-language learners. *Learning Disabilities Research & Practice*, *19*, 214–224.

Martins, M. A., & Silva, C. (2006). The impact of invented spelling on phonemic awareness. *Learning and Instruction*, *16*, 41–56.

Muter, V., Hulme, C., Snowling, M. J., & Stevenson, J. (2004). Phonemes, rimes, vocabulary, and grammatical skills as foundations of early reading development: Evidence from a longitudinal study. *Developmental Psychology*, *40*, 665–681.

National Reading Panel. (2000). *Teaching children to read: An evidence-based assessment of the scientific research literature on reading and its implications for reading instruction: Reports of the subgroups* (NIH Publication No. 00-4754). Washington, DC: U.S. Government Printing Office.

Newcomer, P., & Barenbaum, E. (2003). *Test of phonological awareness skills (TOPAS)*. Austin, TX: PRO-ED.

Nicholson, T. (1997). Closing the gap on reading failure: Social background, phonemic awareness, and learning to read. In B. Blachman (Ed.), *Foundations of reading acquisition and dyslexia: Implications for early intervention* (pp. 381–407). Mahwah, NJ: Erlbaum.

Patti's Electronic Classroom (Klein, A.). Sponsored by the Los Angeles County Office of Education. Retrieved from http://teams.lacoe.edu/DOCUMENTATION/classrooms/patti/k-1/teacher/assessment/tools/tools.html

Pollard-Durodola, S. D., & Simmons, D. C. (2009). The role of explicit instruction and instructional design in promoting phonemic awareness development and transfer from Spanish to English. *Reading & Writing Quarterly*, *25*, 139–161.

Pufpaff, L. A. (2009). A developmental continuum of phonological sensitivity skills. *Psychology in the Schools*, *46*(7), 679–691.

Reading Rockets. A website sponsored by the Corporation for Public Broadcasting. Retrieved from http://www.readingrockets.org/

Ricco, C. A., Imhoff, B., Hasbrouck, J. E., & Davis, G. N. (2004). *Test of phonological awareness in Spanish (TRAS)*. Austin, TX: Pro-Ed.

Roberts, T. A. (2005). Articulation accuracy and vocabulary size contributions to phonemic awareness and word reading in English language learners. *Journal of Educational Psychology*, *97*(4), 601–616.

Roberts, T. A. (2009). *No limits to literacy for preschool English learners*. Thousand Oaks, CA: Corwin.

Robertson, C., & Salter, W. (2007). *The phonological awareness test 2*. East Moline, IL: LinguiSystems.

Schatschneider, C., Fletcher, J. M., Francis, D. J., Carlson, C. D., & Foorman, B. R. (2004). Kindergarten prediction of reading skills: A longitudinal comparative analysis. *Journal of Educational Psychology*, *96*(2), 265–282.

Solari, E. J., & Gerber, M. M. (2008). Early comprehension instruction for Spanish-speaking English language learners: Teaching text-level reading skills while maintaining effects on word-level skills. *Learning Disabilities Research and Practice*, *23*(4), 155–168.

Spira, G. E., Bracken, S. S., & Fischel, J. E. (2005). Predicting improvement after first-grade reading difficulties: The effects of oral language, emergent literacy, and behavior skills. *Developmental Psychology*, *41*, 225–234.

Strattman, K., & Hodson, B. W. (2005). Variables that influence decoding and spelling in beginning readers. *Child Language Teaching and Therapy, 21*, 165–190.

Torgesen, J. K., & Bryant, B. R. (2004). *Test of phonological awareness-second edition: PLUS (TOPA-2+). Austin, TX: Pro-Ed.*

Ukrainetz, T. A., Ross, C. L., & Harm, H. M. (2009). An investigation of treatment scheduling for phonemic awareness with kindergartners who are at risk for reading difficulties. *Language, Speech, and Hearing Services in Schools, 40*, 86–100.

Wagner, R., Torgesen, J. K., & Rashotte, C. (1999). *Comprehensive test of phonological processes.* Austin, TX: Pro-Ed.

Wren, S., & Litke, B. (2006). Reading assessment database for Grades PreK-3. SEDL. Retrieved from http://www.sedl.org/pubs/catalog/items/read02.html

Yopp, H. K. (1995). A test for assessing phonemic awareness in young children. *The Reading Teacher, 49*, 20–29.

CHAPTER 3

Early Word Identification in Preschool and Early Kindergarten

The Strategies of Using Logos, Pictures, Word Shape, and Partial Letter-Sound Associations to Read New Words

This chapter describes four word identification strategies that children use as they begin their journey toward literacy. You will learn how preschool children recognize words by cues in their environment, cues in pictures, or in unusual features of words such as length, shape, or memorable letters. You will find out how children in kindergarten use one- or two-letter names or letter sounds to read new words. You will also learn how these strategies correspond to the development of word learning and conventional spelling and about best practices for teaching children who use one- or two-letter sounds to support word identification. Also

included in this chapter are sections on teaching letter names and a

sound for each letter to English language learners and children at

risk as well as a list of helpful e-resources.

KEY IDEAS

▶ The earliest word identification strategies develop long before children go to school and long before they actually learn to read.

▶ Before children read words, they may associate meaning with cues in the environment, such as logos and product packages.

▶ Early in their journey toward literacy, children may infer meaning from illustrations, often "reading" by saying words that describe the pictures.

▶ As children begin to notice words, they may look for cues in a word's unique shape and length, or an eye-catching letter.

▶ When children first pay attention to the letters and sounds in words, they associate a letter sound (or a letter name) with a whole written word.

KEY VOCABULARY

Configuration cues

Emergent spellers

Environmental print cues

Letter name-alphabetic spellers

Partial alphabetic cues

Partial alphabetic word learners

Picture cues

Prealphabetic word learners

The word identification strategies explained in this chapter develop before children go to school, when children are in kindergarten, or, at the very latest, in early first grade. As children become interested in print, they realize that print represents meaning, they recognize words in the context of familiar everyday surroundings, or they pretend to read by using pictures to cue memory or tell a story. Cues in the environment and pictures do not call for knowing anything whatsoever about the alphabetic principle or letter-sound relationships. When kindergartners do begin to consider letter- and sound-based cues, they typically focus on only one or two of the letters in unfamiliar words. Although these early strategies are not reliable ways to identity or spell unfamiliar words, preschoolers and kindergartners use them, and so it is important for you to understand how they work. With insight into these early strategies, you are in a position to guide children as they move toward using more efficient and effective strategies for reading and spelling new words.

ENVIRONMENTAL PRINT: ASSOCIATING MEANING WITH PRINT IN EVERYDAY SURROUNDINGS IN PRESCHOOL

Children of preschool age often associate meaning with the signs, package labels, and logos in their everyday surroundings. This strategy is one of the first steps toward literacy. Collectively, signs, package labels, and logos are called **environmental print.** The use of cues in environmental print is one of several strategies that five-year-old John uses to make sense of print. When reading, John associates meaning with familiar signs and logos and, when writing, copies the words *California, October, no, stop,* and *soap* from the wall chart in his kindergarten classroom, as shown in Figure 3-1.

Associating meaning with familiar objects and signs in the environment gives preschoolers like John a measure of control over their lives. The preschooler who recognizes the box of Raisin Yum Yum cereal on the grocery shelf might be able to talk her mother into buying that particular breakfast food. Though she quickly recognizes the cereal box, this same child cannot read the word *raisin* on the package of raisins her mother buys for midday snacks. While this preschooler might not be able to tell what the writing *Raisin Yum Yum* actually "says," in all likelihood she can give an approximation that is both meaningful and contextually acceptable. Children give feasible approximations because they connect meaning with the everyday settings in which the print appears, not with the specific words in print.

Figure 3-1   John enjoys copying the words he sees displayed in his kindergarten classroom.

PICTURE CUES: INFERRING MEANING FROM PICTURES IN PRESCHOOL AND EARLY KINDERGARTEN

Like the print in children's everyday surroundings, the pictures in storybooks are an avenue to meaning that does not call for phonemic awareness, understanding the alphabetic principle, recognizing specific words, remembering letters, or knowing letter-sound associations. Long before children read storybooks on their own and well before they go to school, they read their favorite books by inferring and predicting meaning from pictures. For instance, four-year-old Thomas used the strategy of inferring meaning from **picture cues** when he proudly held up a poster of a race car his father brought home from a business trip to Detroit and announced that the poster said: "Gentlemen, start your engines." The fact that the words on the poster bore not the slightest resemblance to the message Thomas read was of little consequence to him; he focused entirely on the rich picture context.

Children who have been read to at home or in childcare programs expect pictures to signal meaning. Turning the pages and cueing on pictures, these children say words that could have been written by the author but are not necessarily on the page. Children who use picture cues to "read" their favorite books may also use pictures when writing their own stories. Kesha, a beginning kindergartner, drew the picture story in Figure 3-2 after hearing her teacher read and reread

Figure 3-2   As children like Kesha begin to pay attention to written language, they may draw pictures to represent the events in familiar storybooks, and they may include in the stories they write pictures, letters, and words copied from their classroom.

Arthur's Halloween (Brown, 1982). Notice how Kesha faithfully renders the big scary house that is so prominent in *Arthur's Halloween*, including a smiley face on the door to show the house is not frightening. Kesha clearly understands the picture–meaning connection. When Kesha read her picture story to her teacher, she described the house that she drew, and she described the events that she remembered from *Arthur's Halloween*. From Kesha's writing, we can infer that she is searching for a medium through which she might effectively communicate with her audience, as yet unaware of the way that our alphabetic writing system represents speech. Eventually Kesha and other beginning readers will turn their attention to print. However, Kesha will not abandon attention to pictures. Rather, she will continue to use picture cues along with her knowledge of print, the reading context, and her background experiences to understand text.

CONFIGURATION CUES: USING WORD LENGTH, WORD SHAPE, AND EYE-CATCHING LETTERS TO READ AND SPELL NEW WORDS IN PRESCHOOL AND EARLY KINDERGARTEN

In their search for ways to bring meaning to print, children look beyond cues in the environment and in pictures. In so doing, they move closer to print, discovering and using the **configuration cues** in words. Configuration consists of a word's shape, its length, or an eye-catching letter. These cues are incidental to alphabetic writing inasmuch as they do not call for connecting letters and sounds. This said, these cues do require that children actively think about written words. Even though these cues essentially bypass the alphabetic principle, children who use them must be able to identify some letters and find words in print. To find words in print, children must understand the purpose of the white spaces between words and, if words are written in sentences, the left-to-right and top-to-bottom orientation of print on the page. Configuration cues consist of word length, word shape, or memorable letters. You can expect children to use word configuration cues before they use letter-sound cues.

Jesse puts one letter or letter after another across the page, as seen in Figure 3-3. He writes his name and copies the words *yellow* and *me*, as well as the letters of the alphabet, from the print in his kindergarten classroom. He also includes numbers and a picture. What Jesse does not do is link the letters in written words to the sounds in spoken words. However, his careful copying suggests that he attends to some of the words he sees in school and is aware of the importance of the words in his classroom. As Jesse carefully notices the words that surround him in his kindergarten classroom, he looks at word configuration and uses these cues to help him identify important words.

Figure 3-3 Jesse knows that words and letters are important, and he explores written language by copying the many different types of print that he sees in his classroom.

Word Shape

A word's shape is formed by letters that may be on, above, or below the line. The word *hat*, for example, has two ascending letters separated by a letter that stays on the line, so its shape looks like:

cat looks like:

pat looks like:

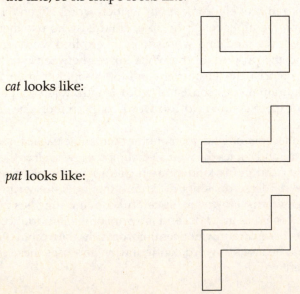

Word shape is frequently unreliable because so many words have virtually identical patterns of upward and downward sloping letters (*pat*, *got*, *jet*). Children who use shape to recognize the word *hat* are bound to be confused when they try to read other words that have the same shape, such as *bat*, *fit*, and *had*.

Word Length

Though *hand* and *homework* are the same shape, a quick glance at word length tells us that *hand* and *homework* are different. It is not surprising, then, that sometimes children cue on word length alone. Length seems to be an important cue only when words differ considerably, such as the difference in length between *hand* and *homework*, or *elf* and *elephant*. Even without paying attention to letter and sound cues, children are far less likely to confuse *eat* with *elephant* than they are to confuse *eat* with *elf*.

Letter Shape

In using letter shape, children pay attention to the circles, arcs, humps, and lines of the letters in words. Children might, for instance, remember the word *nail* because the letter *n* has one "hump"; *took* because the two circles look like eyes. Only paying attention to letter shape can create all sorts of confusion. Take *g* and *j* as an example. Both *g* and *j* have "tails," so children may not think of *g* and *j* as different letters. Children who recognize *game* because it has a "tail" may misread *juice* because the letter *j* has a "tail," too.

All things considered, the configuration cues that are so helpful in one reading condition are frequently not at all helpful in another condition. As long as there is an unusual characteristic like a distinctive shape, length, or letter, children may easily identify words. However, because configuration cues have no predictable, logical association with the sounds that letters represent, these cues are very fragile and often lead to misidentifications as well as confusion and frustration.

PREALPHABETIC WORD LEARNERS AND EMERGENT SPELLERS IN PRESCHOOL AND EARLY KINDERGARTEN

The children in your classroom who use environmental, picture, and configuration cues to identify new words are in **prealphabetic word learners** (Ehri, 2005). The prealphabetic stage of word learning begins in preschool and usually ends early to mid-kindergarten. Children in this stage cannot name the letters of the alphabet or, at best, can name only a few letters. They do not know the letter sounds of phonics and lack phonemic awareness. Not surprisingly, these children seldom read words when the words are outside familiar environmental contexts, when there are no picture cues, or when words do not have a distinct configuration. Also, not surprisingly, these children cannot read their own stories a day or so after writing them because children's writing does not systematically represent speech.

Prealphabetic word learners are also in the *emergent spelling* stage (Henderson, 1990; Bear & Smith, 2009; Bear, Invernizzi, Templeton, & Johnston, 2007). Prealphabetic learners and **emergent spellers** do not understand the alphabetic principle and lack letter knowledge. At the beginning of the emergent spelling stage, children may scribble when writing. As children have more experiences with print, their writing is characterized by pictures, letter like forms (mock letters), and numbers. Still later, children may use a letter to represent the most prominent sound in a word, but their writing does not contain enough sound-symbol correspondences for the teacher to read children's writing. As a prealphabetic word learner and emergent speller, Warren strings letters together, as shown in Figure 3-4, unaware of speech and print connections. Warren knows that writing goes in a left-to-right direction across the page. While he uses several letterlike shapes in his story, Warren has not yet developed the understanding that white spaces separate words, words contain specific letters, and one written word represents one spoken word.

From a word identification perspective, it is important for prealphabetic word learners and emergent spellers to develop an understanding of (1) the alphabetic principle, (2) the use of white spaces to separate words, and (3) the concept that one written word represents one spoken word. It also is important for

Figure 3-4   As a prealphabetic word learner and emergent speller, Warren combines mock letters with real letters, and strings them across the page, unaware of speech and print connections.

children to learn letter names and a sound for each letter. In learning the letter names, children discover how one letter differs from another. Learning letter names also can help children learn letter sounds, provided that the name of the letter (such as *s*) contains part of the letter sound (/ess/). Generally speaking, children tend to learn the names of common letters more easily than the less common letters. Additionally, some children will mistakenly call a letter they are learning by the name of a common letter they know. When teaching the letters of the alphabet, give children plenty of experiences with letters and letter names, especially letters that look similar or have names that sound somewhat similar.

Partial Alphabetic Word Learners and Early Letter Name-Alphabetic Spellers in Kindergarten and Early First Grade

When children begin to use letter-sound cues, they typically take a rather simplistic route to word learning (Ehri, 2005; Ehri & McCormick, 1998). **Partial alphabetic word learners** read and learn new words by connecting a single letter-sound cue (maybe two) or a letter name with the pronunciation of a whole word. For example, if a child sees the word *honey* in a storybook and knows the sound associated with the letter *h*, the child may then identify *honey* by associating the letter *h* with the /h/ sound heard in /honey/. A letter name may be used as a cue if the name includes a portion of the sound heard in the word. For example, the name of the letter *s*, /ess/, includes a portion of the sound the letter represents and, therefore, children may associate the name (/ess/) with the word *sandwich*. Generally speaking, the use of **partial alphabetic cues** emerges in kindergarten and, for some children, in early first grade.

At a *minimum*, children are aware of at least one sound in the spoken words, though their phonemic awareness may well be greater than this. You can expect these children to be aware of the beginning sounds in words and to separate the beginning sound from the rhyming sounds (the vowel and remaining consonants). For instance, children can separate the /s/ from the /at/ in /sat/, and the /m/ from /mat/, as explained in Chapter 2. Children also know the features that distinguish one letter from another and therefore identify individual letters consistently and reliably. They know that written words consist of letters, and they also know or are learning letter names and a sound for each letter. It stands to reason, then, children in the early part of the **letter name-alphabetic spelling** stage use their letter knowledge to spell new words. For example, children may hear /n/ in /nut/, associate the /n/ with the name of the letter *n* (/enn/), and write an *n* to spell *nut*. As children move through the letter name-alphabetic spelling stage, they develop the ability to segment short words into sounds; they learn to associate a letter with each sound they hear in words; and they learn to spell words that include the short-vowel pattern. (See Chapter 5 for an explanation of short vowels.)

Lexi, a partial alphabetic word learner, writes from left to right, uses white spaces to separate words, fluently recognizes a few often-used words, and can read and write her own name, as we can see in Figure 3-5. She approaches word identification systematically. In reading new words, Lexi uses letter names when the names give sound clues, or she uses one, possibly two, letter-sound cues. Lexi might identify *father* because she hears the /eff/ in the name of the letter *f*; she might identify *monkey* because she knows the sound associated with the letter *m*. However, because Lexi does not pay attention to all the letters in words, she is likely to confuse words that begin and/or end alike. You will notice that children in the partial alphabetic stage like Lexi misidentify and confuse words like *father*, *family*, and *funny* because these words all begin alike and, additionally, *family* and *funny* end alike.

Just as Lexi uses partial alphabetic cues when reading, so too does she use limited alphabetic cues when spelling. From her writing in Figure 3-5 we can see that Lexi uses letters to represent some, but not all, of the important sounds in words. She uses consonant letters such as *w* to represent *want* and *swim*, and *p* to represent *park*. Lexi conventionally spells words in her reading vocabulary (*I*, *to*, *go*, *the*, *play*). Notice how she spells *playground*: *play* is among the words she instantly

Figure 3-5   Lexi conventionally spells words in her fluent reading vocabulary and uses the beginning consonant to spell other words. Lexi often struggles when identifying new words because she does not know enough letter-sound associations to fully translate words into speech. Her story reads: I want to go to the park. I want to go for swim. I want to play on the playground.

recognizes in print. The portion of *playground* that she does not know how to read, *ground*, she represents with the letter *g*, resulting in *playg*.

Children like Lexi frequently guess at words using the context cues, picture cues, and beginning and/or ending letter-sound cues. As long as context and picture cues are robust, these children may successfully read new words. Rich context and excellent, descriptive pictures related to the story are most conducive to accurate word identification; weak context and weak picture cues may result in guesses that do not make sense in the story. This explains why partial alphabetic word learners may sometimes be inconsistent in reading words. Some of the words they correctly read when context and picture cues are high may be misread in another book or on another page in the same book when the context and picture cues do not give children strong hints for word identification.

Alecia writes about her favorite things, as shown in Figure 3-6, using a blend of conventional and unconventional spelling. Alecia correctly spells words she recognizes on sight. The words she does not conventionally spell are not yet in her reading vocabulary. In comparing Lexi's and Alecia's writing, we see that Alecia has more known words in her story (*I*, *have*, *green*, *and*, *blue*, *a*, *my*, *is*, *love*, *dog*, *see*),

Figure 3-6   Alecia is phonemically aware of beginning and ending sounds and is developing awareness of middle sounds. She uses letters to represent the beginning and ending sounds as well as some middle sounds in words. She is moving into the use of more sophisticated letter and sound relationships. Her story reads: "I have green and blue eyes. I have brown hair. I have a twin sister. My favorite color is pink. My favorite food is corn. My favorite restaurant is Chick-Fil-A®. I like to see my friends."

and she typically uses two or three consonants for words she unconventionally spells (some examples are *bn* for *brown*, *sdt* for *sister*, and *lk* for *like*). Alecia's use of letters to represent some of the sounds in words (for example, *clr* for *color*, *fd* for *food*, and *rt* for *restaurant*) suggests that she is carefully thinking about letter-sound relationships.

Further evidence comes from her use of the vowel letter *i* in *pink* (spelled *pik*). In contrast to Lexi who uses only beginning sounds to spell, Alecia frequently writes both beginning and ending sounds and includes some middle sounds as well (*sdt* for *sister* and *clr* for *color*). We have additional evidence that Alecia is looking carefully at print in the way she uses hyphens to spell her favorite restaurant, Chick-Fil-A®—spelled as *C-F-a*. From her story, we can infer that Alecia is phonemically aware of beginning and ending sounds, that she is developing awareness of the middle sounds in words, and that she is moving toward using more complex letter-sound relationships than simple partial alphabetic cues.

Perhaps the greatest advantage of using partial cues is that children like Lexi and Alecia have opportunities to develop, test, and revise hypotheses about how the alphabet works. As children experiment with even a single letter-sound cue, they refine their phonemic awareness and extend their knowledge of how letters represent sounds. Though the use of partial cues is relatively short lived, it eases children into strategically using alphabetic writing and as such is the precursor to the development of more advanced word identification strategies.

BEST PRACTICES FOR TEACHING PARTIAL ALPHABETIC WORD LEARNERS

You will be a more effective teacher of children in the partial alphabetic stage when you use the following best practices to improve children's ability to read and spell new words.

1. *Teach the names of all the letters* (Kim, Petscher, Foorman, & Zhou, 2010). Children are more likely to know the letter sounds when they know the names of the letters. Furthermore, phonemic awareness has a greater effect on learning letter sounds when children also know the letter names. Some letter names give clues to the letter sounds. For instance, the name of the letter *s*, /ess/, tells children something about the sound the letter *s* represents. The names of other letters, *g* for example, does not give a clue as to this letter's sound. Children taught letter names and sounds learn the sounds of more letters with names that give clues to letter sounds as compared with letter names that do not give children clues to letter sounds (Piasta & Wagner, 2010). Therefore, you will want to use the names of letters that give clues to the letter sounds to bootstrap letter-sound learning.

2. *Teach phonemic awareness of all the sounds in words—first, middle, and last* (National Reading Panel, 2000). At this point in their development as readers, children have some awareness of the sounds in words but lack

sufficient awareness to separate words into each and every sound. Use the activities in Chapter 2 to develop the ability to separate words into sounds and to blend sounds together. When teaching phonemic awareness, combine instruction with activities in Chapter 5 that teach phonics letter-sound patterns.

3. *Teach both consonant and vowel letter sounds.* The vowels in English are *a, e, i, o,* and *u.* All the remaining letters are consonants. (See Table 5-1 and Appendix A for more detailed explanations.) It is important to teach a name and a sound for each letter. Most English words begin with a consonant letter; but the vowels are important, too. Every English word contains at least one vowel sound. Consequently, children cannot read or write words if they have not learned the vowel letter sounds. Teach one sound for each vowel. Most teachers teach the short sounds first, as the /a/ heard in /apple/. The short-vowel pattern, as illustrated by *cat, bed, sit, mop,* and *tug,* is the easiest to learn because this pattern is not as complicated as the long-vowel patterns—*same, boat, seed,* and *rain,* for instance. Additionally, short vowels often appear in words spelled with the same letter pattern, such as *fat, hat, sat.* (You will learn more about this in the next chapter.) In teaching letter names and a sound for each letter, be sure to read alphabet books, point out letters in words, and have children make their own alphabet books or ask children to work together to make a classroom alphabet book.

4. *Have children read easy, meaningful text.* Surround children with print in your classroom and then use that print to engage children in reading. For example, you might use shared reading with big books to familiarize children with words and letters and help to develop comprehension strategies. Shared reading occurs when the teacher reads aloud, and children follow along and participate when they recognize words, phrases, or sentences. Encourage children to read the small versions of big books, to read and reread familiar books with a buddy, and to read for pleasure. Have children read familiar text together in chorus. Put labels in prominent places in your room and, as children become familiar with the labels, ask one child to bring you a label and another child to put it back. Keep a storehouse of books available and encourage children to read them in their spare time and to take books home to share with their families.

5. *Ask questions that help children demonstrate and extend their knowledge of written language.* It is important at this stage of children's development to give them opportunities to demonstrate and extend their knowledge of written language and to actively participate in reading aloud. While reading aloud, ask children to use their word and letter knowledge to do things like find words, point to letters, and find letter-sound patterns in familiar words.

6. *Explore words.* Call attention to the vowel-consonant combinations at the ends of words (the *op* in *hop, shop,* and *drop,* explained in Chapter 4) and to letter-sound relationships (explained in Chapter 5). Make lists of rhyming words that share a similar spelling (*time-dime,* not *time-climb*) and lists of

words with the same beginning, middle, or ending letter sounds. Select some of these words to add to your classroom word wall; have children keep personal boxes of words they want to learn or words they need when writing; talk about how letters represent sounds in the words that children see on the word wall, in books, and in children's personal word boxes. You also might ask children to sort words according to particular letter-sound patterns and to build words from the letter sounds they know (as explained in Chapter 5).

7. *Have children write every day and ask them to think about letters and sounds when spelling new words.* When children cannot conventionally spell a word they wish to write and cannot find the word on the word wall, encourage them to write letters that represent the sounds they hear in the word. This helps children focus on sound, which enhances phonemic awareness, and also helps children focus on letter-sound relationships, which enhances phonics knowledge.

8. *Read aloud to children.* Reading aloud to children has a long-lasting, beneficial effect on reading achievement. Read to children every day and read a variety of genres. When you read aloud, pause occasionally to ask questions that prompt children to interact with the book by doing or saying something (Justice, Weber, Ezell, & Bakeman, 2002). For instance, you might ask children to find words in text or to point to letters in familiar words, or you might engage children in discussing the structure of stories, including the setting, the characters, the problem, and the solution in the story.

TEACHING LETTER NAMES AND A SOUND FOR EACH LETTER TO ENGLISH LANGUAGE LEARNERS

When you begin to teach letter names and sounds, start by teaching the letters in children's names and the sound of the first letter. Have children write their names and read the names of their classmates, display children's names in your classroom, and play games that feature children's names. Bear in mind that some names will begin with letters that are associated with sounds that differ from the sounds associated with letters in the English alphabet. For instance, *J* in the Spanish name *José* is pronounced as /h/ in English, and *I* in the French name *Inès* (or *Inez*) is pronounced as a long *e* (e.g., the sound at the beginning of *each*). Therefore, rather than asking José to find or point to something that begins with the sound of *j* (/j/), you might ask him, "Point to the first letter in your name on the alphabet strip or word wall." We also like to teach José, and other children like him, the letter name and sound of the first letter in his last name. The English learners we teach are fascinated when they learn the letter name and sound of the first letter in their parents' names. So, for children whose names begin with letters that represent sounds other than those we associate with the letters of our alphabet, select last names or the names of family members.

Use key words when teaching English learners letter names and a sound for each letter. Key words are words in children's English vocabulary, or words you preteach, that are spelled with the letter sounds children are learning. Key words are paired with pictures to help children remember letter names and the sound each letter represents. Good key words are easy to visualize and the letter sound is prominent in pronunciation. The words on alphabet strips are examples of key words. The words prominently featured in alphabet books, such as "Bb bear" or "Hh horse" are another example of key words. When it comes to selecting your own key words, a word like *ball* is a good choice for *b*: Ball begins with /b/, it is easy for English learns to visualize a ball, and English learners are likely to understand the meaning of ball. When English learners think of the key word *ball*, they (1) associate *ball* with the letter *b*, (2) use the word *ball* to help them remember the name of the letter *b*, and (3) associate /b/ with the letter *b*. Other examples of key words are *pig* for *p*, *dog* for *d*, and *moon* for *m*. When selecting key words and other words to use in teaching letter names and a sound for each letter, choose words that English learners need to know in order to communicate in English. For instance, connecting the letter *z* and the sound /z/ with *zipper* is a better choice than connecting the letter name and sound with the word *zebra*. Although *zebra* is easy to visualize and an interesting English word, *zipper* is a far more useful word for English learners to know.

English learners learn best when lessons and activities involve physical movement. For example, in combining physical movement with teaching the name and sound of the letter *b*, you might give each child in a small group several plastic letters. Then show the children a small ball and a large card with the word *ball* on it. Read "ball," and pronounce /b/ while you place your finger under the *b*. Give the ball to a child in the group, show children the card with *ball*, and ask, "What is Carlos holding?" What is the beginning sound in *ball*?" Then ask everyone, "Hold up the letter that comes at the beginning of *ball*." "What is this letter's name?" "What is the /b/ sound?" "What is something in our room that begins with *b*?" If a child says "book," have that child get a book and bring it to the group. Last, have the group join you in reading *ball* aloud in chorus, and say the letter name (*b*) and sound (/b/). Last, ask the whole group to say the letter sound followed by the key word: "/b/-/b/ ball."

When children write the letters, they pay attention to the features that make one letter different from another. Understanding the features that distinguish letters, in turn, helps children accurately recognize the letters. Multimodal activities that combine touch and movement are good choices for reinforcing letter knowledge and for practice in writing letters. For example, children might write letters in finger paint or shaving cream, make letters out of clay or Play-Doh®, or make letters from found objects, such as gluing buttons in the shape of an uppercase *B*. Writing letters in shaving cream is a good activity to prepare for Open House night. Children need just a dab of shaving cream on their workspace. Shaving cream letters are easily erased by swiping the hand over the shaving cream, so children can write many letters at one sitting. In cleaning up the shaving cream, children's workspaces get a good sprucing up, which makes this a great activity before events like an open house. We find that sand and salt are also good mediums for practice writing letters.

Pour a bit of sand or salt in shallow container with a lid. Children write the letters you dictate. You might ask children to "Write a *b* (letter name)." "Write the letter that makes the /b/ sound." or "Write the letter that comes at the beginning of *ball*." When children are finished writing the letter, have them tell you the name and the sound. A simple shake erases letters. Another medium to use with English language learners is writing letters with a damp sponge. A sturdy sponge and a dusty chalkboard or cement is all you need for this activity. Ask children to write a letter whose name or sound you pronounce. Letters disappear as the water evaporates.

Take advantage of the normal daily activities in your classroom routine to teach letter names and a sound for each letter to English language learners and others in your class. For instance, morning message—the time set aside at the beginning of the day to talk about the date, weather, and important events—is a good time to review the names and sounds of the letters. Combine phonemic awareness with letter learning by asking children, "What is the beginning sound in rain?" "Point to the first letter in rain." "What is the name of the first letter in rain?" Or you may wish to use letter names and sounds to call the roll as children line up for lunch, dismissal, or going to specials. To do this, give each child a letter card, and have children tell you the letter name and/or sound before lining up. Another choice is to have children get in line when they hear the name or sound of the first letter in their name.

Alphabet books are excellent resources, provided that these books are designed to promote learning letter names and sounds. Since all alphabet books feature letters and words that begin with the letters, it would be logical to assume that all alphabet books are equally good for teaching the ABCs to English learners, but this is not the case. In selecting alphabet books, look for books that (1) show upper- and lowercase letters (Aa, Bb, Cc), (2) place letters and words in the upper-left corner or, at the very least, put them in a predictable place on each page, (3) have pictures that are easy to identify, (4) connect letters and their sounds with many different, but familiar words, and (5) include many words English learners already know. When alphabet books have words children already know, you can focus on letter learning rather than on teaching word meaning. Should you decide to use the words in alphabet books to expand children's English speaking vocabularies, look for books that feature words that are useful to know. For instance, *zither* is not particularly useful, but *zero* and *zoo* are quite helpful—*zero* for math and *zoo* for stories children are likely to read about zoo animals. There are many alphabet books available in other languages, as well as books that feature letters and sounds in English and in another language. These books bring in to your classroom children's native language and culture, and offer many exciting ways to help the English-only children learn more about the spoken language and culture of their classmates who speak a language other than English at home.

In teaching letter names and a sound for each letter, give English learners ample opportunities to talk, have English learners work with English-only buddies, and use hands-on activities when possible. Use direct instruction and set aside extra time to help English learners to learn letter names and sounds. Find books that feature children's cultures, put some of the words in these books on your classroom word wall, and use these words in learning activities. Make paper and pencils available and read aloud often. Point out letters and words that begin with the sounds children are learning for each letter. Consider making an alphabet book with VoiceThread and flip cameras, and using the Learning Phonics Game on the Fisher-Price® website, as explained in the e-resources section.

TEACHING LETTER NAMES AND A SOUND FOR EACH LETTER TO CHILDREN AT RISK

Alphabet knowledge is a good predictor of early success in learning to read, so you can expect kindergartners with high alphabet knowledge to be better readers later in school than their classmates with low knowledge (Keppänen, Aunola, Niemi, & Nurmi, 2008). Children at risk who begin school without rich experiences with print as preschoolers may not begin kindergarten with a clear understanding of the terms *letter* and *sound*. These children need to learn, for instance, that *Gg* and *Ss* are letters, and that /guh/ and /s/ are the sounds these letters represent. Learning would be more straightforward if children needed to learn only 26 letters. But children at risk need to learn 52 letters—26 uppercase letters and 26 lowercase letters. The difference in form between the upper- and lowercase letters may be problematic for some at-risk learners. Consistently using the term *letter* when referring to a letter (*Ss*), and sound when referring to the letter sound (/s/) makes it easier for children to understand your explanations. For example, in calling attention to the letter name, say: "*Goat* begins with the *letter* Gg (the letter name)." Or you might ask children to "Point to the *letter* Gg." When referring to the letter sound, say something like, "*Goat* begins with /guh/." Or you might ask children, "What *sound* does this letter make in *goat* (pointing to the *g* in *goat*)?" Later, when children understand the distinction between the letters and the sounds they represent, you will not need to be so careful in your use of these terms.

Keep in mind that in learning the letters, *recognition* (pointing to a letter when the teacher says the name) precedes *production* (saying the letter name without cues). In other words, children will *recognize* a letter before they can *tell* you the letter name (Lafferty, Gray, & Wilcox, 2005). This explains why a child may be able to find a letter you name but cannot tell you the name of the same letter. For example, a child may be able to point to the letter *Mm* when you say the letter name, but this same child may not be able to tell you the letter name, on her own, without prompting. Do not be surprised if you ask this child, "What is this letter?" and the child cannot think of the name. You may prompt the child, perhaps by referring to a key word, *moon*, or asking the child to refer to the alphabet strip in your classroom. Later in the day, however, the child may have difficulty naming the *Mm* when prompts are not available. Make teaching and learning letter names less stressful by beginning with activities that ask children to find or point to letters ("Find the *letter Gg* in *goat*." "Point to the *letter* Gg."); then, when children are successful identifying the letters you name, ask children to say the letter names when they see letters ("What is the name of this letter?").

Teach first the letter names that give hints to their letter sounds (de Jong, 2007; Piasta & Wagner, 2010). Some letter names include part of the letter sounds. For instance, when we pronounce the name of the letter *Ss* (/ess/), we hear part of the letter sound, /s/. Consonant letter names that give clues to the letters' sounds are *Bb, Dd, Ff, Jj, Kk, Ll, Mm, Nn, Pp, Ss, Tt,* and *Vv*. The vowel letters are a bit different. The majority of kindergarten programs teach children the short-vowel sounds first, as heard in *apple, edge, itch, octopus,* and *up*. The names of the vowels do not give readers hints for learning the short-vowel sounds. However, vowel letter names do help children learn the long-vowel sounds, as heard in *ate, each, I, over,* and *use*, because the names and the sounds are exactly the same. This explains why beginning readers often use letter names when spelling. For example, Lexi (Figure 3-5) used the name of the letter *Pp* (/puh/) to spell *park*; Alecia (Figure 3-6) used the names of the letters *Ff* (/eff/) and *Tt* (/tee/) to spell *favorite*. In both examples, these readers and spellers relied on cues to the sound they heard in the letter names. In teaching children at risk, encourage them to listen for hints to the letter sounds in letter names, and help them use these hints to make it easier to learn a sound for each letter. Use the activities already described for developing alphabet knowledge in English language learners as well as the activities described in the paragraphs below.

Some of the at-risk children you teach will confuse letters that look similar long after their classmates have learned to name the letters. The letters are formed by lines, circles, and curves. Some letters stay on the line (*n*), others extend above (*f*) or have "tails" that go below the line (*g*), and still others face different directions (*b-d*). It is harder for children to differentiate letters that share many of the same features such as *b-d, p-q, c-o, v-w,* and *m-n*. Generally speaking, part of the reason children have difficulty learning letter names is that they get tangled up in differentiating letters that look similar. For children who confuse b, d and p, try the Fishing Bowl interactive game on the Literactive website (see e-resources) If children are to learn letter names, they must be able to recognize the letters without confusing one for another. If you have the freedom to choose the order in which you teach the letters to children at risk, avoid teaching letters that look similar together. Likewise, in teaching a sound of each letter, separate letter sounds that are hard to discriminate. Chief among the hard-to-discriminate sounds are the short sound for /i/ (/i/ as in /it/) and /e/ (/e/ as in /edge/), as well as /p/ and /d/, /p/ and /b/, /v/ and /t/, and /p/ and /t/.

Hidden letter rubbing is especially useful for helping children at risk discriminate and name letters. To use hidden letter rubbing, place a dye cut letter under a piece of construction paper. The paper needs to be thick so that children cannot see the letter underneath. Children use crayons to scribble over the letter, beginning at the top. Hidden letter rubbing is a multimodal activity because children feel the letter under the paper, see the colored crayon slowly reveal the letter, and use movement—scribbling—to reveal a letter's shape. Encourage children to guess the letter after they have revealed the top third. If children do not get the answer, have them scribble a bit more and ask them to guess again. Continue until children name the letter. Then have children scribble to reveal any remaining portions of the letter. Ask children to say the sound of the letter and to find words in your classroom that begin with the "hidden" letter. In "guessing" the letter's identity, children exhibit an understanding of the features that distinguish the hidden letter from all other letters.

Children at risk will need more practice and reinforcement activities than their classmates who quickly learn letter names and a sound for each letter. Activities that call for sorting, matching and writing, chanting, finding alphabet stickers, and playing alphabet games reinforce learning and give children the practice they need to be successful. Children might sort (1) uppercase letters, (2) lowercase letters, (3) upper- and lowercase letters that go together, or (4) by letter shapes—those that have circle (*o, p, g*), lines (*l, t, k*), arcs (*c, e, s*), stay on the line (*m, a, e*), go above line (*t, b, l*), or go below the line (*y, g, p*), for example. Have children sort plastic letters, letters on cards, and Alpha-bits® cereal letters. Ask children to find letters on cereal boxes and in the words in your classroom. Hide uppercase letters in your classroom; give each child one or more lowercase letters. Then have children hunt for the hidden uppercase letters that match the lowercase letters. Talk about the features that differentiate the letters, and call children's attention to circles, to curves and to lines, and to letters that stay on the line, go above the line, or have tails below the line. Use the activities described above to give children many opportunities to learn the features that make up each letter.

In teaching a sound for each letter, have children sort pictures that begin with the letter sounds, such as putting pictures of a boat, ball, and baby into the Bb pile, and pictures of a moon, mop, mouse, and man in the Mm pile. In addition to sorting, we use an activity called Big Letter Stenciling to help children associate a sound with an individual letter. Children first stencil from one to four big letters on a sheet of construction paper. Once letters are dry, children think of a word that begins with each of the stenciled big letters, or look at the word wall for words that begin with the big letters. Children then tell you a word that begins with the letter. You write (or have children write) the word beside each big stenciled letter. We use activities like ABC ladders, finger hopscotch, and letter walks to reinforce letter knowledge and to give children at risk extra practice naming letters and associating sounds with letters. These activities are easy for you, the teacher, to prepare and call for the active involvement of learners. To use ABC ladders, draw a ladder and write a letter on each rung. Then have children climb up and down the ladder by saying letter names and sounds. For finger hopscotch, draw a hopscotch form on paper, on a white board, or on cement. Write a different letter in each square. Children take turns using their fingers to jump through the pattern on paper or white board or hop through the pattern on cement. As children move from square to square, have them say each letter's name and sound. Letter walks are another way to give children at risk extra practice. Draw a large, winding path on a hard surface such as a sidewalk or cement surface. Divide the path into sections at least a foot apart, and write a letter 10 inches high in each section. Have children take a letter walk by stepping on a letter and saying its name and sound, or thinking of a word that begins with the letter. Consider interactive games like the Phonics Learning game (found on the Fisher-Price® website and explained in e-resources) with different levels that provide from easy to more challenging practice learning letter names and sounds.

Spend more time developing the letter knowledge of children at risk than children who begin school with a good deal of letter knowledge. Make sure that children are able to discriminate one letter from another. Realize that recognition proceeds production, and plan activities that first focus on recognition ("Which one is the letter *Mm*?") and then on production ("What is the name of this letter?"). Plan lessons that use several modalities—sight, touch, movement—to give children many different ways to learn letter names and sounds. Make provision for ample practice and reinforcement. Teach letter names and sounds in small and large groups and throughout the day whenever opportunities arise. The more opportunities children at risk have to associate names and sounds with letters, the greater the learning and the sooner they will use their letter knowledge to read and spell. When children know letter names and associate a sound with each letter, they are in a position to begin to look for letter groups in unfamiliar words that are present in familiar words. When children do this, they use existing information to construct and acquire new knowledge. Using parts of known words to identify unknown words that share some of the same letters is the key to reading new words with analogy-based phonics, which is the topic of the next chapter.

E-RESOURCES FOR TEACHING LETTER NAMES AND A SOUND FOR EACH LETTER

Voice Media

VoiceThread Interactive Alphabet Book (*www.voicethread.com*):

VoiceThread is a means of adding voice to media presentations. To make an interactive alphabet book, begin by creating a PowerPoint that features the letters and pictures that begin with the letter sounds. Use VoiceThread to record your voice saying the letter names and sounds. Then have individual children use VoiceThread to record their own voices saying the letter names, the sounds of the letters, and the names of the pictures on each PowerPoint alphabet page. This example is only one of many ways you might create and use interactive VoiceThread alphabet books in your classroom. VoiceThread may be purchased by an individual or schools may purchase a site license for one year.

Video Media

Flip Camera Alphabet Book:

Flip cameras are handheld camcorders with the capacity to record video for up to four hours. These small cameras are easy to use and light enough for young children to handle. Show children how to operate a flip camera; then send them around the school to find examples of words that begin with letters they are currently learning. For each letter, have children use their flip camera to capture the word and their voices saying the word and the name of the letter at the beginning of the word. It is more effective to have children make their own flip camera alphabet books by filming letters in alphabetical order. Filming in alphabetical order reinforces the order in which letters are sequenced in the alphabet and also gives you (and children) a good way to keep track of which letters are already in the book and which letters need to be added. When finished, burn a DVD for each child to preserve their personal, electronic alphabet book. Flip cameras can be purchased for $100 to $300, depending on features.

Websites with Activities, Games, or Lessons for Computers or Interactive Whiteboards (IWBs)

SMART Exchange™ Activities for an IWB (*http://exchange.smarttech.com/#tab=0*):

Look for a downloadable, interactive alphabet book with animals whose names begin with the letters and letter sounds. Each page features a letter, a picture of an animal, and a colored square covering the animal's name. Children touch a colored square to reveal the name of the animal.

ReadWriteThink (*http://www.readwritethink.org*):

Look on this website for a variety of lesson plans and interactive games to teach letter recognition, letter names, and a sound for each letter such as ABC Match, Picture Match, and My Amazing Alphabet. ABC Match calls for matching letters with pictures that begin with the letter sound, and Picture Match for matching pictures to beginning letters or short- or long-vowel sounds. My Amazing Alphabet Book is a lesson with a downloadable template for making an alphabet book.

PBS Kids™ (*http://pbskids.org/games/alphabet.html; http://pbskids.org/lions;* and *http://pbskids.org/whiteboard*):

The PBS site offers many interactive games. Some options are described below. Look at the website for other games to share with the children in your classroom. Examples of games on the whiteboard page are (1) Sesame Street: Cookie's Letter of the Day, which asks children to feed Cookie Monster; (2) Sesame Street: Letters to Big Bird, a game where children match pictures to letters; (3) Super Why! Alpha Bricks, which calls for matching letters; and (4) Super Why! Alpha Pig Bingo, which gives children practice identifying letters. The Between the Lions page includes two games for recognizing and matching letters. Sky Riding helps children to recognize and discriminate among letters in five different fonts. Monkey Match asks children to match upper- with lowercase letters, match letter sounds with pictures of words that begin with the same sound, or match rhyming pictures. Games for learning a sound for each letter include (1) Between the Lions: Theo's Puzzles, a click-and-drag game where children complete a puzzle showing an object and its beginning letter. After the picture is complete, children watch a short video of words that begin with the letter. (2) Super Why! Princess Presto Spectacular Sounds Bingo, which calls for matching letters to sounds. (3) Sesame Street Oscar's Bumper Cars where children find words that begin with specified letters. (4) WordWorld: Dog's Letter Pit, which calls for spelling words by clicking on letters that represent sounds. (5) Sesame Street: Abby's Adventures asks children to identify pictures with names that begin with the same sound. (6) Super Why! Amazing Alphabet Match Up, which calls for matching letters to words that begin with the letter-sound. (7) Sesame Street: Cookie Monster's Alphabet Soup where children click on letters to spell words. Games for letter recognition on the alphabet page include (1) Super Why! Alpha Pig Paint by Letter; (2) Super Why! Alpha Pig's Lickety Letter Bingo; and (3) WordWorld: Alphabet Falls. ABCD Watermelon reinforces knowledge of alphabetical order.

ABC Ya! (*http://abcya.com/*):

Look on the first grade page for interactive alphabet activities such as (1) ABC: Put the Alphabet in Order, (2) Alphabet Match, and (2) Uppercase and Lowercase Letter Match.

Bembo's Zoo (*http://www.bemboszoo.com*):

Children click on letters that transform into animals with names that begin with the letter sound.

e-Learning for Kids (*http://www.e-learningforkids.org/index.html*):

This site for global learning is sponsored by a U.S. nonprofit and a Dutch nonprofit. The site offers two interactive alphabet games under Learning Letters. One is a click-and-drag game for matching letters and the other is an electronic alphabet book where children click and drag letters that begin with picture names. Proficiency at moving the mouse is a must. Course tutorials help children develop the computer skills they need. This site would be especially appealing to older children at risk, say first or second graders who have not learned the alphabet. Activities for the alphabets of four languages are available—English, Spanish, French, and Dutch.

Starfall™ (*www.starfall.com* and *http://www.starfall.com/n/N-info/scope.htm?n=educators*):

This site offers a variety of free resources. Look for an interactive learning activity accessed by clicking on the ABCs icon. The top of the page shows letters written on blocks. When the child clicks a letter, the upper- and lowercase versions appear, the child hears the letter name and sound, and then sees a picture of an object that begins with the letter. Clicking the icon of a hand at the bottom of the ABCs page brings up a page with uppercase letters. Clicking on one of five vowel letters at the bottom of the ABCs page brings up a vowel letter accompanied by the short-vowel sound and a song featuring the sound. This site also includes the complete alphabet song accompanied by the American Sign Language signs for the letters. Downloadable, printable alphabet pages present upper- and lowercase letters and pictures of objects that begin with the letter and have space for children to trace and write the letter. The second address links directly to the Scope and Sequence page, where you will find an inventory of the resources on this website. The creators of *starfall.com* also make available for purchase CD-ROMs, teaching materials, and kindergarten curriculum.

Learning Planet (*http://www.learningplanet.com/act/abcorder.asp*):

This features an ABC order game that asks the child which letter comes next to complete a sequence of three letters. This colorful game shows letters on a train and the child selects the letter that comes next. A correct answer results in a "choo-choo" sound. This game does not teach letter sounds, only ABC order. Access to other activities requires a membership fee.

Owl & Mouse (*http://www.yourchildlearns.com/learnletters.htm*):

This site has two downloadable alphabet activities (1) Learn Letters and (2) Letter Sounds. Learn Letters calls for clicking on circles, lines, and curves to make letters. This activity could be useful for children who have difficulty distinguishing one letter from another. Letter Sounds calls for dragging a picture to the letter that begins with the picture name. This activity can be used online or downloaded. There are three levels: (1) Level 1 asks children to match a letter to a picture. (2) Level 2 calls for picture-letter matching. Following correct matches, children see and hear the word. (3) In Level 3, children match a picture to a letter and then see and hear the word.

Chateau Meddybemps™ (*http://www.meddybemps.com/letterary/index.html*):

An activity for learning to draw letters encourages children to write upper- and lowercase letters. Children may watch and then copy a moving pencil or try their hand at moving the mouse to write their own letters on a lined page.

Literacy Center (*http://www.literacycenter.net/*):

The Education Literacy Center Network is a nonprofit organization that provides educational materials suitable for preschoolers or children at risk in kindergarten who are having difficulty learning the alphabet. The materials are offered in English, Spanish, French, and German. Available are two click-through alphabets of lower- and uppercase letters accompanied by the name of each letter, and games for matching upper- and lowercase letters, including a memory-type version. Clicking the writing icon brings up pages of upper- and lowercase letters. When children click on a letter, a pencil writes the letter and a voice pronounces the letter name. Watching the pencil form each letter could be helpful for children who have a difficult time remembering the differences among letters or for children who need more instruction in how to form letters when they write.

Scholastic™ (*http://teacher.scholastic.com/whiteboards/languagearts.htm*):

This site has IWB-ready activities featuring Clifford the Big Red Dog.™ Letter Match, a sorting game, asks children to drag words to sacks that show the beginning letters. Children can listen to four Clifford books read in English or Spanish. Look in Building Language for Literacy for a letter matching game called Leo the Letter-Loving Lobster.

Internet4Classrooms (*http://www.internet4classrooms.com*):

This searchable website links to many free resources for teaching letter recognition and alphabetical order. Resources include interactive games and printable resources.

A short explanation for each activity indicates whether it is an interactive game with or without sound, a printable resource, or a lesson plan.

Jump Start Knowledge Adventure (*http://www.knowledgeadventure.com/games/ abc-game.htm*):

Children click on a letter to hear the sound and the name of a picture that begins with the sound. The sounds are clearly enunciated and easy to understand.

ict Games (*http://www.ictgames.com/literacy.html*):

Examples of games for associating letters and sounds include (1) Phoneme Pop Letters and Sounds and (2) Letter Lifter. In Phoneme Pop Letters children listen to a sound and click on bubbles with letters that match the sound. Letter Lifter calls for clicking a Start Belt button, listening to a picture name, typing a letter that corresponds to the beginning sound and clicking on a Lift button to remove the picture. This game would be suitable for English speaking, end-of-year first-graders and second-graders who have not learned the sounds that letters represent.

Literactive (*http://www.literactive.com/Home/index.asp*):

Literactive is a free site once you register. Click on Learning Activities to bring up a menu of interactive games. Look in ABC activities for (1) Match Capitals, (2) Match Smalls, and (3) Letter Formation. Match Capital Letters and Match Smalls ask children to associate letters and sounds. The Letter Formation game demonstrates how to write letters and the sounds associated with letters. The Level 1 page includes games like (1) Mouse House, (2) Rubber Ducks, and (3) Fishing Bowl. Children match uppercase and lowercase letters in the Mouse House game. The Rubber Ducks game asks children to associate sounds with letters. In Fishing Bowl children sort the letters *b*, *d* and *p*. Fishing Bowl is suitable for children who confuse *b*, *d* and *p* long after their classmates correctly read and write these letters. Level 2 includes (1) Flying Kites where children identify one out of four words that end in a different letter, and (2) Swings where children identify ending sounds. The Laying Hens game, found in Level 3, is an oddity game where children identify words that differ in middle letters. Other resources on the Literactive website include books for English language learners and guided reading in kindergarten, and an interactive phonics program.

Game Goo™ (*http://www.earobics.com/gamegoo/gooey.html*):

Click on Paw Park Kangaroo Confusion for a game where children match kangaroos wearing uppercase letters to kangaroos wearing lowercase letters. Paw Park Alphabet Bears is a game where children place letters in alphabetical order.

Printable Materials

Reading A-Z (*http://readinga-z.com*):

This website features downloadable resources for teaching the alphabet, including chants, alphabet books, flashcards, worksheets, and a strategy bank with tips for effectively teaching letter names and sounds. The activities help children develop alphabet knowledge. A paid membership is required to access this site.

DLTK Growing Together (*http:/dltk-teach.com/*):

The AlphaBuddies Alphabet Section features a wide variety of crafts as well as games, activities, rhymes and songs for letters of the alphabet. Look for bingo cards and bookmarks you can customize for the children in your classroom.

SparkleBox (*http://www.sparklebox.co.uk/index.html*):

Free, downloadable, colorful materials include sets of pictures with letters that represent a sound in the picture name, and letter sound activity books. There are many themed sets from which to choose, such as food, space, animals and transportation. This site, developed and maintained in the United Kingdom, features the lowercase letters written in D'Nealian®.

Alphabet Avenue (*http://www.alphabetavenue.net/*):

Alphabet Avenue, a project of Cherry Carl, has a wide variety of alphabet activities. Examples of resources on this website include printable worksheets, puzzles, flip books for each letter, alphabet songs, games, word wheels, posters, stickers and activities for every letter. This site includes tips for teaching letter knowledge, a PowerPoint to use in staff development, and research in support of teaching activities.

Florida Center for Reading Research (*http://www.fcrr.org/Curriculum/pdf/GK-1/P_Final_Part1.pdf* and *http://www.fcrr.org/curriculum/pdf/GK-1/P_Final_Part2.pdf*):

This site, sponsored by the Florida Center for Reading Research, has two links that the classroom teacher will find useful. The first link has four printable activities for naming and matching letters, and seven activities for identifying letters. The second link has printable activities and games for teaching a sound for each letter at the beginning, middle and end of words.

Apps for iPhone™ and iPad™

Examples of apps parents might wish to share with their children.

PBS: Super Why! games (*http://pbskids.org/mobile/apps.html*):

Download for a fee from iTunes the Super Why! games for iPad or iPhone.

REFERENCES

Bear, D. R., & Smith, R. E. (2009). The literacy development of English learners: What do we know about each student's literacy development? In Lori Helman (Ed.), *Literacy development with English learners: Research-based instruction in grades K-6* (pp. 87–116). New York: Guilford Press.

Bear, D. R., Invernizzi, M., Templeton, S., & Johnston, F. (2007). *Words their way: Word study for phonics, vocabulary, and spelling instruction* (3rd ed.). Upper Saddle River, NJ: Pearson Education.

Brown, M. (1982). *Arthur's halloween.* Boston: Little, Brown.

de Jong, P. F. (2007). Phonological awareness and the use of phonological similarity in letter-sound learning. *Journal of Experimental Child Psychology, 98,* 131–152.

Ehri, L. C. (2005). Learning to read words: Theory, findings, and issues. *Scientific Studies of Reading, 9,* 167–188.

Ehri, L. C., & McCormick, S. (1998). Phases of word learning: Implications for instruction with delayed and disabled readers. *Reading & Writing Quarterly, 14,* 135–163.

Henderson, E. (1990). *Teaching spelling* (2nd ed.) Boston: Houghton Mifflin.

Keppänen, U., Aunola, K., Niemi, P., & Nurmi, J.-E. (2008). Letter knowledge predicts grade 4 reading fluency and reading comprehension. *Learning and Instruction, 18,* 548–564.

Kim, Y. S., Petscher, Y., Foorman, B. R., & Zhou, C. (2010). The contributions of phonological awareness and letter-name knowledge to letter-sound acquisition: A cross-classified multilevel model. *Journal of Educational Psychology, 102*(2), 313–326.

Justice, L. M., Weber, S. E., Ezell, H. K., & Bakeman, R. (2002). A sequential analysis of children's responsiveness to parental print references during shared book-reading interactions. *American Journal of Speech-Language Pathology, 11,* 30–40.

Lafferty, A. E., Gray, S., & Wilcox, M. J. (2005). Teaching alphabetic knowledge to pre-school children with developmental language delay and with typical language development. *Child Language Teaching and Therapy, 21,* 263–277.

National Reading Panel. (2000). *Teaching children to read: An evidence-based assessment of the scientific research literature on reading and its implications for reading instruction: Reports of the subgroups* (NIH Publication No. 00-4754). Washington, DC: U.S. Government Printing Office.

Piasta, S. B., & Wagner, R. K. (2010). Learning letter names and sounds: Effects of instruction, letter type, and phonological processing skill. *Journal of Experimental Child Psychology, 105*(4), 324–344.

CHAPTER 4

Analogy-Based Phonics in Late Kindergarten and First Grade

The Strategy of Using the Predictable Patterns in Known Words to Read New Words

This chapter describes the strategy of using the parts in known words to read and spell new words. As you read this chapter, you will learn how syllables consist of onsets and rimes, how words that share rimes form word families (*at*, *cat*, *sat*, *rat*), and how we teach analogy-based phonics. You will find best practices for teaching analogy-based phonics as well as activities for teaching children to use the analogy strategy to read and spell new words. Also included in this chapter are suggestions for teaching English language learners and children at risk, and a list of e-resources for teaching word family words.

KEY IDEAS

- In analogy-based word identification, children use parts of familiar words to read unfamiliar words.
- Syllables have a two-part structure, consisting of an onset, which is the consonant that comes before the vowel, and a rime, which is the vowel and all the letters thereafter.
- Words that share a common rime form word families.
- Children who know how to read a rime in a known word have a clue to the identification of any word that is spelled with the rime.

KEY VOCABULARY

Early alphabetic word learners

Letter name-alphabetic spellers

Onset

Phonogram

Rime

Word family

What do you notice about the following sets of words?

at	ock	ing
cat	lock	sing
fat	rock	ring
hat	sock	bring
chat	clock	swing

A quick glance is all it takes to realize that the same letter patterns occur in many different words. Once readers discover that the words in each of these three sets share a common pattern, readers have a way to organize their thinking so as to use the parts of known words to read and spell unknown words. An analogy-based approach to phonics teaches children how to find a shared letter pattern in words, such as the *ing* in *bring*, and then to use this similarity to read and spell unfamiliar words with the same pattern, such as *ring* and *swing*.

LOOKING INSIDE SYLLABLES TO FIND ONSETS AND RIMES

Lucy sets a decidedly lighthearted tone as she ruminates about school in the poem in Figure 4-1. Lucy repeats words and rhymes words. What's more, all the words she uses have only one syllable. Looking inside the syllables in Lucy's poem

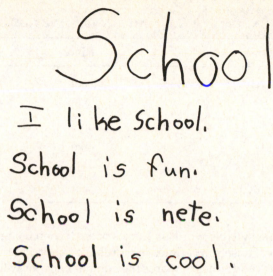

Figure 4-1   Some of the one-syllable words in Lucy's poem consist of an onset and a rime; others consist of a rime only.

reveals a two-part structure that consists of an onset and a rime. **Onsets** are the consonants that come before the vowel in a syllable or one-syllable word, such as the *sch* in *school*. Similarly, the *s* in *sit*, the *sl* in *slit*, and the *spl* in *split* are onsets. Onsets are always consonants; there can be as many as three clustered together in *common* words (*sch* and *spl*, for example).

   Rimes are the vowel and everything thereafter. The *ool* in *school* is a rime. Correspondingly, the *ent* in *tent* is a rime consisting of the vowel (*e*) and the consonants that follow it (*nt*); the rime in *scream* is *eam*; in *black*, it is *ack*. We can see, then, that in dividing one-syllable words into onsets and rimes, we split the beginning sound(s) from the part of the word that begins with the vowel (*s-at, sl-at, spl-at*). Two-syllable words are divided the same way. For example, *pencil* would be divided into *p-en* and *c-il*; habit is *h-ab* and *it*. Some words and syllables do not begin with an onset. Words like *at*, *it*, and *in* consist of a rime but no onset. Remember, too, that the rime has one and only one vowel sound. Although a rime may have more than one vowel letter in spelling, we hear just one vowel sound. For instance, *ice* has two vowels, *i* and *e*, but only one sound /i/. Likewise, *heat* has two vowel letters, *e* and *a*, but only one vowel sound, a long /e/.

   Rhyming words like *school* and *cool* share a rime—in this case, the rime *ool*. When rime is common to two or more words, then the words usually share a rhyming sound. However, this is not always the case, as we see in *know* and *now*, which share the *ow* pattern but do not rhyme. And, of course, sometimes rhyming words do not share a common letter pattern (*sheep* and *leap*). In this case, the words rhyme, but the rhyming sound is spelled differently (*eep* versus *eap*). In this chapter we are interested in words that both rhyme (*sheep—deep*) and have the same vowel and ending letter pattern (*eep*). Table 4–1 shows the onset-rime structure of the

TABLE 4–1		*Onsets and Rimes in Lucy's Poem*		
Onset	**+**	**Rime**	**=**	**One-Syllable Word**
sch	+	ool	=	school
c	+	ool	=	cool
	+	is	=	is
l	+	ike	=	like
f	+	un	=	fun
n	+	eat	=	neat

one-syllable words in Lucy's poem. When using the analogy strategy, readers connect onsets and rimes in words they already know how to read with the same onsets and rimes in words they do not know how to read. The analogy-based method teaches children to associate the onsets and rimes in known words with the onsets and rimes in new words. In teaching analogy-based phonics, you will encounter three related terms: rimes, phonograms, and word families. Rimes and **phonograms** refer to the vowel and any letter that comes after it in a syllable (the *at* in *cat*). **Word families** are word groups that share the same rime or phonogram (*cat, rat, fat, sat, bat*). The essential points for you to keep in mind are (1) rimes and phonograms both refer to the vowel and any letter thereafter (*un*), and (2) word family refers to word groups that share the same rime or phonogram (*run, sun, fun*). Thus, the *ool* in *school* and *cool* in Lucy's poem are rimes or phonograms; *school* and *cool* are part of the same word family.

TEACHING ANALOGY-BASED PHONICS WITH WORD FAMILIES

Analogy-based phonics is taught in late kindergarten and first grade. This method involves teaching children the sounds that onsets and rimes represent, how to identify rimes in words, and how to substitute onsets. Children must be skilled at (1) separating spoken words into beginning sounds (onsets) and rhyming sounds (rimes) and (2) blending beginning sounds and rhyming sounds together to pronounce meaningful words. Refer to Chapter 2 for teaching ideas.

In kindergarten, children typically learn to associate one sound with each letter. Therefore, children should already know the sounds that single consonants (onsets) represent. The main teaching focus is on the rimes. The premise is that if words share onsets and rimes, then words must share similar pronunciations. Rimes are taught in the context of known word family words, such as the *ap* in *map*. When generalizing the rime in one word (*map*) to the pronunciation of another word with the same rime (*cap*), teachers show children how to look for shared letter patterns.

Once children realize that *ap* says /ap/, children are taught how to read and spell words that belong to the same word family and are spelled with the *ap* rime.

When you help children notice onsets and rimes in new words that are also part of familiar word family words, you are teaching analogy-based phonics and helping children use the analogy strategy. Suppose that a child sees the new word *kind* in a sentence in the text. You might guide the child in making an analogy to the rime in the familiar word family word *find* by saying, "Look at this word (pointing to the new word *kind*). Now, look at this word (pointing to the familiar word family word *find*). If this is /find/, what do you think this word might be (pointing to *kind*)?" Another way to guide readers as they apply analogy-based phonics to read word family words is to say, "Can you think of another word that ends with *ind*?"

Think aloud as you demonstrate and model using the analogy strategy, perhaps by saying something like, "I know the word *find*. The *ind* in *find* says /ind/. So to read this new word (pointing to *kind*), I will change the *f* (/f/) to a *k* (/k/), which makes /kind/. Now you try it with me." It is also important to help children develop a metacognitive, or conscious, awareness of their own ability to use the analogy strategy. Encourage children to reflect on their own strategy use by asking, "What word do you already know that can help you figure out this new one?" This type of reflection helps readers become metacognitively aware (Chapter 1) of what they know about making analogies from known words and word parts to new words. Metacognitive awareness, in turn, improves readers' knowledge of when, why, and how to use analogy to read and spell new words.

How Children Use the Onsets and Rimes in Known Word Family Words to Read New Words

Readers who remember the sounds associated with onsets and rimes in word family words will tell you, their teacher, that *ap* represents /ap/ in *map*, *tap*, and *nap*. Likewise, children will tell you that *m* represents /m/, *t* represents /t/, and *n* represents /n/. Suppose that Tamara, a first-grader, does not automatically recognize the word *tent* in the sentence *Jane saw a large tent in the campground*. Suppose further that Tamara cannot figure out *tent* from picture cues or the reading context. However, Tamara brings to reading the knowledge of onsets and rimes in words she already knows. Here is how Tamara uses the analogy strategy:

1. Tamara notices a familiar onset and a familiar rime in *tent*. She recalls that the *t* represents /t/, and that the *ent* represents /ent/ in *went*, a word she already knows how to read.
2. Tamara now substitutes (Chapter 2) the /w/ in *went* for the /t/, which leaves /t/ + /ent/.
3. Tamara then blends /t/ + /ent/ to pronounce /tent/.
4. Last, Tamara checks to make sure that /tent/ is a good fit for the sentence. She asks herself: "Does *tent* sound and look right? Does *tent* make sense in the passage? Do I know what the author means?" If the answers to these

questions are yes, Tamara continues reading. If the answers are no, Tamara tries once again to figure out *tent*.

In spelling *tent*, Tamara begins by saying "tent" to herself. As she says the word she listens for sounds. When she hears the beginning sound, she associates /t/ with *t*, and writes a *t* on her paper. On hearing /ent/ writes *ent*, thus spelling *tent*. Tamara can now spell and read any word that begins with an onset she knows and ends with the *ent* rime.

EARLY ALPHABETIC WORD LEARNERS AND LATE LETTER NAME-ALPHABETIC SPELLERS

As children transition from partial alphabetic word learners into the early part of the alphabetic stage, they begin to focus on reading and spelling word family words, as we see in Anna's writing. Anna wrote the word list in Figure 4-2 when her teacher asked her to write as many words as she could. Anna is an early alphabetic word learner. We can infer from Anna's list that she thinks about the rime in words, for the 20 word family words are made up of only four rimes: *op*, *ox*, *ad*, and *am*. Anna's teacher emphasizes word families, so it is no surprise that Anna thinks of word family words when she writes.

Figure 4-2   When Anna's teacher asked her to write as many words as she could, Anna wrote 20 words using only four rimes—*op*, *ox*, *ad*, and *am*.

Early alphabetic word learners like Anna understand the alphabetic principle. When readers first begin to use letters and sound associations to read new words, they often do so by associating sounds with beginning letters and rimes. Children make analogies from words they know how to read, *pet* for example, to words they do not know, such as *wet*. These children are in the early part of the alphabetic stage. While they understand and use the alphabetic principle, they do not associate a sound with each letter. Rather, they would associate a sound with onset (*h* = /h/), and whole groups of sounds with a single rime (*im* = /im/), to read *him*. Later, as children move farther into the alphabetic stage, they learn to read and spell new words by associating a sound with each individual letter (or letter pattern) in an unfamiliar word (*him* = /h/, /i/, /m/). Children in the early part of the alphabetic stage of word learning are in the latter part of the letter name-alphabetic spelling stage (Henderson, 1990; Bear, Invernizzi, Templeton, & Johnston, 2007). Late **letter name-alphabetic spellers** become increasingly aware of the match between the sounds they hear in words and the letters they see in words. By the end of the letter name-alphabetic spelling stage, children know how to spell many rimes and words that contain the rimes as well as words with short-vowel sounds.

HOW RIMES MAKE IT POSSIBLE FOR EARLY ALPHABETIC WORD LEARNERS TO READ NEW WORDS

Identifying words by their analogous onsets and rimes is easier than decoding or spelling words letter-sound by letter-sound. First, learning that *ent* represents /ent/ is far less taxing than learning that the *e* represents the sound of /e/, *n* the sound of /n/, and *t* the sound of /t/. Second, blending onsets and rimes is much easier than blending individual sounds, because with onsets and rimes there are only two items to blend. In the example of *tent*, children would blend only /t/ + /ent/ in comparison with the four phonemes /t/ + /e/ + /n/ + /t/ associated with individual letters. Having fewer items to blend, in turn, decreases the probability of reversing sounds, deleting sounds, or adding sounds during blending. Consequently, readers who might not be successful sounding out and blending *tent* as /t/ + /e/ + /n/ + /t/ may be able to read *tent* when it is divided into /t/ + /ent/. Likewise, spellers who may have difficulty writing a sound for each letter in *tent* are more likely to be successful associating a sound with the letter *t* and sounds with the *ent* to write *tent*.

As Lilly writes about her pet cat (see Figure 4-3) she conventionally spells words in her reading vocabulary and spells other words by adding different onsets to the *at* rime. We can infer from her story that Lilly is thinking carefully about speech-to-print relationships, resourcefully combining her knowledge of onsets and rimes, her memory for known words, and her understanding of letter-sound associations. When Lilly reads, she uses frequently occurring rimes as well as the letter-sound patterns of phonics to identify new words. It is quite typical for children like Lilly to use both analogy-based decoding and letter-sound decoding. Children like Lilly look for consistency in written and spoken language relationships. They learn and remember words by paying attention to recurring letter

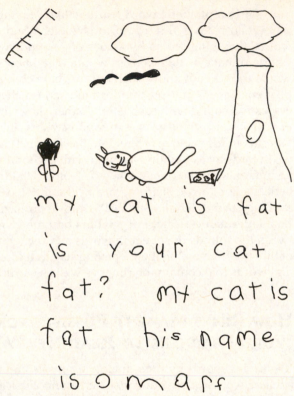

my cat is fat
is your cat
fat? my cat is
fat his name
is o marf

Figure 4-3   When writing, Lilly uses her knowledge of rimes and her ability to substitute beginning consonants (onsets).

patterns, and hence they can write and read words that consist of onset-rime combinations they already know (*p* + *et* = *pet*). Classroom reading programs typically introduce the different rimes in word family words at approximately the same time as they introduce the short-vowel letter-sound pattern, as the short *e* in *pet*. Consequently, depending on the sequence followed by the classroom reading program, children like Lily will learn to use the onset-rime patterns in word family words at about the same time as they begin to use the letter-sound patterns of phonics (*p* + *e* + *t* = *pet*).

Bear in mind that the beneficial effect of rimes may be more important in English than in other languages that have more consistent sound-letter matches. The consonant letters are relatively dependable, but this is not true for vowels. Each vowel represents more than one sound, as with the *a* in *track*, *bake*, *saw*, and *car*. Vowels are more easily remembered, decoded, and spelled when learned as part of rimes (Goswami, 2001). Because the vowels in rimes are learned as part of a chunk of letters and sounds, readers do not have to understand why the *a* in *track* is pronounced one way and the *a* in *bake* another way. Instead, readers remember that the *ack* in *track* represents /ack/ and the *ake* in *bake* represents /ake/. Learning rimes sidesteps the need to learn exceptions to the conventional way letters represent sounds. Take the *ind* in *find*, for example. We would expect the *i* in *find* to represent the same sound as the *i* in *dish*, since there is only one vowel (the *i*) in a short word followed by consonants (*ind–ish*). Children would be confused if they tried to read *find* as though the *i* represented the sound in /dish/. However, the *i* in *find* is not at all troublesome when remembered as part of the whole rime *ind*. Early alphabetic word learners who know how to read the rime in *find* have a cue to the identification of any word in the *ind* word family, for example, *mind*, *kind*, *blind*, and *find*. The net effect is that even vowels that stand for a variety of sounds are more easily remembered and decoded when learned within the context of word family words.

BEST PRACTICES FOR TEACHING ANALOGY-BASED PHONICS WITH WORD FAMILY WORDS

If you teach children like Lilly, you can expect them to recognize and use the rimes in word family words when you directly teach analogy-based phonics and when you provide reading and writing activities like those described later in this chapter.

1. *Use word family clue words.* Readers are more inclined to use the analogy strategy when they learn clue words that contain rimes. A clue word is a familiar word that contains an often-used rime in word family words. Examples include *cat* for the *at* word family, *pig* for the *ig* word family, *fan* for the *an* word family, *jet* for the *et* word family, *sun* for the *un* word family, and *night* for the *ight* word family. Clue words like these help children remember the sounds and spellings of word family rimes. Make sure readers can readily refer to clue words by putting them on the word wall, writing them on charts, taping them to the tables where children read and write, or writing them on the board.

2. *Show children how to use the analogy strategy to read and spell words.* We cannot assume that children will naturally begin to use analogous onsets and rimes. Significantly, while some children may be able to figure out the identity of word family words with known onsets and rimes without their teachers' help, most children need guidance from their teachers and structure in learning.

3. *Teach rimes from large, often-used word families.* From a practical perspective, we want to teach children those rimes that are the most helpful—that is, the more common rimes that make up many different word family words. The rimes with an asterisk in Table 4–2 are part of almost 500 words in books for beginning readers.

4. *Teach rimes along with the letter-sound relationships within rimes* (Juel & Minden-Cupp, 2000). Children who know the sounds that the individual letters in rimes represent are better able to use analogy-based phonics as compared with children who do not understand the letter-sound relationships within rimes. For example, the reader who knows that

TABLE 4–2 *Word Family Rimes for Reading and Spelling*

ab*+	cab	ace	race	ack*+	back	ad+	had
ade	made	ag*+	bag	ail*	mail	ain*	train
ake*	make	ale*	sale	all*	ball	am*+	ham
ame*	came	amp	lamp	an*+	can	and+	hand
ane	plane	ang+	sang	ank*+	drank	ap*+	cap
ark	dark	ash*+	cash	at*	cat	ate*	late
aw*	saw	ay*	play	eam	dream	ear	near
eat*	seat	eck	deck	ed*+	red	eed*	need
eep	sleep	eet	meet	eer	cheer	ell*+	bell
en+	ten	end	send	ent	went	est*+	best
et*	let	ew*	knew	ice*	nice	ick*+	quick
id+	hid	ide*	ride	ig+	pig	ight*	light
ill*+	hill	im*+	him	in*+	grin	ind	kind
ine*	nine	ing*+	bring	ink*+	think	ip*+	ship
it*+	fit	ob*+	job	ock*+	clock	og+	hog
oil	spoil	oke*	broke	old	told	ong+	song
onk+	honk	op*+	shop	ore*	more	orn	torn
ot*+	hot	ought	bought	out*	shout	ow**	snow
ub+	tub	uck*+	duck	ug*+	bug	um*+	hum
ump*+	jump	un*+	fun	ung+	hung	unk*+	trunk
ust	must	ut	cut	y*	by		

*Rimes with an asterisk are part of many different words, according to Cheek, Flippo, and Lindsey (1997) and/or Fry (1998).

** Word family *ow* is pronounced with a long /o/ as in /know/.

+ Rimes with a short-vowel sound.

at represents /at/ and who also knows that the *a* in *at* represents /a/ (the short *a*) and the *t* represents /t/ is more likely to effectively use the analogy strategy than the child who knows only that *at* represents /at/. In fact, readers may need to know something about the manner in which individual letters represent sound before they can successfully use analogy-based phonics (Ehri & Robbins, 1992). Good readers use several word identification strategies and change strategies, going between analogy and letter-sound decoding with phonics, depending on the reading circumstances (Walton, Walton, & Felton, 2001).

CLASSROOM ACTIVITIES FOR TEACHING ANALOGY-BASED PHONICS WITH WORD FAMILY WORDS

The following activities help children to learn onsets and rimes as well as apply the analogy decoding strategy. You can use these activities to teach any rime you think beneficial for the children in your classroom. Be sure to adapt the activities so that they are compatible with your teaching style. Combine these activities with activities in Chapter 5 for teaching letter sounds. Provide word family clue words to help children make analogies from known to unknown words and include in your balanced classroom reading program a generous amount of time devoted to reading and writing, including the reading and writing of word family words.

4.1 *Pocket Chart Word Families*

Skill: Using onsets and rimes to read and spell word family words.

In this scaffold activity, the teacher supports children in spelling words by lining up small cards with onsets and rimes on them. This activity is suitable for children working in small groups.

Things You'll Need: One set of large 3 × 5 inch onset and rime cards that combine to spell often-seen and often-used word family words; sets of small onset and rime cards; a pocket chart.

Directions: Use a pocket chart (a hanging chart with lines of clear compartments to hold cards) and the large onset and rime cards to demonstrate spelling, as shown in Figure 4-4. Put an onset and a rime card side by side in a pocket chart (*s* and *at*, perhaps) and push the cards together to spell a word family word (*sat*). Pronounce the sound of the onset and the rime as you point to each card. Demonstrate blending by sound stretching /sat/ as you push the cards together (/sssaaat/). Then say the whole word, /sat/. Use a different onset and the same rime to spell another word from the same family (*fat*, for instance). Line up word family words, thus creating opportunities to compare and contrast the rimes in words and to develop an understanding of how word family words sound alike and look alike. Once the children understand how to spell word family words, they are ready to try the next activity, Word Family Spelling, which entails less teacher support than Pocket Chart Word Spelling.

4.2 *Word Family Spelling*

Skill: Using onsets and rimes to read and spell word family words.

Use this activity with small groups of children who are ready to spell words with slightly less teacher guidance than present in the Pocket Chart Word Families activity.

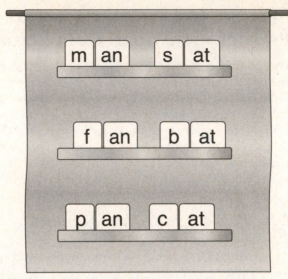

Figure 4-4   The use of a pocket chart to build words helps children gain insight into the sound that analogous rimes represent in word family words.

Things You'll Need: Onset and rime cards.

Directions: Give children onset-rime cards and ask them to work individually or with a partner to spell the word family words you specify. Once children are familiar with word family word spelling, ask them to spell as many words as they can from the same set of onset-rime cards. Have children share the word family words they spell, write the words on the board, and compare and contrast words from different families.

4.3   *Rewrite Familiar Poems*

Skills: Predicting rhyming words; using knowledge of word family rimes to write.

Children in small groups predict rhyming words in familiar poems and then use their knowledge of rimes to add their own new and creative endings to the poems.

Things You'll Need: Sticky notes; familiar poems written on large charts. Use only poems with words that both rhyme and share a rime (*might-light*, not *might-write*).

Directions: Use a sticky note to cover up one or more rhyming words in a familiar poem. Have children read the poem aloud. When the children come to a covered-up word, have them predict the word under the sticky note. Once children make their prediction, take off the sticky note to reveal the word family word. After children are thoroughly familiar with the poem, ask them to write their own versions by adding new endings. The endings in Figure 4-5 were written by first-graders after their teacher shared the big book *Oh, A-Hunting We Will Go* (Langstaff, 1989). Once children share their poems with the class, you may want to bind the poems together to make a class poetry book.

Figure 4-5   Writing new endings for familiar poems helps children gain insight into words that share letter and sound patterns.

Figure 4-5 (continued)

4.4   *Sticky-Note Word Family Flip Books*

Skill: Reading and writing word family words.

Children working in small groups, with a partner, in a learning center, or literacy station use sticky notes to make their own word family word books, such as those in Figure 4-6.

Things You'll Need: Sticky notes; pencils; stapler.

Directions: Have children join you in making lists of word family words. Give each child a few sticky notes, and ask them to write one word family word on each sticky note. Children put their sticky notes together to form a flip book; staple the pages to keep them together (see Figure 4-6). Children flip the pages to read their sticky-note word family books. Have children share their sticky-note flip books with their classmates and then take the books home to read with their families.

Figure 4-6   Children make sticky-note word family (or beginning letter-sound) books and then flip the pages to read their books.

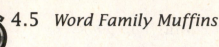

4.5 *Word Family Muffins*

Skill: Using onsets and rimes to read and spell word family words.

This word spelling activity is especially good for learning centers or literacy stations and yields a permanent record of the words children spell with onsets and rimes.

Things You'll Need: A muffin tin; small cards or tiles with onsets and rimes; muffin word guide. Put an assortment of onset-rime cards in each compartment of the muffin tin. Tape a small label above each compartment to tell which onset or rime cards are inside.

Make a muffin word guide (see Figure 4-7) by drawing several circles on a sheet of blank paper to simulate a row on a muffin tin. Write a word family clue word above each of the simulated muffins. The clue words on the muffin word guide should be the same clue words that help remind children of word family rimes, consistent with best practice. Underline the rime in each word family clue word.

Directions: Children in centers or literacy stations read the word family clue words on the muffin word guide and use onset and rime cards to spell word family words (see Figure 4-7). Then children write the words they built in the "muffins." If children spell more words than fit in the blank muffins on the muffin word guide, ask them to write the extra words underneath the muffins.

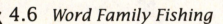

4.6 *Word Family Fishing*

Skill: Substituting onsets.

Children in a small group fish for words in a bucket "pond." Instead of simply reading words, as is the procedure in the traditional version of the word fishing activity, children substitute one beginning letter sound for another to read words with familiar rimes.

Things You'll Need: A plastic bucket to serve as a pond; a pole (a ruler works well); string; paper clips; a magnet; fish made of laminated construction paper; a marker.

To make the fishing pole, tie a string to a ruler and fasten a small magnet to the end of the string. To make the fish, cut colored construction paper into fish shapes. Write a different word with a familiar rime on one side of each fish—the word *band*, for instance. On the other side, write an onset, such as *s*, that creates a word when substituted for the beginning letter in the word on the reverse. Laminate the fish. Last, fasten a large paper clip to each fish and dump all the fish in the pond (the plastic bucket).

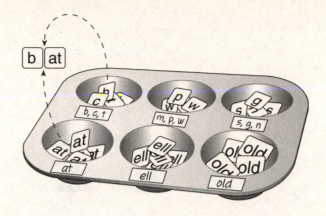

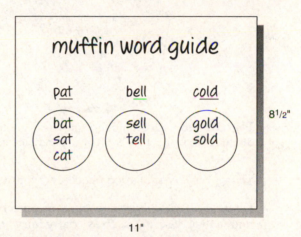

Figure 4-7 The muffin word guide that children fill in when they combine onset with rime cards placed in a muffin tin is a permanent record for the words that children build.

Directions: Children catch a fish, read the word on one side (*band*), substitute the beginning sound written on the reverse side (*s*), and then make a new word (*sand*), as shown in Figure 4-8. Correctly identified words are removed from the pond. *If the word is not correctly identified, the fish is thrown back into the pond for another try later in the game.*

4.7 *Hink Pinks*

Skill: Using onsets and rimes to read and spell word family words.

Hink pinks are two-word rhymes consisting of an adjective and a noun that share a rime.

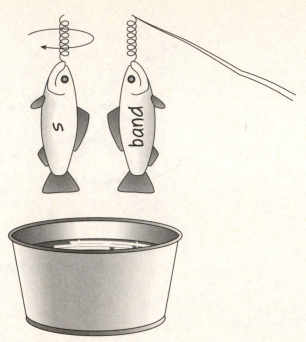

Figure 4-8 Children substitute one beginning sound (onset) for another to discover the words they catch in a "pond" made from a bucket or pail.

Things You'll Need: Paper; pencils; crayons or markers.

Directions: Ask children to think of adjectives with the same rimes as the nouns they describe, such as "dairy fairy" or "smelly belly." Write examples on the chalkboard to serve as illustrations. Children create and illustrate their own hink pinks. Figure 4-9 shows hink pinks and pictures created by a multiage group of second- and third-graders. You may want to ask children in second grade and above to write definitions for their hink pinks. For example, "soggy doggy" is a hink pink for "a drippy pet" or "a wet pet." You also may want to prop the definitions on the chalk tray and have children match the definitions with the hink pinks and pictures.

4.8 *Tongue Twisters*

Skill: Reading and writing short sentences with the same onset.

Tongue twisters are sentences in which all (or nearly all) the words begin with the same letter sound. Use this activity to give children practice paying attention to onsets.

foggy doggy

STUPID CUPID

Figure 4-9   Children think about rime and word meaning when they create and illustrate words that share the same rime.

Things You'll Need: Tongue twisters remembered from childhood or a good book with lots of twisters, such as *World's Toughest Tongue Twisters* (Rosenbloom, 1986) or *Tongue Twisters* (Keller, 1989).

Directions: Write a tongue twister on the board and have children read and reread the twister in chorus for fluency. Ask a volunteer to underline the words with the same beginning letter sound (onset). Then have children write their own tongue twisters. You may designate the onset each child is to use in writing, or children may decide for themselves which beginning sound they would like to use. Share the alliterative tongue twisters children write (see Figure 4-10), read twisters aloud in chorus, and put them on wall charts. To develop fluency, have children tape-record tongue twisters. Fasten together children's alliterative sentences and illustrations to make a book of playful, alliterative language created by the readers and writers in your classroom.

happy
pappy

Figure 4-9 (*continued*)

Horribal Harry hits hippos
on a hill on a happy
holiday in Hairballville.

Figure 4-10 Writing and illustrating tongue twisters gives children opportunities to identify the onsets in words and to creatively use this knowledge.

4.9 *Word Family Eggs*

Skill: Using onsets and rimes to read and spell word family words.

Children working with a partner or individually in centers or literacy stations spell words by putting together two halves of colorful plastic eggs—one half with an onset written on it and the other with a rime.

Things You'll Need: A permanent marker; plastic eggs; a basket (optional). Write an onset on one half of a plastic egg and a rime on the other half.

Directions: Put the eggs in a basket; separate them into halves; scramble the halves. Have children fasten together two halves of colored plastic eggs with a rime and an onset (see Figure 4-11). If children work with a partner, ask the partners to read the words to each other. You may want to ask children to write the words they spell.

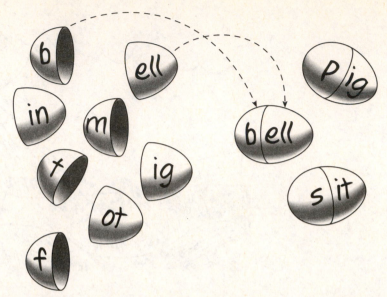

Figure 4-11   Children build words by putting the halves of plastic eggs with onsets on them together with the halves that have rimes written on them.

4.10 *Word Family Chains*

Skill: Using onsets and rimes to read and spell word family words.

Children make brightly colored paper chains of word family words.

Things You'll Need: Colorful construction paper cut into strips about one inch wide; stapler or tape.

Directions: Children look for word family words on the word wall, charts, and bulletin boards. Children write word family words on construction paper strips. Tape or staple the ends of strips into a circle, linking the circles with one another to form a giant chain. Before hanging the chains, count the number of words children chained together, and make a list of the words. Drape chains over bulletin boards, hang them from one corner of the room to the other, or tape them to desks, windows, and walls.

4.11 *Rime Pick-Up*

Skill: Reading often-used rimes.

In this gamelike activity, children pick up sticks—such as popsicle sticks or tongue depressors—with rimes on them (see Figure 4-12). This activity works

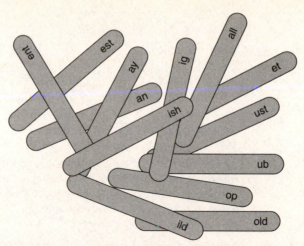

Figure 4-12 Children get lots of practice thinking of the recurring rime in words when they pick up craft sticks with rimes written on them and then think of a beginning sound to make a word.

best when two or three children play together and fits nicely into literacy stations or learning centers.

Things You'll Need: Popsicle sticks, craft sticks, or tongue depressors with rimes on them, and cards with onsets.

Directions: Scatter several sticks with rimes on a table of floor and place onset cards close by. Taking turns, children pick up a stick, read the rime, check to see if one of the onsets cards, when combined with the rime on the pick-up stick, makes a word family word. If the child makes a word, the child puts the rime stick in his or her own personal pile. Each rime stick is worth one point. The player who gets the most sticks (the most points) wins.

4.12 *Word Family Tic-Tac-Toe*

Skill: Using rimes to read and spell word family words.

This old standby works well in learning centers or literacy stations and is played much like the original version of the game, except word family words are written in tic-tac-toe squares instead of Xs and Os.

Things You'll Need: Oak tag tic-tac-toe cards; markers. Make tic-tac-toe cards by drawing on sturdy oak tag the traditional nine-box design and writing two word family clue words with different rimes above the boxes. Underline the rime in each word family clue word (*c̲a̲t̲*, *r̲a̲n̲*). Laminate tic-tac-toe cards and have players use erasable markers when they play.

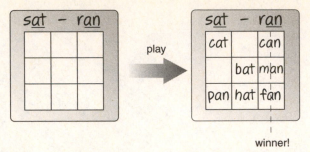

Figure 4-13 Tic-tac-toe challenges children to think of words that share the same rime. This activity can also be adapted for often-used prefixes and suffixes (Chapter 6) or for words that have specific letter-sound patterns, such as long vowels or r-controlled vowels (Chapter 5).

Directions: Two children play. Each writes a word with the same rime as that at the top of the playing card (see Figure 4-13). In this example, one player writes *at* family words, while the other writes *an* family words. The traditional rules hold—any three words joined in a horizontal, vertical, or diagonal direction win. Use this game for letter-sound patterns (Chapter 5), prefixes (Chapter 6), or suffixes (Chapter 6) by writing two words with different letter-sound patterns (such as b<u>oa</u>t and t<u>ai</u>l for long *o* and long *a*), prefixes (<u>un</u>happy and <u>re</u>play), or suffixes (play<u>ing</u> and look<u>ed</u>) at the top of the tic-tac-toe cards.

4.13 *Word Family Trains*

Skill: Using onsets and rimes to read and spell word family words.

Children make their own train tickets by writing word family words on cards and then putting them inside train cars with a word family rime clue word.

Things You'll Need: An engine and train cars made of colorful construction paper; large envelopes with a word family clue word on each. Staple a large envelope with a word family rime, flap side out, to each car. Fasten everything to a bulletin board (see Figure 4-14).

Figure 4-14 Getting on board this train calls for writing word family words (or words with the same beginning sound) and putting them inside the proper car. When the train leaves the station, all the cards are read and returned to the children, who then take them home for additional practice.

Directions: Children make their own "tickets" by writing word family words on index cards. Children then put the "tickets" inside the car with the word family clue word on it. When the train is ready to leave the station, take out the tickets, read and discuss the words, and return tickets to their makers so children can take them home to share.

4.14 *Word Family Slides*

Skill: Reading word family words by substituting onsets.

Children read word family words by pulling a strip of oak tag through a slide, as shown in Figure 4-15. This activity fits nicely into learning centers or literacy stations.

Things You'll Need: Although slides can be purchased, they are extremely easy to make. Write onsets on a strip of oak tag. Then cut a medium-size shape out of another piece of oak tag to serve as the body of the slide. Write a rime on the slide and cut a window (two horizontal slits) beside the rime. Make the window large enough so that the strip with onsets can be threaded through it.

Directions: Children pull the strip through the slide. As children do this, different word family words are formed. Because the onsets change but the rime stays the same, children get practice changing or substituting beginning

Figure 4-15 Word family slides give children practice identifying word family words that are formed when different onsets are combined with the same rime.

letter sounds (onsets). (Refer to Chapter 2 for an explanation of substituting beginning consonant sounds.) Ask children to read the word family words. If children are working in pairs, ask them to read the words to each other. For a more permanent record of the word family words, you may want to have the children write the words they make. Include the word family words on the slides in the word spelling activities (4.1, 4.2, and 4.5) described earlier.

4.15 *Word Family Towers*

Skill: Reading word family words.

Children in a small group or working with a partner build towers of word family words by reading words written on blocks.

Things You'll Need: Blocks with word family words. Make blocks by covering tissue boxes with drawer liner paper, and writing words on the blocks.

Directions: Children read the words on each block, select words that belong to the family, and then stack the blocks one on top of the other (see Figure 4-16). In reading different words on the blocks, children get repeated practice reading the same words, which helps to develop fluency reading word family words. Ask children to suggest other words that share the same rime; add some of the words to your classroom word wall. Connect this activity to math by having children count the words in the towers, and decide which tower has more or less blocks.

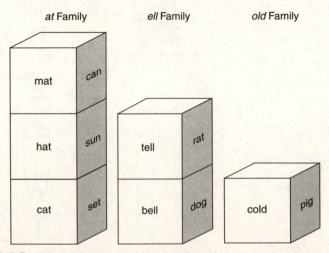

Figure 4-16 When children make word family towers, they have opportunities to read and reread the same words, which helps familiarize children with onsets and rimes, and helps to develop fluency in reading often-used words.

4.16 *Word Family Sorts*

Skill: Reading word family words.

Children sort words that belong in the same family or have the same vowel sound. Sorting is appropriate for children working individually or in pairs and is an excellent center or literacy station activity when children are familiar with the word family rimes in the words they are to sort.

Things You'll Need: Cards with word family words.

Directions: Have children sort words according to word family, such as sorting *cat*, *sat*, *mat*, and *fat* into one group; *hot*, *not*, *dot*, and *shot* into another; and *big*, *pig*, *rig*, and *wig* into a third group. Alternatively, you may ask more advanced children to sort words according to shared vowel sounds. In this sort children would group *hat*, *sad*, *pan*, and *back* together because these words contain a short *a*; and *dig*, *win*, *bit*, and *did* into the short *i* group. You may wish to forego telling children how to sort, opting instead for "open" sorting in which children choose the categories. During or after sorting, ask children to explain why they sorted the way they did, and talk about the families and, importantly, about the sounds that the vowels represent and the patterns children observe.

4.17 *Word Family Blocks*

Skill: Using onsets and rimes to spell word family words.

Children in a small group, in pairs, or working individually spell by lining up blocks horizontally and then turning blocks with onsets and rimes so that the combined onsets and rimes form word family words. This activity fits nicely into learning centers or literacy stations.

Things You'll Need: Onset blocks and rime blocks. Onset blocks have different onsets on six sides; rime blocks have a different rime on each of the six sides. For example, the six sides of an onset block might have *c*, *m*, *h*, *r*, *s*, and *t*. A word family rime block might have *ap*, *op*, *en*, *at*, *ot*, and *ug*. The blocks should have the onsets and word family rimes children are learning in your classroom. If children have not learned as many as six rimes, you may put the same rime on more than one side of a rime block.

Directions: Give each child one onset block and one rime block. To spell words by substituting onsets, have each child turn the rime block so that the same rime, say *ap*, faces toward them. Then ask each child to place the onset block next to the *ap* rime block, and turn the onset block to spell word family words. *Cap*, *rap*, *sap*, and *tap* are possible words spelled with these blocks. In order to spell by substituting the rime, have children place *t* face up, and then turn the rime block to make *ten*, *tug*, *top*, *tap*, and *ten*. If using this activity with a small group, write the words children build on the board and then compare and contrast the different word family rimes.

4.18 *Word Family Hunts*

Skill: Identifying and reading word family words.

Children search for word family words. In the process, children learn to look for, recognize, and read words with the rimes you are teaching.

Things You'll Need: Cards with word family words; each word should be written on two cards to form two identical decks.

Directions: Divide the cards into two decks of the same words. Hide one stack of cards in your classroom. Distribute the cards from the identical deck to children in your classroom. Write word family rimes on the board. Have children search the room to find cards that match. When a child finds a match, the child writes the word under the appropriate rime on the board to create lists of word family words.

SPARE-MINUTE ACTIVITIES FOR TEACHING ANALOGY-BASED PHONICS WITH WORD FAMILY WORDS

4.19 *Riddles*

Skill: Substituting onsets in word family words.

Write two words on the board, *rice* and *bug*, perhaps. Children then use the clue words to solve a riddle. For example, you might say, "The word starts like *rice* and rhymes with *bug*. What is it?" Have children write the solution on small white boards which they hold up to show you their solution to each puzzle.

4.20 *Buddy Words*

Skill: Using onsets and rimes to spell word family words.

Tape an onset or a rime to individual children. Children find a buddy who is wearing an onset or rime that, when combined with the onset or rime worn by both children, makes a word family word.

4.21 *Duck, Duck, Goose*

Skill: Using onsets and rimes to spell word family words.

Give each child sitting cross legged in a circle a white board and marker. One person is "It." *It* has one card with a word family rime, but keeps the rime hidden. *It* walks around the circle tapping each child gently on the shoulder while saying, "Duck." Without warning, *It* stops in front of a child, taps the person on the shoulder, says, "Goose," and shows the tapped child the rime card. The tapped child then has a few seconds to write a word with the rime. If successful, the tapped child becomes the new *It*. Give the new *It* a card with a new word.

4.22 *Beach Ball Roll*

Skill: Spelling word family words with onsets and rimes.

Use a permanent marker to write onsets on a beach ball. Write a rime on a small white board or on the chalkboard. Children sit in a circle and gently roll the beach ball. The child who catches the ball pronounces a word by blending the consonant closest to his or her right hand with the rime on the small whiteboard you are holding (or the rime on the chalkboard). Write the word family word on a large whiteboard, chalkboard, or chart. When finished rolling the beach ball, have children read together in chorus the beach ball words they made (the lists on the board).

4.23 *Word Family Spelling Race*

Skill: Spelling word family words with onsets and rimes.

Give each child or pair in a small group an envelope containing onset and rime cards. At the word "Go," children combine onsets and rimes to make words. For a competitive game, the first child or pair to use all the onset-rime cards wins.

4.24 *Word Family Lists*

Skill: Reading word family words.

Children make long lists of words that begin with the same rime. Encourage children to actively participate in list making, to help write the words, and to read and reread the lists to develop instant word recognition.

Teaching Analogy-Based Phonics with word Family Words to English Language Learners

Learning word family words by analogy is more effective when words spelled with rimes are in English learners' speaking vocabularies. For example, an English learner can use the *ip* in *ship*, a known word, to read *trip*, a new word, when the child knows the spoken word, /trip/. If the child does not know this spoken word, then you will need to teach word meaning either before reading or during reading through the use of context clues and discussion. We can see, then, that the more English words a child knows the greater the potential for that child to use the onsets and rimes in known words to read words he or she has never seen before. Give children many examples of words and their meanings, and demonstrate word meaning when possible with gestures, pictures, and objects. Encourage English learners to use language in your classroom, and have children work with native English speaking buddies in small groups. Use English words children already know to explain words children do not yet know. If children do not know some of the English words you wish to use in analogy lessons, preteach those words.

Rimes that occur in many different words are more useful than those that occur infrequently. English learners are more likely to have words in their English speaking vocabularies when the words occur with some regularity. Moreover, the more often certain rimes occur, the more often children can use their knowledge of rime to read and spell new word family words. The rimes in Table 4–2 with an asterisk (*) are useful to teach because these rimes are part of many different words. Activities like sticky-note flip books (4.4) and word family slides (4.14) give children practice reading word family words, and activities like word family muffins (4.5) and pocket chart spelling (4.1, 4.2) give children practice spelling words that share the same rime. Have children read books with word family words, write stories, and play games. As you plan reading and writing experiences, also provide ways for children to learn words that contain these rimes.

Children draw on their memory of a rime in a known word to make an analogy to a new word. The use of clue words is a way to support and promote decoding by analogy. Clue words are especially helpful for English learners because clue words remind English learners of the rimes they already know, and prompt children to use the rimes when reading and spelling. In selecting clue words for use with English learners, look for words that are (1) in children's English speaking vocabularies, (2) useful for reading and writing, (3) the names of objects, (4) easy to depict in pictures, and (5) short, consisting of only one syllable so the rime is obvious. *Pig* is a good clue word for the *ig* rime. *Pig* is likely to be a word in English learners' speaking vocabulary; *pig* is a word young English learners are likely to come across as they read stories; *pig* is a concrete noun; *pig* is easy to picture; and *pig* is a short word. In contrast, *wig* is not a good choice. While the *ig* rime is obvious in this short word, *wig* is more difficult to depict in a picture, less likely to be in children's English speaking vocabulary, and less likely to occur in the stories children read and write.

Look for clue words in the books children read. Select clue words from the words children use when they talk and write. Display word family clue words in your classroom in plain view; make them available in learning centers or literacy stations and in other places where children read and write. Be sure English learners know where the clue words are located. Talk about word family clue words and underline the rime when you display these words in your classroom. In calling attention to clue words, write word family clue words on a special bulletin board on or a large chart. Make a word family word wall in your classroom that features clue words followed by examples of words that contain the clue word rimes. For instance, if *clock* is the clue word for *ock*, words underneath *clock* on the word wall might be *sock*, *lock*, and *block*. Write a word family clue word on chart paper, put the paper in a place where children have access to it, and encourage children to add word family words to the chart. Count the word family words in your classroom. Have each English learner make a personal word family clue word book. Ask children to illustrate the clue words and to keep the books on hand at their work spaces or in learning centers or literacy stations.

TEACHING ANALOGY-BASED PHONICS WITH WORD FAMILY WORDS TO CHILDREN AT RISK

Learning word family words by making analogies from rimes in known words to rimes in unfamiliar words is a gateway to decoding for the children at risk whom we teach. Learning word family words requires less phonemic awareness and less code knowledge than decoding words letter-sound by letter-sound (Chapter 5). With respect to phonemic awareness, children need to be aware of beginning sounds and rhymes. Beginning sound and rhyme awareness develop before the ability to segment words into individual sounds (Chapter 2). Children at risk are more likely to segment and blend word family words into onsets and rimes (/cat/ = /c/ + /at/) than to segment and blend all the individual sounds in words (/cat/ = /c/ + /a/ + /t/). As for rimes, the brain naturally looks for patterns, and rimes are relatively easy patterns to recognize in words. It is simpler to learn the sounds associated with a whole rime (at = /at/) than to learn the sounds associated with individual letters (a = /a/ + t = /t/). Fewer sounds to segment and blend, and fewer letter groups to associate with sounds, make it possible for children with low phonemic awareness and relatively modest code knowledge to successfully read and spell word family words. These same at-risk children, however, may struggle with letter-sound decoding (Chapter 5) because their phonemic awareness and letter-sound knowledge are too limited to support the skill.

Activities like pocket chart word family spelling (4.1), word family fishing (4.6), and word family slides (4.14) strengthen the ability to substitute beginning consonants (see sound manipulation, Chapter 2). Point out and underline the onsets and rimes when children rewrite familiar poems (4.3). Use word family spelling (4.2) and word family blocks (4.17) to give children at risk practice, under your guidance, in spelling and reading words that consist of several different rimes. Activities like word family muffins (4.5), word family eggs (4.9), and word family chains

(4.10) give children practice building words with onsets and the rimes they are learning. And, as you use these and other activities, refer to clue words to remind children of the rimes they already know. Additionally, talk about the individual sounds in clue words and the rimes children know. Develop phonemic awareness through activities in Chapter 2 that ask children to listen for sounds, identify sounds, and blend the sounds in word family words. Children read and spell more words through analogy when their teachers use clue words and develop children's awareness of all the sounds in rimes (Ehri, Satlow, & Gaskins, 2009).

After children have some familiarity with rimes, ask children to think about the commonalities and differences among rimes. The short-vowel pattern is the most important commonality to explore. Let us take a closer look at the short-vowel pattern. A vowel (*a*, *e*, *i*, *o*, or *u*) represents a short sound when it is the only vowel in a word that ends with a consonant sound (Chapter 5). *Cat*, *met*, *sit*, *hot*, and *hut* are examples of this pattern. The short-vowel pattern is typically the first vowel pattern children learn as they move into letter-sound decoding (Chapter 5). The short-vowel pattern is straightforward, and, insofar as the vowel letters are concerned, is arguably the most dependable of the vowel patterns. The majority of classroom reading programs teach the short vowels well before the more complex long vowels. In our experience, children at risk find the short-vowel pattern is easier to understand and use when children first learn the short-vowel rimes. Write letters in the same color that stand for the same vowel sound in different rimes (Hines, 2009). For instance, write the short *a* rimes in Table 4–2, such as *at*, *am*, and *an*, in green; the short *e* rimes in red; the short *i* rimes in blue; the short *o* rimes in orange; and the short *u* rimes in purple. Phase out the color when children demonstrate that they know the sounds the different short vowels represent in rimes. For these reasons, when teaching decoding by analogy, call attention to vowel sounds and the short-vowel pattern in rimes and support children as they generalize this knowledge to read many different words spelled with the short-vowel pattern. Use the activities in this chapter to increase children's use of onsets and rimes to read and spell word family words, and the activities in Chapter 5 to develop the ability to read and spell with letter-sound phonics.

E-RESOURCES FOR TEACHING ANALOGY-BASED PHONICS WITH WORD FAMILY WORDS

Voice and Graphic Media

VoiceThread (*www.voicethread.com*) and
Wordle™ Word Clouds (*http://www.wordle.net/*):

Wordle™ is a tool for creating word clouds displaying words provided by you or the children whom you teach. Identify a word family and have children make a list of word family words. Decide on the most common words. Enter the words on the website and select the font, color and direction for the display. The more often a word appears on the list, the larger the word will appear on the finished display. Combine VoiceThread and Wordle™ to make talking word families. After children create their own word family Wordles, have them use VoiceThread to read their Wordles. Share the VoiceThread Word Family Wordles with the class. Subscriptions to VoiceThread are available online.

Video Media

Flip Camera: Word Family Words and Word Family Book

Flip cameras are small handheld cameras that are easy to use and readily available in retail stores. Use flip cameras to record children's work samples showing word family words. Record the class or individual children reading word family books. Have children find word family words in your school and record themselves identifying the family and reading the words they find. Consider, too, making large word family books with the whole class and then recording the class or individual children reading the books. Upload the video clips and save them on CDs or make movie DVDs that can be viewed on DVD players. Send the CDs or DVDs home for children to share with their families.

Websites with Activities or Lessons for Computers or Interactive Whiteboards (IWBs)

Smart Exchange™ (*http://exchange.smarttech.com/#tab=0*):

Examples of IWB word family rime activities include(1) Under the Sea, for the *ight* word family; (2) a lesson on the *an, et, in, op*, and *ug* word families; (3) a lesson on the *ap, est, it, ot*, and *uck* word families; and (4) Catch of the Day, for *ang, ing, ong*, and *ung* word families.

Cricketweb (*http://www.crickweb.co.uk/*):

The Cricketweb site has two interactive games: (1) Word Wheel 1 gives children practice building words with onsets and rimes. (2) The CVC Word Maker game has two levels. The first level, Wordplay, calls for building words with onsets and rimes, and the second level, Wordmatch, asks the player to match words. Lesson plans are available for Word Wheel and CVC Word Maker.

PBS Kids™ (*http://pbskids.org/whiteboard/, http://pbskids.org/lions/games/pounce.html*, and *http://pbskids.org/superwhy/index.html#games*):

The PBS Kids™ website has two IWB-ready games: (1) Super Why: Wonder Red's Freeze Dance Rhyming, which calls for finding words that share a rime, and (2) Between the Lions: The Problem with Chickens, where children build words with onsets and rimes. Examples of games that call for identifying words with the same rimes are (1) Super Why! Wonder Red's Rhyme N' Roll, and (2) Super Why! Wonder Red's Rhyme Time Bingo. Super Why!: Rhyming Match Up asks children to remember onsets and rimes that make words.

ReadWriteThink (*http://www.readwritethink.org*):

This site, co-sponsored by the International Reading Association and the National Council of Teachers of English, has an interactive, click-and-drag game called Construct-a-Word that includes building words by adding onsets to rimes and sorting words by word family and Word Family Sort for identifying words that belong to the same family. The site has many free lesson plans for teaching reading and spelling with onsets and rimes, research in support of lessons, and teaching standards met by the lessons.

BBC Little Animals Activity Center (*http://www.bbc.co.uk/schools/laac/menu.shtml*):

Sponsored by the British Broadcasting Corporation, this website includes a Little Animals Activity Center where you will find the Digby Mole. This game includes options for matching written words that rhyme and for matching words to beginning or ending letter sounds. Each option has three levels. The first two levels of the rhyming option are appropriate for children who understand rime and need more practice recognizing rime. The beginning sounds and ending sounds options are suitable for children who have experience associating letters and sounds and would benefit from additional practice. The voice in this game adds an /uh/ when pronouncing individual sounds. The extra /uh/ has the potential to confuse some children (see Chapter 2 for an explanation).

Roy the Zebra (*http://www.roythezebra.com*):

This site has many lessons and activities for teaching beginning readers. There are stories for guided reading, downloadable worksheets, and a selection of interactive games. Click on Interactive Reading Games and then click on Words that Rhyme games. These games ask children to find words with that rhyme (sound alike) and are spelled with the same rimes. Look for the Consonant Vowel Consonant Words: Make Words worksheet for practice combining onsets and word family rimes to spell words.

Story It (*http://www.storyit.com/*):

Look on this site for a game called Odd One Out. In this online game, the player clicks on a word that is spelled with a different rime. Clicking on the odd word encourages the player to carefully attend to the rimes in words.

Starfall™ (*www.starfall.com*):

Select option 2—Learn to Read—on the main index to access word family activities. This site offers interactive word building activities where the child clicks and drags an onset to combine with a rime to make a word that matches a picture. Look, too, for printable sheets for reading and writing word family words that feature the short vowels. To access printable worksheets click on the Download Center at the bottom of the main index and then click on Online Book Printouts.

ict Teaching Games (*http://www.ictgames.com*):

Click on Literacy on the home page, then on Rhyming Rockets. In the first two levels of this game, players shoot down rockets that are spelled with the same rime. The third level presents words that share a rhyming sound but are not necessarily spelled the same, such as *bread*, *said*, and *red*. The sound effects, exploding rockets and World War II bombers, may be more likely to appeal to children who are interested in shooting games. Review this game to determine whether the violence is suitable for the children in your classroom.

Internet4Classrooms (*http://www.internet4classrooms.com*):

This website offers a plethora of teaching and learning activities, games, and print-outs for children PreK–12. You will find on this site many different links, all of them categorized according the grade-level expectations. This is a good resource for all teaching areas and a quick way to access websites the developers have already screened.

Literactive (*http://www.literactive.com/Home/index.asp*):

The resources on this site are free once you register. On the home page click on Download Activities and then on the level you wish to access. The Weighing Scales game, found in Level 1, asks children to combine onsets and rimes to build word family words. Look in Level 2 for (1) Sandpit Trucks and (2) Garden Leaves. In Sandpit Trucks, children match words that share a rime. Garden Leaves calls attention to the ending letters in word family words. Level 3 has a Lovebirds game where children identify birds that belong to the same word family. In Rhyming Fish, a Level 4 game, children sort word family words. The resources are free after you register on the Literactive site.

PowerPoint Presentations with Words, Pictures and Sound:

Begin Create PowerPoint presentations that feature word family words, pictures and sound. Presentations can be created by teachers and children. PowerPoint presentations can be shared with the class with a digital projector and shared with families by copying them onto CDs. You may also want to use PowerPoint presentation as an alternative to posting children's work online.

Printable Materials

Word Way (*http://www.wordway.us.com/*):

This site, created by Cherry Carl, offers free, downloadable activities for classroom use. Examples of activities and resources germane to word families are Word Family Posters that feature lists of word family words, Word Building Mats for use in learning centers or literacy stations, Recording Pages where the child adds an onset to a rime to form a word family word, Word Family Kid Cards to remind children of word families, Word Family Lists, Welcome to the Neighborhood mats and cards for sorting words, Word Family Slides, and Word Family Cut and Paste for matching word family words with pictures. There are also Cloze the Gap worksheets where children fill in word family words to complete sentences. Other resources include books and games. The downloadable resources on this website are free and useful for group instruction, literacy stations or centers, homework, and materials for children to take home.

Kidzone (*http://www.kidzone.ws*):

Kidzone includes 14 sets of printable worksheets, activities word lists, and flashcards for reviewing and reinforcing over 30 rimes, and printable worksheets of beginning sounds, ending sounds, and vowels.

REFERENCES

Bear, D. R., Invernizzi, M., Templeton, S., & Johnston, F. (2007). *Words their way: Word study for phonics, vocabulary, and spelling instruction* (3rd ed.). Upper Saddle River, NJ: Pearson Education.

Cheek, E. H., Flippo, R. F., & Lindsey, J. D. (1997). *Reading for success in elementary schools.* Dubuque, IA: Brown & Benchmark.

Ehri, L. C., & Robbins, C. (1992). Beginners need some decoding skill to read words by analogy. *Reading Research Quarterly, 27,* 12–28.

Ehri, L.C., Satlow, E., & Gaskins, I. (2009). Grapho-phonemic enrichment strengthens keyword analogy instruction for young readers. *Reading & Writing Quarterly, 25,* 162–191.

Fry, E. (1998). The most common phonograms. *The Reading Teacher, 52,* 620–622.

Goswami, U. (2001). Early phonological development and the acquisition of literacy. In S. B. Neuman & D. K. Dickinson (Eds.), *Handbook of early literacy research* (pp. 111–125). New York: Guilford Press.

Henderson, E. (1990). *Teaching spelling* (2nd ed.) Boston: Houghton Mifflin.

Hines, S. J. (2009). The effectiveness of a color-coded, onset-rime decoding intervention with first-grade students at serious risk for reading disabilities. *Learning Disabilities Research & Practice, 24,* 21–32.

Juel, C., & Minden-Cupp, C. (2000). Learning to read words: Linguistic units and instructional strategies. *Reading Research Quarterly, 35,* 458–492.

Keller, C. (1989). *Tongue twisters.* New York: Simon & Schuster.

Langstaff, J. (1989). *Oh, a-hunting we will go.* Boston: Houghton Mifflin.

Merrill linguistic reading program (4th ed.). (1986). Upper Saddle River, NJ: Merrill/ Prentice Hall.

Rosenbloom, J. (1986). *World's toughest tongue twisters.* New York: Sterling.

Walton, P. D., Walton, L. M., & Felton, K. (2001). Teaching rime analogy or letter recoding reading strategies to prereaders: Effects on prereading skills and word reading. *Journal of Educational Psychology, 93*(1), 160–180.

CHAPTER 5

Letter-Sound Phonics in Late Kindergarten, First, and Second Grade

The Strategy of Using Letter and Sound Associations to Read and Learn New Words

This chapter explains the letter-sound relationships of phonics and how children strategically use letter-sound associations to read new words. You will learn why the left-to-right sequencing of letters in words is important for reading and spelling words, how to sequence phonics instruction, the appropriate place for decodable books in your classroom reading program, and best practices for teaching phonics. Here you will also find activities for teaching letter-sound relationships, suggestions for teaching English language learners and children at risk, and a list of e-resources for teaching letter-sound phonics.

KEY IDEAS

▸ Readers who use phonics associate sounds with letters and then blend sounds together to pronounce familiar words that make sense in reading contexts.

▸ Readers use phonics to teach themselves new words; they do this independently without help from better readers.

▸ In spelling new words, children listen for the sounds in the words they want to spell, associate letters with those sounds, and then write the letters.

▸ Decodable books—those that include the same letter-sound patterns you are teaching in your classroom—may give some children beneficial practice using phonics when used as supplementary reading.

▸ Phonics is taught in the kindergarten, first, and second grades, and may be reviewed in the third grade if children are not already skilled at decoding. We expect children to be able to read and learn new words on their own when they begin third grade.

KEY VOCABULARY

Consonant

Consonant blend

Decodable books

Digraph

Diphthong

Full alphabetic word learners

Invented spelling

Letter-sound pattern

Phonetically regular word

Vowel

Vowel team

Within word pattern spellers

Unlike the turtles in Wen Ting's drawing in Figure 5-1, the alphabet is not a jumble of topsy-turvy letter-sound combinations. Readers do not aimlessly tumble as they learn how letters represent sounds, nor do they stand on their heads when using letter and sound relationships to read unfamiliar words. For readers who do not automatically recognize *topsy*, *turvy*, and *turtles*, the strategy of using letter sounds is a quick and sure route to pronunciation. Letter-sound-based phonics instruction teaches readers how to take advantage of the alphabetic principle—the principle that letters of the alphabet represent the sounds in words.

The children in your classroom are likely to be successful readers only when they understand and use this principle. Children who learn phonics early and well are better readers and better comprehenders than children who do not learn phonics (Blachman et al., 2004; Christensen & Bowey, 2005; National Reading Panel, 2000). This is true regardless of children's social or economic background (Armbruster, Lehr, & Osborn, 2001). Good readers use their in-depth knowledge of letter and sound patterns with strategic flexibility and resourcefulness. They *think* while using phonics to read and spell. They always focus on meaning. They use their knowledge of phonics to support comprehension through decoding words they do not instantly recognize, and to support writing through spelling new words.

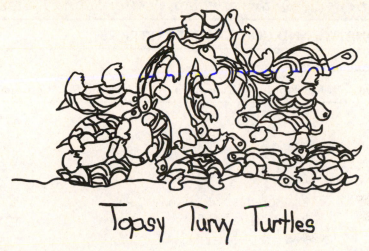

Topsy Turvy Turtles

Figure 5-1   Unlike the jumbled turtles in Wen Ting's drawing, letters represent sounds in predictable ways and are, therefore, a useful pathway to word identification.

PHONICS LETTER-SOUND PATTERNS

The 26 letters in our alphabet are a hardworking bunch. This small group of 26 is systematically arranged, rearranged, and sequenced to build tens of thousands of words. With all this arranging and sequencing, it is inevitable that certain letters routinely appear right next to one another in spelling. This creates a type of spelling context in which certain letters are frequently and predictably adjacent to other letters. These letters form patterns. **Letter-sound patterns** represent one or more sounds in words, such as the *t* in *tap*, the *th* in *this*, the *thr* in *three*, the *oi* in *soil*, or the *ai* in *sail*. As children become familiar with the letters that appear together in spelling, they associate sounds with those letters and hence begin to use the letter-sound patterns of phonics.

We divide letters of our alphabet into 21 **consonants** (represented with a C) and 5 **vowels** (represented with a V). The vowels consist of *a, e, i, o,* and *u;* occasionally *w* and *y* also act as vowels. Consonants are the remaining 21 letters, as explained in Table 5–1 and Appendix A. Because there is almost always more than one way to group the consonant and vowel letters in a new word, readers must consider which letters combine to form patterns and which do not. For example, *me* forms a consonant-vowel (CV) long-vowel pattern in *me* (see Table 5–1 and Appendix A). This same sequence (*me*) does not constitute the letter-sound pattern in *met* because the *e* belongs to the vowel-consonant (VC) short-vowel pattern. Experienced readers know this and therefore look for predictable and frequently occurring patterns in words they have never seen before. Consonant patterns consist of consonant letters. Vowel patterns consist of sequences of vowel and consonant letters that indicate the sound represented by the vowel. Table 5–1

TABLE 5–1 *Summary of Phonics Letter-Sound Patterns**

CONSONANTS AND CONSONANT PATTERNS

Single Consonants

Consonant	Key Word	Consonant	Key Word	Consonant	Key Word
b	boat	k	kite	s*	sun
c*	cat	l	lion	t	turtle
d	dog	m	moon	v	van
f	fish	n	nut	w*	wagon
g*	goat	p	pig	x*	fox
h	hat	q(u)*	queen	y*	yellow
j	jeep	r	ring	z	zipper

*The single consonants *c*, *g*, and *x* represent more than one sound. The *w* and *y* may act as consonants or vowels. The *q* is followed by *u*. Look in Appendix A for explanations.

Consonant Blends (or Clusters)

The sounds represented by the letters in a consonant blend are joined together during pronunciation. The two-letter blends can be divided into three four groups: (1) blends with the letter *Ll*; (2) blends with the letter *Rr*; (3) blends with the letter *Ss*; and (4) blends with the letter *Ww*.

Two-Letter Blends

L Blends	Key Words	R Blends	Key Words	S Blends	Key Words	W Blends	Key Words
bl	black	br	broom	sc	scarf	dw	dwell
cl	clown	cr	crab	sk	skate	tw	twig
fl	flag	dr	dress	sm	smile		
gl	glass	fr	frog	sn	snail		
pl	play	gr	grape	sp	spider		
sl	sled	pr	pretzel	st	star		
		tr	train	sw	sweep		

Two-Letter Blends That Occur at the End of Words or Syllables

Final Blends	Key Words	Final Blends	Key Words
ld	gold	nt	tent
lk	walk	sk	desk
mp	lamp	sp	wasp
nd	hand	st	nest

Three-Letter Blends That Represent Three Sounds

Blends	Key Words	Blends	Key Words
scr	scrap	squ	squirrel
spl	splash	str	stripe
spr	spring		

Look in Appendix A for three-letter blends that represent two sounds.

Consonant Digraphs

Digraphs are two consonant letters that represent one sound.

Digraph	Key Word	Digraph	Key Word	Digraph	Key Word
ch	chair	sh	shoe	th (voiced)	that
th (unvoiced)	thumb	wh	whale		

See Appendix A for more information on the consonant digraphs.

Hard and Soft Cc and Gg Consonants

ca, co, cu: When *c* precedes *a, o,* and *u,* the *c* usually represents the /k/ heard in *kite* (called a hard sound).
ce, ci, cy: When *c* precedes *e, i,* and *y,* the *c* usually represents the sound associated with the /s/ in *soap* (called a soft sound).

Hard C	Key Word	Soft C	Key Word
ca /k/	cat	ce /s/	cent
co /k/	coat	ci /s/	city
cu /k/	cut	cy /s/	cycle

ga, go, cu: When *g* precedes *a, o,* and *u,* the *g* usually represents the sound associated with the /g/ in *gate* (called the hard sound).
ge, gi, gy: When *g* precedes *e, i,* and *y,* the *g* usually represents the sound associated with the /j/ in *jelly* (called the soft sound).

(continued)

TABLE 5–1 *Continued*			
Hard G	**Key Word**	**Soft G**	**Key Word**
ga /g/	game	ge /j/	gem
go /g/	got	gi /j/	giant
gu /g/	gum	gy /j/	gym

VOWEL PATTERNS

Short-Vowel Sounds and Key Words

The short-vowel sounds are shown below. VC is the major short-vowel pattern. VCCe also indicates that the vowel letter usually represents a short sound.

Short Vowel	**Key Word**
Short *a*	apple
Short *e*	edge
Short *i*	igloo
Short *o*	octopus
Short *u*	umbrella

Short-Vowel Patterns

VC Short-Vowel Pattern

This pattern consists of one vowel followed by one or more consonants in a one-syllable word or in a single syllable.

Short Vowel	**Example**
VC short *a*	<u>fan</u>
VC short *e*	n<u>et</u>
VC short *i*	<u>fin</u>
VC short *o*	mo<u>p</u>
VC short *u*	n<u>ut</u>

VCCe Short-Vowel Pattern

In the VCCe pattern, the vowel generally represents a short sound and the *e* is silent.

Short Vowel	**Example**
VCCE short *a*	ch<u>ance</u>
VCCE short *e*	<u>dense</u>
VCCE short *i*	br<u>idge</u>
VCCE short *o*	bl<u>onde</u>
VCCE short *u*	n<u>udge</u>

Long-Vowel Sounds and Key Words

Teachers often describe the long sounds as vowels that "say their names."

Long Vowel	Key Word
Long *a*	apron
Long *e*	eraser
Long *i*	ice
Long *o*	overalls
Long *u*	unicorn

Long-Vowel Patterns

The long-vowel patterns consist of VCe, VV vowel team, and CV.

VCe Pattern

The final *e* is silent and the preceding vowel usually has a long sound.

VCe Long Vowel	Example
VCe long *a*	b<u>ake</u>
VCe long *e*	th<u>eme</u>
VCe long *i*	sm<u>ile</u>
VCe long *o*	h<u>ome</u>
VCe long *u*	c<u>ube</u>

VV Vowel Team

A vowel team consists of two adjacent vowels (VV) that represent one vowel sound when they are in the same syllable. In the vowel teams of *ai, oa, ay, ee, ey,* and *ea*, the first vowel usually represents a long sound and the second is silent.

VV Vowel Team Long Vowel	Example
ai long *a*	s<u>ai</u>l
ay long *a*	pl<u>ay</u>
ea long *e*	l<u>ea</u>f
ee long *e*	f<u>ee</u>t
ey long *e*	k<u>ey</u>
oa long *o*	b<u>oa</u>t

(continued)

TABLE 5–1 *Continued*

CV Pattern

In the CV pattern, the vowel usually represents a long sound. The CV is an open syllable, described in Chapter 6.

CV Long Vowel	Example
CV long *a*	la̱bel
CV long *e*	me̱
CV long *i*	ti̱ger
CV long *o*	no̱
CV long *u*	mu̱sic

Other Vowel Patterns

Other patterns consist of the r-controlled pattern, diphthongs, *oo, au, aw, ew* and *eu*.

R-controlled Vowel – Vr - Pattern

The *r* affects pronunciation so that vowels cannot be classified as short or long.

R-control Vowel	Example
Vr *ar*	ca̱r
Vr *er*	he̱r
Vr *ir*	bi̱rd
Vr *or*	fo̱rt
Vr *ur*	tu̱rn

Vowel Diphthongs

Ow, ou, oi, oy: Ow, ou, oi, and *oy* are vowel diphthongs. These patterns often represent the following sounds in pronunciation: *ow* in *cow; ou* in *out; oi* in *oil; oy* in *boy.*

Double oo

The double *oo* usually represents the sound heard in *school* or the sound heard in *book* with about equal frequency.

Au and Aw Patterns

The *au* generally represents the sound in *fault.* The *aw* usually represents the sound in *straw.*

Ew and Ue Patterns

The *ew* and *ue* patterns usually represent the sounds in *blew* and *blue.*

Look at Appendix A for more detailed explanations.

summarizes consonant and vowel letter-sound patterns; Appendix A gives more complete explanations of patterns.

Left-to-right letter order is important. The left-to-right order of letters in words affects the sounds the letters represent. If children are to be successful using letter-sound phonics, they absolutely must pay attention to letter order. Let us use the letter *a* as an illustration. The *a* represents one pronunciation when followed by a consonant in *mat*, a different pronunciation when followed by a consonant plus an *e* in *mate*, and still another when followed by an *r* in *mart*. If we were to look at only the first two beginning letters, *ma*, we might conclude that the *a* in each of these words—*mat*, *mart*, and *made*—is pronounced the same. If we were to look only at the beginning and ending letters of *m* and *t* in *mat* and *mart*, we would not realize that the *a* represents different sounds in these words. On closer inspection we notice that the letters following the vowel, the letters to the right of the *a*, provide the clue to the vowel sound. Thus, the *a* in *mat* is situated in a short-vowel (VC) pattern, the *a* in *made* is in a VCe pattern, where the *a* is long and the *e* is silent, and the *a* in *mart* is part of a Vr or r-controlled pattern. Each pattern—short-vowel VC, VCe, and Vr—is a letter-sound pattern. Readers must look to the right of the vowel, in this example the letter *a*, to identify the pattern in which the *a* is placed. Each word—*mat*, *mate*, and *mart*—is easily decoded and spelled when and only when readers take the left-to-right order of letters into account. This is why it is so important to encourage the children in your classroom to look all the way through new words, beginning with the first letter and ending with the last. Left-to-right inspection reveals the consonant and vowel patterns in words. Furthermore, in associating sounds with letters from left to right, children are well positioned to recall and blend sounds in their proper sequence. You will learn more about what happens when readers do not analyze words from left to right when you read the section on teaching children at risk.

WHICH LETTER-SOUND PATTERNS TO TEACH AND WHEN TO TEACH THEM

You may be surprised to learn that research does not support the use of any one particular sequence for teaching letter-sounds over another sequence. If you use a commercial set of teaching materials or your school district has a prescribed sequence, by all means follow that plan. But if you have some flexibility in how you sequence instruction in letter-sound patterns, begin with the most useful and the easiest patterns followed by increasingly more difficult patterns, as described in this section.

Single Consonant and Vowel Letters

Children are introduced to the sound of the letters in kindergarten or preschool. It is common practice to teach the names of the letters and the sound the letter represent at the same time or in close succession. The sounds associated with the consonants and vowels are explained in Table 5–1 and Appendix A.

- *Single consonants.* Teach a sound for each consonant in kindergarten, as explained in Chapter 3. Then, when readers know a sound for a consonant letter, teach readers to use that letter sound to identify words. Once children use beginning consonant letter sounds to identify unfamiliar words, show them how to use a combination of beginning and ending consonants. As it turns out, far more English words begin and end with consonants than begin and end with vowels. Beginning consonants are especially obvious and can be readily combined with sentence structure and context clues, which keeps decoding meaning based. It is not surprising, then, that many readers first pay attention to the single consonants at the beginning of words. When children are comfortable using beginning consonants, prompt them to use both beginning and ending consonants, saying something like, "Look at the beginning and ending letters. What word makes sense (in the reading context) that begins and ends with these sounds?" In so doing, children are apt to keep decoding meaning based. After children develop the ability to use beginning and ending consonant letter sounds, they notice the middle letters in short words (h*a*t), which brings us the vowel letters.
- *Single vowels.* Teach the short sound for each vowel. Examples of short vowel sounds are /a/ in *apple*, /e/ in *edge*, /i/ in *itch*, /o/ in *octopus*, and /u/ in *up*. The letter *y* at the end of a word acts as a vowel, as in *try*, when combined with an *a* (*stay*) or an *e* (*key*), or when acting as a suffix (*pricey*, *nicely*). Teach a sound for each vowel before you teach *all* the consonant letter sounds. It is important to teach a mixture of vowels and consonants because every English word has at least one vowel. When you teach a handful of consonants and vowels, children can begin to read and spell three-letter words made up of those consonants and vowels. For instance, if you teach *s*, *n*, *a*, *i*, *p*, and *t*, children can read and spell words like *sat*, *tip*, *pan*, *pin*, *tan*, *sip*, and *snap*. This makes it possible for children to begin to use phonics right away.

VC Short-Vowel Pattern (Vowel-Consonant)

Teaching a *short sound* for each vowel letter (described above) sets the stage for teaching the VC *short-vowel pattern*, which is the first vowel pattern you should introduce. The short-vowel pattern consists of a single vowel followed by one or more consonant sounds. In the VC pattern one consonant (*at*, *bat*), two consonants (*bath*), or three consonants (*batch*) can follow the vowel. Similarly, one or more consonants may precede the single vowel (*cat*, *chat*, *splat*). Teach the short-vowel pattern *after* children know a short sound for each single vowel (Chapter 3) and a few short-vowel rimes (Chapter 4). Once children know a few short-vowel rimes, encourage them to look inside the rimes to find and learn the VC pattern.

Consonant Blends (Clusters) and Digraphs

Many words begin with consonant blends and digraphs; therefore, children notice these while reading and spelling. Introduce consonant blends and digraphs while you are teaching the short-vowel and the VCe long-vowel patterns. You can expect children to have learned all the consonant blends and digraphs before the end of first grade.

- *Consonant blends (or clusters).* The letters in **consonant blends** (such as the *cl* in <u>cl</u>am or the *st* in <u>st</u>op) represent the same sounds as the individual consonants, with one big difference: The sounds of letters in consonant blends are pronounced by sliding them together—blending—rather than saying each sound separately. This means that the consonant blends are pronounced somewhat differently than the individual sounds. For instance, when we pronounce the *sl* in <u>sl</u>ip we glide or blend the /s/ and /l/ together such that one sound almost flows into the other /sl/. Because the sounds represented by blends are the same as the sounds represented by the single consonants, children have relatively little new information to learn. This said, we find that the consonant blends are challenging for some children. These children try to pronounce the *sl* in <u>sl</u>ip as two separate sounds, /s/ + /l/, rather than two blended sounds, /sl/, and hence mispronounce this consonant blend. When you teach the consonant blends, start with the two-letter blends (*st*) and then move to three-letter blends (*str*). Teach the blends that include a digraph (such as the *th* portion of *thr* in <u>thr</u>ow) after children have learned the digraphs (see Table 5–1 and Appendix A).
- *Consonant digraphs.* The consonants in **digraphs** represent a different sound from that which the letters represent separately. For example, *sh* represents /sh/ in <u>sh</u>oe, a different sound from the *s* in *sat* or the *h* in *hat*. Surprisingly, many of the children we teach find the consonant digraphs easier to learn and use than the consonant blends. Learning something new, as in /sh/ for the digraph *sh*, may be somewhat less confusing than learning to pronounce familiar consonant sounds somewhat differently (consonant blends).

Long Vowels

Teach the long-vowel patterns after children know and use the short-vowel (VC) pattern to read and spell. Begin with the VCe pattern, then move to VV vowel team and CV (open syllable) patterns. Long vowels "say their names." That is, the long sound is the vowel letter name, as the *a* in *cake*, the *e* in *bee*, the *i* in *nine*, the *o* in *rose*, and the *u* in *cube*.

- *VCe long vowel (vowel-consonant-e pattern).* Teach the VCe pattern *after* children know the VC short-vowel pattern. Though the final *e* is a good visual reminder of the VCe long-vowel pattern, as in *same* and *time*, children may overlook the final *e*, thus treating letters as if they are in a VC short-vowel pattern. In this example, children would mistakenly read *same* as

/sam/ and *time* as /tim/. Tell children to be on the lookout for the final *e*. Some teachers help children remember the effect of the final *e* by calling the *e* "bossy" because it makes the preceding vowel "say its name" or call the final *e* "magic" because the *e* magically makes the first vowel long. There are some obvious exceptions to the VCe pattern, as we see in *have* and *come*. When children meet a word in text that they do not instantly recognize, advise them to try the long-vowel sound first; if that does not make a sensible word that fits the reading context, then try a short sound.

- *VV vowel teams pattern.* **Vowel teams** are formed when two vowels (VV) are adjacent to one another and represent a long-vowel sound. The most reliable teams are *ai* (*sail*), *ea* (*cream*), *ee* (*seed*), *oa* (*boat*), *ay* (*stay*), and *ey* (*honey*). We teach the vowel teams after children recognize, understand, and use the VC and VCe patterns. Some teachers help readers remember the *vowel teams* (VV pattern) by telling them, "When two vowels go walking, the first one does the talking and the second does the walking." While the vowel team pattern usually represents a long-vowel sound, there are some exceptions (see Appendix A). Teach readers to try the long-vowel sound first and then, if necessary, to try the short-vowel sound as a backup.

- *CV long vowel (consonant-vowel) pattern.* CV represents a long-vowel sound, as in *me* and *spider* (refer to Table 5–1 and Appendix A). The CV is an open syllable pattern. An open syllable ends with a vowel sound (see Chapter 6). We typically introduce the CV pattern after children are comfortable reading and spelling words that contain the *vowel team* pattern. The long-vowel, open syllable pattern has some exceptions (particularly in unaccented syllables) and hence takes children more time to learn than the CVe and VV *vowel team* long-vowel patterns (look for a detailed explanation of syllables in Chapter 6).

Other Vowels

The other vowels consist of *oo*, Vr (r-controlled vowels), vowel diphthongs, and *au*, *aw*, *eu*, and *ew*. Teach the Vr, vowel diphthongs, and *au*, *aw*, *eu*, and *ew* after children understand the long-vowel patterns.

- *Double oo pattern.* The *oo* pattern almost always represents one of two sounds: the sound heard in *school* or the sound heard in *book*. You may teach *oo* after children have learned long vowels or you may sandwich *oo* into the teaching of long-vowel patterns.

- *Vr pattern.* The r-controlled pattern Vr is challenging to learn and use because the *r* changes the sound represented by the vowel letter. The sound of the vowel is almost lost in the /r/. This is so regardless of which vowel precedes the letter *r*. Some children mistake the Vr combination for the VC short-vowel pattern because, after all, *r* is a consonant letter. Readers must learn to pay special attention to the *r* and anticipate its effect on the vowels it follows, as in *car*, *her*, *sir*, *for*, and *fur*. It is important to introduce this pattern after the long- and short-vowel patterns because a good many words include the Vr. Do not be surprised if some end-of-year second-graders still need practice and targeted instruction to efficiently and effectively use the Vr pattern.

- *Diphthongs.* The *ow*, *ou*, *oi*, and *oy* are **diphthongs.** The *ow* represents the sounds heard in <u>cow</u>, *ou* the sounds in <u>out</u>, *oi* the sounds in <u>oil</u>, and *oy* the sounds in <u>boy</u>. Diphthongs represent sounds that are different from the sounds the letters represent individually or in short and long patterns. Hence, children must learn totally new letter-sound associations for them. Added to this, *ow* sometimes represents the long *o* sound, as heard in *crow*. For these reasons, diphthongs may take more attention and more experience with print to learn to read and spell. Since fewer words contain diphthongs than the other previously described vowel patterns, we prefer to teach the diphthongs after children have been introduced to the short- and long-vowel patterns, and the Vr patterns.

- *Au, aw, ue, and ew.* The *au*, *aw*, *ue*, and *ew*—as in *haul*, *draw*, *due*, and *blew*—can be quite challenging for some children. Some one-syllable words might be learned by analogy—*saw*, *draw*, *law*, *flaw*. However, *au*, *aw*, *ue*, and *ew* are also part of many words that do not readily fit into a word family structures (*faucet*, *dawdle*, *jewel*). Therefore, it is important for children to recognize these letter patterns when they see them and to know how to spell them when writing. These combinations may take a good bit of practice and, not surprisingly, emerge later in both reading and writing. Teach these patterns last. Give readers lots of practice reading and writing words with these letters.

In the final analysis, children learn the letter-sound relationships when we teach these patterns directly and when they have many opportunities to read all sorts of books, poems, articles, and stories, and many opportunities to spell and write. Point out and explore patterns, help children become sensitive to these patterns through spelling, and use the activities described later in this chapter to support readers as they use their letter-sound knowledge to read and spell new words.

TEACHING LETTER-SOUND PHONICS IN YOUR CLASSROOM READING PROGRAM

All the letter-sound patterns in Table 5–1 and Appendix A are taught from kindergarten through the second grade. Generally speaking, kindergarten teachers spend about 30 minutes a day teaching phonics and phonemic awareness. First-grade teachers devote approximately 30 to 35 minutes to instruction. Second-grade teachers spend a bit less time, say around 25 to 30 minutes. Bear in mind that these are general guidelines. The classroom reading programs in your school may set aside more or less time for teaching phonics in these grades. Regardless, some children will require extra help, and you must consider their needs when planning instruction.

Kindergarten

Kindergarten teachers usually teach phonics, phonemic awareness, and perhaps high-frequency words during the time set aside for word study or word work. Generally speaking, kindergarten classroom reading programs usually apportion about 30 minutes a day for direct instruction in word work, although this may vary depending on the classroom reading program, the daily schedule, and the teacher's philosophy. If you teach kindergarten, you will teach letter names and a sound for each letter, including a sound for each vowel letter. Your classroom reading program may also include teaching beginning and ending consonants, the VC short-vowel pattern, and rimes or phonograms in word family words. The kindergarten teachers in your own school may teach more phonics or less phonics, depending in large measure on the needs of the kindergartners in their classrooms. At the end of kindergarten, children should know all the letter names, associate a sound with each letter, recognize some onsets and rimes, and read and spell some word family words. Some children will understand the VC short-vowel pattern. In addition, children should bring to first grade a cache of words known by sight, the ability to spell some words conventionally, and the ability to spell new words by associating letters with sounds.

First Grade

First-grade teachers spend a bit more time for word work (or word study), usually over 30 minutes, depending on the classroom schedule. Word work or word study in first-grade classroom reading programs usually includes direct instruction in phonics, phonemic awareness, spelling, and high-frequency words. First-grade teachers integrate phonics throughout and across subjects, so first-graders get much more instruction and have many more opportunities to use phonics while reading and spelling than is provided in the time set aside for word work.

If you teach first grade, you will begin with the VC short-vowel pattern. If children learned this pattern in kindergarten, you may review the pattern for a short time to refresh memory and then move on to teaching the long-vowel patterns, usually beginning with the VCe pattern (*cap–cape*). You will continue teaching consonant letter sounds, picking up where the kindergarten teacher left off. You will teach nearly all the digraphs (*thing*, *charm*, *shell*) and all of the consonant blends, including digraphs at the end of words (*blast*, *dish*). By the end of first grade, the children will have been introduced to almost all of the letter-sound patterns in Table 5–1 and Appendix A.

Second Grade

Second-grade teachers spend slightly less time teaching phonics and spelling each day, perhaps around 25 minutes. Phonics and spelling are taught during this time in second-grade classroom reading programs, and, depending on children's development as readers, programs also may teach high-frequency words. If you are a second-grade teacher, you will continue to teach the phonics patterns covered in first grade. You will review and reteach the vowel and consonant patterns through-out the year. You will spend proportionally more time teaching r-controlled (Vr), diphthongs, and long-vowel patterns that children need to know to be successful readers and spellers. You will also teach children how to add suffixes to words, with particular attention to doubling the last consonant letter when adding a word ending (*biggest*, *sipping*). (See Chapter 6 for an explanation of suffixes and the conventions for adding them to words.) By the end of the second grade, the children in your classroom will have learned a great deal about phonics. Children will know all the vowel and consonant patterns; their reading vocabulary will be growing rapidly; and they will be independent readers. At the end of the year, average second-graders *only* sound out words they do not know; they read many words instantly; their reading vocabularies are growing by leaps and bounds; and they read faster and more efficiently than ever before. Additionally, children will be developing, or on the brink of developing, the ability to recognize many different multiletter chunks in word structure (explained in Chapter 6).

Third Grade

Third-grade teachers spend about 15 minutes a day on word work. This time may be devoted to phonics, spelling, or structural analysis (see Chapter 6). Phonics is not taught every day. Most third-grade classroom reading programs provide for reteaching, reviewing, and revisiting selected phonics letter patterns. Reviewing and reteaching ensure that the children have ample opportunities to master any phonics patterns they did not completely master by the end of second grade.

If you teach third grade, your classroom reading program may teach phonics and spelling together. To teach phonics and spelling together, teachers ask children to spell words that include the phonics patterns children are reviewing. However, it is fair to say that more time is spent on structural analysis than on phonics letter-sound patterns. As a matter of fact, teachers build on children's knowledge of vowel patterns to develop knowledge of syllables in longer words, as explained in Chapter 6. By the end of the year, the average third-graders in your classroom use letter-pattern knowledge to read and spell new words with minimal effort. Added to this, children are well on their way to using the multiletter groups in word structure to read and spell new words (explained in Chapter 6).

Fourth and Fifth Grades

If you teach fourth or fifth grade, you will not set aside specific time during the school day to teach phonics. You will fold phonics into the teaching of spelling. In teaching spelling, you will remind children of the patterns they already know and then have children spell words with those patterns. This helps children appreciate how knowing phonics makes it easier to spell and read long words. Classroom pro-grams in the fourth and fifth grades focus on teaching the structure of long words (explained in Chapter 6). By the time children go to the sixth grade, they are good spellers and good readers. They have a large and growing reading vocabulary and read independently. These children do not need further review or reteaching of any of the patterns, whether that review is through spelling or direct instruction.

Classroom reading programs vary, of course, so your program may have different expectations than the sequence described. We expect some flexibility in teaching phonics. Instead of being tied to a specific grade-by-grade teaching sequence, we want to consider children's individual needs and then adapt and adjust phonics instruction to meet those needs. Some children will learn phonics early, well ahead of the expectations for their grades. Other children will make good, average progress, while still others will fall behind. We would teach children with excellent phonics skills how to use the multiletter chunks in word structure (Chapter 6); we would provide grade-level phonics instruction to average learners; we would provide extra instruction to children who struggle. The advantage of knowing the patterns, understanding best practice, and having teaching activities at your fingertips is that you have the tools to be an effective phonics teacher for all children.

How Children Use Letter-Sound Phonics to Read New Words

Readers who use the letter-sound strategy have the full strength and power of the alphabet at their fingertips. Thanks to their constant self-monitoring, self-correcting, and cross-checking, readers identify and pronounce real words that match the reading context. These children have good phonemic awareness and, of course, a solid working knowledge of letter-sound patterns (Ehri, 2006).

As an illustration of this strategy, we will consider how Leslie decodes the new word *tree* in the sentence *Rosie and Rita sat under the tree*. In using the letter-sound strategy to read *tree*, Leslie reaps the full benefit of reading a language written in an alphabet, and here is how she does it:

1. Leslie realizes that *t* and *r* (*tr*) belong in one pattern (a consonant blend) and that the *ee* is an example of the vowel team (VV) pattern. Noticing the vowel team gives Leslie the clues she needs to figure out the vowel pronunciation.
2. Leslie then associates *tr* with /tr/ and *ee* with the long /e/ sound.
3. Now she blends /tr/ + /e/ (long *e*) to pronounce /tree/.
4. Last, Leslie cross-checks to make sure that /tree/ fits the reading context. She asks herself: "Does *tree* sound and look right? Does *tree* make sense in the passage?" If the answers are yes, Leslie stops decoding and turns her full attention to *meaning*, finishing the page, and reading the rest of the chapter. If the answers are no, she returns to decoding.

Interestingly, readers do not have to be segmenting and blending experts like Leslie to begin to use letter sounds to read and learn new words. Readers need only enough phonemic awareness to separate and blend the sounds in short words. Likewise, readers need only enough knowledge of letter-sound patterns to associate sounds with the letters in short, uncomplicated words.

Sounding out a short word like *big*, which has only three sounds and a predictable VC short-vowel pattern, is far less taxing than sounding out a long word like *hippopotamus*, which has 12 letters, many phonics patterns, and a whopping five syllables. For this reason, it is quite possible, and indeed highly likely, that some children who have no difficulty sounding out short words like *big* will have trouble sounding out a long word like *crayon*.

The strategy of associating sounds with letters only works when readers connect the meaning of printed words with the meaning of spoken words. In the preceding example, *tree* is among the words children recognize in spoken language. If the words children sound out are not in their speaking vocabularies, sounding out will help with pronunciation, but not with meaning. So, when you teach letter-sound phonics (and previously described strategies), make sure that the words children identify are already in their speaking or listening vocabularies. If readers do not know the meanings of the words they are to decode, help children add these words to their speaking vocabularies before they decode them.

Leslie successfully sounds out *tree* because the letter patterns in *tree* represent sounds in a predictable way. However, English spelling often strays from the sounds the reader expects. *Where* is an example of an often-used word that cannot be easily identified through associating sounds with letters. While the *wh* gives children a partial clue to identity, children will have to remember, through repeated reading and writing experiences, the print-to-speech connection between *where* and /where/. Some teachers call words like *where* outlaw words; others call them rule breakers. The point is to call the children's attention to the fact that this word has to be memorized; there is no letter-sound shortcut to fully pronouncing this type of word.

Correcting Misidentifications

Given the complexity of our English alphabetic writing system, there is no guarantee that the first try will result in a meaningful word. If the sounds Leslie blends together do not make a sensible word, self-monitoring, self-correcting, and cross-checking (explained in Chapter 1) bring the misidentification to light. There are three ways Leslie might self-correct. Leslie might:

1. Reblend the same sounds, perhaps gliding sounds together more smoothly, and then cross-check for meaning.
2. Associate different sounds with the same letter groups and then reblend to pronounce a new word that is then cross-checked for meaning.
3. Redo the entire process—regroup letters into patterns, associate sounds with the letters in patterns, blend, and cross-check all over again.

The children whom you teach are bound to prefer easier, less attention-demanding ways to self-correct over energy-draining alternatives. You will notice that successful word identifiers often try reblending as their first attempt to correct mistakes. Then, if re-blending does not work, they may try a different sound for a specific letter, often the vowel. Only when all else fails do readers typically redo the entire process of re-identifying every letter-sound pattern.

Minor Mistakes

Readers may take minor mistakes in stride. Minor mistakes may not derail decoding because readers actively look for sensible connections between the words they recognize in everyday language and the words in the reading context. Accordingly, as readers self-monitor, self-correct, and cross-check, they find words in their speaking vocabularies that sound similar to minor decoding mispronunciations. When this happens, readers associate minor mispronunciations with real words that make sense in the reading context. Once plausible words are identified, readers automatically adjust mispronunciations so that the sounds in the words they decode match the words in their speaking vocabularies. The net effect is that slight letter-sound mistakes and minor blending miscalculations do not require great effort to repair.

BEST PRACTICES FOR TEACHING LETTER-SOUND PHONICS

You will be a more effective phonics teacher when you follow these best practices:

1. *Teach letter-sound patterns early* (National Reading Panel, 2000).   Effective phonics instruction begins early and uses learning activities that are appropriate for a child's age and development as readers. Introducing the patterns of phonics early, in kindergarten and first grade, is more effective than introducing instruction later in the elementary grades, say second grade and above.

2. *Teach directly* (Shankweiler & Fowler, 2004).   Teaching phonics directly is more effective than teaching phonics indirectly or on an as-needed basis (Shanahan, 2005).

3. *Follow a logical, planful sequence* (de Graaf, Bosman, Hasselman, & Verhoeven, 2009).   Teaching should be sequenced so that kindergarteners, first-graders, and second-graders learn the phonics patterns in Table 5–1 and Appendix A well enough to use them when reading and spelling new words.

4. *Teach phonemic awareness, when needed.*   Programs that combine phonics with phonemic awareness are more beneficial for kindergartners and first-graders than programs that teach these two skills alone (Christensen & Bowey, 2005).

5. *Pace instruction to the needs of each child.*   Children learn phonics patterns at different paces. Some quickly grasp letter-sound patterns and how to use them, while others take more time, more instruction, and more reading and spelling practice. Move children along at a pace that is comfortable for them—fast enough to cover the patterns children need to learn and slow enough to ensure that children are competent users of the letter-sound strategy. Recognize, too, that the amount of time you devote to phonics is related to achievement. First-graders are better readers when their teachers spend more time on phonics and phonemic awareness than on noninstructional and nonreading activities (Foorman, Schatschneider, Eakin, Fletcher, Moates, & Francis, 2006).

6. *Teach the same letter-sound patterns in spelling as you teach in reading.*
Teaching the same patterns in reading and spelling ensures that instruction in reading and spelling supports and reinforces each other. Children use their understandings of letter-sound patterns when they read and their understandings of sound-letter patterns when they spell. Added to this, spelling helps children read whole, intact words when the words contain phonics patterns children have learned (Conrad, 2008).

7. *Integrate phonics into your classroom reading program.* Phonics is a means to an end, not the end itself. The goal of phonics instruction is to develop independent readers who are skilled at learning new words and who are fully capable of using reading as a learning tool. Balance phonics teaching within your classroom program and measure success in many ways and by many barometers, including word learning, comprehension, the ability to use reading as a learning tool, love of reading, and interest in books.

DO PHONICS RULES BELONG IN YOUR CLASSROOM READING PROGRAM?

Researchers have put tremendous energy into finding out which letter-sound patterns are dependable and which are not. In their quest, researchers investigated 45 phonics rules (Bailey, 1967; Clymer, 1963; Emans, 1967). Take the rule that says, "A vowel in the middle of a one-syllable word represents the short sound." Let us think about this middle vowel "rule," which is a way of explaining the VC short-vowel pattern. We would agree that words like *man* and *red* are examples of the VC short-vowel pattern and, coincidentally, follow the rule. Surprisingly, researchers find this rule to be relatively unreliable. In a sample of primary grade reading material, both Clymer (1963) and Emans (1967) report that the middle vowel rule applies only 62 percent and 73 percent of the time, respectively. Examining materials for grades one through six, Bailey reports that this rule is useful a mere 71 percent of the time.

Some of the examples these authors cite as exceptions to the middle vowel rule reflect a narrow interpretation of this "rule." Narrow interpretations make our alphabetic system seem more complicated than it really is. In this example, a narrow interpretation overlooks the fact that some vowels in the middle of one-syllable words are not in a VC short-vowel pattern. Emans (1967) cites the word *hew* and Bailey (1967) the word *her* as examples of exceptions to the middle vowel rule. It is not reasonable to consider either word—*hew* or *her*—as an exception because the vowels in these words represent two different patterns: The *e* in *hew* is part of the *ew* pattern found in words like *jewel*, *chew*, and *threw*, as explained in Table 5–1 and Appendix A. The *e* in *her* is perfectly regular, too, for the *e* in this word is part of an r-controlled pattern (Vr), and so the sound it represents is characteristic of this pattern, as in *germ* and *clerk*, as described in Table 5–1 and Appendix A.

While most readers cannot recite the "rules" of phonics word for word, they do have mental representations—mental images—of the way that phonics patterns represent sound. Their in-depth knowledge of phonics patterns gives them a powerful resource that, when combined with cross-checking, self-monitoring, and self-correcting, enables them to pronounce any word that is spelled like it sounds.

Perhaps you are wondering whether you should teach children the "rules" in your classroom reading program. Just because children recite rules does not mean that they know when and how to apply them. Children who memorize rules without connecting them to reading and writing may not be able to use the rules to support word identification or spelling. In fact, some children are quite skilled at reciting phonics rules yet do not have the foggiest notion of how to use the rules they put so much effort into memorizing. These children learn to "parrot" rules—they recite the wording of rules but do not relate the rules to the words they read and write.

Rather than focus on teaching the rules themselves, a more beneficial approach is to sensitize children to the way letter-sound patterns affect pronunciation and to ground patterns in the spelling of words children encounter as they read and write. Does this mean that you should never ever say a rule? Of course not. Sometimes it is helpful to tell children about a rule, especially when children need some clarification. In fact, explaining a rule from time to time can speed learning along, provided that the rule is solidly related to the words children read and spell. Encourage children to analyze left-to-right letter order and to learn how letter order affects the sounds that letters represent. As a result, children will learn how patterns look and sound in real words and create mental pictures of words in which the letter-sound patterns appear. This, in turn, contributes to word recognition and supports development of a large vocabulary of instantly recognized words.

FULL ALPHABETIC WORD LEARNERS AND WITHIN WORD PATTERN SPELLERS

Full alphabetic word learners associate sounds with all the letter-sound patterns in words. In the early part of the alphabetic stage, children use onsets and rimes to read and spell new words. Later, as readers understand how vowel patterns represent sound, children develop the ability to take full advantage of all the letter-sound relationships in words (Ehri, 2005). As children move through the alphabetic word learning stage, they become increasingly adept at learning words on their own and at spelling words in ways that others can read. We can infer from the spelling in Logan's story, shown in Figure 5-2, that he understands how many different patterns represent sound, including vowel patterns. He has enough phonemic awareness and letter-sound knowledge to completely pronounce many new words, his vocabulary is rapidly expanding, he enjoys reading, and he can read easy books by himself without help. Logan is a **within word pattern speller.** Children move into the within word pattern spelling stage when they begin to spell words with long-vowel patterns (Bear, Invernizzi, Templeton, & Johnson, 2007). Within word pattern spellers like Logan are learning how to spell words with the VCe, VV vowel teams, CV, Vr, and other patterns. These children conventionally spell many words. Notice that when Logan spells unconventionally, *you* and *I* can

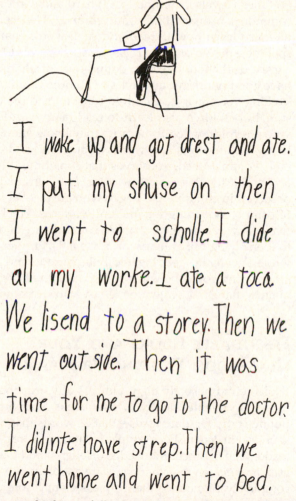

I woke up and got drest and ate.
I put my shuse on then
I went to scholle I dide
all my worke. I ate a toca.
We lisend to a storey. Then we
went outside. Then it was
time for me to go to the doctor.
I didinte have strep. Then we
went home and went to bed.

Figure 5-2   Logan thinks carefully about letter-sound patterns when writing. As he considers which letters represent sound, he sometimes substitutes incorrect letters for correct ones, adds incorrect letters after correct ones, and uses the letter-sounds he hears to represent past tense.

read what he writes. When Logan figures out the spelling of new words on his own, he represents all essential sounds in words, even though there may not be a correct match between letters and sounds (*shuse*, for example). This type of spelling is called **invented spelling,** or phonetic or temporary spelling. It is an early problem-solving stance to spelling in which children write a letter for each sound heard in a word (*lisend* for *listened*). Logan thinks carefully about the sounds in words and has enough phonemic awareness to associate letters with the sounds he wants to spell.

As Logan moves through the full alphabetic reading stage, he will learn how to read words with (1) long vowels, (2) r-controlled vowels, (3) diphthongs, (4) other vowels including *oo*, (5) hard and soft *c* and *g* (see Appendix A), (6) less common consonants like *ng* and *gh*, and (7) less common vowels like *eu* and *aw*. He will also learn how to read and spell words that are exceptions to conventional spelling, such as *have* and *come*. And, as we would expect from children who know a great deal about the letter-sound code of phonics, full alphabetic word learners have good phonemic awareness. Children rapidly add words to their reading and spelling vocabularies. Children learn to read the words their teachers teach, to be sure, but children also learn to read many words they are not directly taught in school. Children do this because they know enough about the patterns of phonics to teach themselves new words as they read and write.

Logan's teacher observes that sometimes he seems to move slowly through text as he focuses on the words. Slow, almost plodding, reading is frequently observed in children like Logan who are just beginning to develop some measure of competence using letter-sound patterns. For Logan and others like him, relatively slow reading is probably a consequence of dedicating a good bit of attention to identifying unfamiliar words as well as trying to read exactly what the author wrote. As Logan's reading vocabulary grows and his ability to use the letter-sound strategy improves, he will pay less attention to figuring out the words and, consequently, have more attention left over to work out meaning.

DECODABLE BOOKS AND YOUR CLASSROOM READING PROGRAM

Books with unusually high numbers of words that sound like they are spelled are called **decodable books.** These books support word identification by using **phonetically regular words**—that is, words that can be pronounced by associating sounds with letters. For example, *pig* and *sweet* are phonetically regular words because readers can use their knowledge of letter-sound patterns to figure out pronunciation. *Have* and *cafe*, on the other hand, are not phonetically regular because readers cannot completely pronounce them by associating sounds with letters. Many decodable books emphasize one or two patterns by clustering together words that have the same patterns, such as the long *e* spellings in *str<u>ee</u>t*, *tr<u>ee</u>*, *b<u>ee</u>*, *cr<u>ea</u>m*, *l<u>ea</u>ve*, and *r<u>ea</u>l*.

Decodable books support word identification by directing readers' attention to the phonics patterns they are learning in your classroom and by allowing readers to actually use their letter-sound knowledge when reading. These books are beneficial for three types of children: (1) partial alphabetic word learners moving into the use of the letter-sound strategy, (2) alphabetic word learners who lack fluency using particular patterns, and (3) readers who know letter-sound patterns but do not use them. The high number of phonetically regular words not only gives readers practice applying phonics knowledge, but also encourages them to use this knowledge to read new words. The amount and type of phonics instruction are likely to affect the contribution decodable books make to improving decoding ability. Decodable books serve a specific purpose at a specific time in children's development as readers. These books should never replace good-quality literature in your classroom, and their presence in your classroom should not limit children's choices of the books they read. Decodable books are beneficial when they reinforce the patterns children are learning, when they are used selectively, and when they are read by children who are transitioning into the alphabetic stage, lack fluency using letter-sound patterns, or know patterns but do not use them.

CLASSROOM ACTIVITIES FOR TEACHING LETTER-SOUND PHONICS

The following activities help children develop knowledge of letter-sound patterns. You may adapt these activities to focus on the patterns children are learning in your classroom, to meet the specific needs of the children whom you teach, and to create your own teaching style. Some activities are appropriate for large, focused skill groups, others for small groups, still others for pairs or individuals, and still others for learning centers or literacy stations. As you use these activities, stop occasionally to ask children to explain how letter patterns represent sound, when to use patterns to read new words, and how knowing letter sounds helps in spelling. As children reflect on the letter-sound patterns in the words they read and spell, they become more metacognitively (consciously) aware of how, when, and why to use the letter-sound strategy, as explained in Chapter 1. As a consequence, children will learn to use this strategy on their own to read and learn new words.

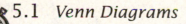 5.1   *Venn Diagrams*

Skill: Associating sounds with the patterns children are learning.

Venn diagrams are overlapping circles with shared characteristics in the overlapping portion and unique characteristics inside each separate circle, as illustrated in Figure 5-3. Venn diagrams illustrate how some of the challenging patterns represent more than one sound. Use Venn diagrams with large or small groups.

Things You'll Need: Chart paper or a chalk or whiteboard.

Directions: Draw two overlapping circles and write a letter pattern that represents more than one sound (*ow*, for instance) in the overlapping portion. Write a word that represents one pronunciation (*cow*, perhaps) in one circle and a word that represents another pronunciation (*snow*, for example) in the other circle, as illustrated by Figure 5-3. Children think of words in which *ow* represents the sounds heard in *cow* and in *snow*; write those words in the appropriate circles. This gives children opportunities to think of words that fit the pattern and helps them become more sensitive to the two sounds that *ow* typically represents.

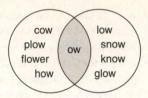

Figure 5-3   Venn diagrams illustrate how some of the more challenging letter-sound patterns represent more than one sound.

5.2 *Spelling for Sounds*

Skill: Associating sounds with the patterns children are learning.

Children in large or small groups spell, with the teacher's help, by listening to sounds and then associating letters with the sounds. You may also use spelling for sounds to give individual children extra practice and assistance.

Things You'll Need: Chart paper or a chalk or whiteboard.

Directions: Pronounce a word children wish to spell. Ask children to listen for sounds and connect letters with the sounds they hear in words they dictate. For instance, in spelling *slip* you would sound stretch /slip/—/sssllliiip/. A child from a small group associates *s* with /s/ and the child (or the teacher) writes *s* on the board. Stretch /slip/ a second time. Have children associate an *l* with the /l/ sound. The third time you, the teacher, stretch *slip*, the children will suggest writing an *i* for the /i/. Call attention to /p/ and write a *p*, thus spelling *slip*.

5.3 *Building Words with Intact Letter Patterns*

Skill: Spelling words with the letter-sound patterns children are learning.

Children spell words you pronounce. This activity is appropriate for children who have been introduced to patterns but who are not sufficiently familiar with the patterns to construct the patterns on their own. Use it with children working in large, small, and flexible groups and for children in any grade. It also can be used with any letter-sound pattern. In this version of word building, children make words with the intact patterns (*oa*, *ee*) they are learning.

Things You'll Need: As many cards with whole letter-sound patterns as there are children in a small group.

Directions: Give children letter cards with a whole pattern on them. For example, you might distribute cards with the VV long-vowel patterns *oa* and *ee*, and the consonants *b, t, f, l, m, d, p*, and *s*. Ask children to arrange and rearrange the single consonants to build words like *boat, beet, feed, seed, feel, foam, seem, soap, load*, and *toad*. Talk about the patterns. Ask the children to explain how they know that *ee* represents long *e* and *oa* long *o*.

5.4 *Single-Letter Word Building*

Skill: Spelling words with the letter-sound patterns children are learning.

In this version of word building, children build words that are spelled with two or more patterns. Use this version of word building with the letter-sound patterns that require a little extra practice before children effectively use them when reading and spelling new words.

Things You'll Need: Cards with letters on them.

Directions: Give children letter cards that combine to make words that are spelled with the patterns children need to practice. For example, you might distribute cards with *r, t, b, s, a, e*, and *m* (see Figure 5-4). Ask the children to use the letters to spell words. For example, you might ask children to build *me* and change it into *meat*, and then build *team, seam, sea, sat, same, tame, tar, star*, and so forth. Have children explain in their own words why they spelled the words as they did and how the patterns represent sound. Also ask children to tell how knowing the letter-sound patterns helps them read new words.

Figure 5-4 Building words helps children think about the way letters form patterns that represent pronunciation.

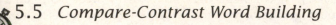

5.5 *Compare-Contrast Word Building*

Skill: Associating sounds with the patterns children are learning.

Things You'll Need: Cards with single letters on them.

Directions: Give the children cards with letters that combine to make words with two or more patterns. Ask children to first build a word with a pattern they already know, and then have them build a new word with a pattern they are learning or need to practice. For example, if children already know the VC pattern and are learning the VCe pattern, you would begin by demonstrating how adding an *e* (*cap* + *e* = *cape*) turns a short-vowel word into a long-vowel word. Next, distribute letter cards with *t*, *r*, *c*, *n*, *p*, *a*, and *e*, and ask children to build *cap–cape*, *can–cane*, *pan–pane*, *nap–nape*, *rat–rate*, and *tap–tape*. Compare and contrast the patterns. Ask children to explain how the finale *e* affects the pronunciation of the first vowel, and why they spelled the words the way they did. Also ask children to tell how knowing the letter-sound patterns helps them read and spell new words. Table 5–2 is a list of VC words that, when the final *e* is added, make VCe pattern words (also see Figure 5-5).

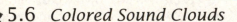

5.6 *Colored Sound Clouds*

Skill: Associating sounds with the patterns children are learning.

In this activity children in small groups or flexible skill groups think of words with the same sound and then circle different patterns that represent the sound.

Things You'll Need: Colored chalk (or colored dry erase markers if your classroom has a whiteboard).

Directions: Children suggest words that have a certain sound, such as the long *e*. You write the words on the board. Draw children's attention to the different ways the pattern is spelled in the words. Give children different colors of chalk, one color for each pattern. Children then take turns drawing lacy clouds around each different pattern. In our example, all the *ee* vowel team (*seem*) words might be circled with blue clouds around them; *ea* vowel team (*bead*) words have green clouds; and CV (*be*) words have red clouds.

Look in e-resources for making Word Clouds with Wordle™, an online source for creating colorful word displays that are an excellent follow-up to this activity.

TABLE 5–2   *VC and Vce Words for Word Building and Other Activities*

VC	VCe	VC	VCe	VC	VCe	VC	VCe
bid	bide	fin	fine	man	mane	shad	shade
bit	bite	gal	gale	mat	mate	sham	shame
can	cane	gap	gape	mop	mope	slat	slate
cap	cape	glad	glade	nap	nape	slid	slide
cod	code	glob	globe	not	note	slim	slime
con	cone	grad	grade	pan	pane	slop	slope
cop	cope	grim	grime	pet	Pete	snip	snipe
crud	crude	grip	gripe	pin	pine	tap	tape
cub	cube	hat	hate	plan	plane	Tim	time
cut	cute	hid	hide	plum	plume	ton	tone
dam	dame	hop	hope	prim	prime	tot	tote
dim	dime	hug	huge	rat	rate	trip	tripe
din	dine	Jan	Jane	rid	ride	tub	tube
dot	dote	kit	kite	rip	ripe	twin	twine
dud	dude	lob	lobe	rob	robe	van	vane
fad	fade	lop	lope	rod	rode	wad	wade
fat	fate	mad	made	Sam	same	win	wine

5.7 People Pattern Words

Skill: Spelling words with the patterns children are learning.

This is a whole body analog of the word-building activities described earlier. Only here, children wearing letter-sound patterns line up one pattern after another to build words with the patterns they are learning, as in Figure 5-6. Use this activity with small, ongoing groups or flexible skill groups.

Things You'll Need: Large cards with letter-sound patterns on them.

Directions: Distribute one card with one pattern to each child. For example, one child might hold a card with *r*, another a card with *ai*, still another a card with an *n*. Children with letter-sound patterns line up to spell the words you pronounce (see the illustration in Figure 5-6). In this example children spell the word *rain*. Talk about the patterns in words; read words in chorus.

Figure 5-5 Comparing a known pattern with a new pattern helps children understand how to identify different patterns and associate sounds with them.

Figure 5-6 People pattern words. Children line up to build words that are spelled with the letter-sound patterns they are learning, read the words in chorus, and then add the words to their personal word boxes.

5.8 *Picking What Works for Me: Decoding Prompts*

Skill: Developing metacognitive awareness of how to use patterns to read new words.

Children select prompts to guide them in reading and spelling new words. The prompts are cues or scaffolds for using the letter-sound strategy to read new words. This activity is useful for small, flexible skill groups.

Things You'll Need: One small plastic flower pot (or disposable container) per child or pair of children; popsicle sticks with flowers that prompt the child to look for different patterns (see Figure 5-7). On the side of the pot, in permanent marker, write, "Does it make sense?"

Figure 5-7   In selecting prompts, children reflect on their own use of the letter-sound strategy and become more metacognitively (consciously) aware of how to use patterns to read new words.

Directions: Give each child or pair of children a pot with flowers that serve as prompts or reminders for letter patterns they have already learned or are currently learning. Demonstrate how to use flower prompts to guide decoding by writing a word on the board and then reading the flower prompts. Compare the prompts with the letter patterns in the word. Select an appropriate prompt, take it out of the pot, and show children how to use it to guide decoding. Model cross-checking by drawing children's attention to the prompt "Does it make sense?" on the side of the pot. Leave flower pot prompts in an accessible place for general use or in a learning center or literacy station for targeted practice. Encourage children to use the flower prompts on their own to help them look for patterns in new words. Add or change flower prompts as appropriate for children's needs.

Examples of prompts:

- Do I see a part I know?
- What is the beginning sound?
- Do I see a silent *e*?
- Are two vowels together?
- Is there an *ou* or *ow*?
- Is there an *oy* or *oi*?
- Do I see *oo*?
- Do I see a vowel before an *r*?

5.9   *Compare-Contrast Charts*

Skill: Associating sounds with the patterns children are learning.

Children working in small groups make large charts that show how several patterns represent the same sounds. Understanding how different patterns represent the same sounds, in turn, gives children valuable insight into word recognition and spelling.

Things You'll Need: As many large sheets of paper as there are pairs or small groups; colored markers.

Directions: Begin by pronouncing a sound—the long *o* sound, for instance. Ask children to suggest words with this sound. Make a list of these words on the board. Call children's attention to the different patterns that represent the long *o*. Distribute chart paper and have children divide the paper into as many sections as there are different spelling patterns for the same sound. In our example, children would divide the chart into four sections, each for a different long *o* pattern. In each section, children write words with one of the patterns and draw a picture of one of the words (see Figure 5-8).

Figure 5-8 In making charts, children compare and contrast different letter-sound patterns that represent the same sounds in words.

5.10 *Pattern Sorts*

Skill: Associating sounds with the patterns children are learning.

Children working with a learning partner, individually, or in learning centers or literacy stations sort words into paper lunch sacks according to the sounds letter patterns represent.

Things You'll Need: As many sets of word cards as there are pairs or individual children; small paper sacks with a letter-sound pattern on them, as shown in Figure 5-9.

Directions: Give children several small paper sacks and a group of word cards or leave the sacks and cards in a learning center or literacy station. Children sort by putting words that have the same letter-sound pattern in the sack with that letter pattern on the front. For example, children might sort for long- and short-vowel patterns or digraphs and diphthongs. When finished sorting, children empty each sack, cross-check with a partner to

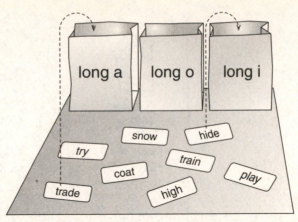

Figure 5-9 Sorting helps children become sensitive to the letter-sound patterns that occur in many different words.

make sure that all the words inside are sorted correctly, and then write each word on the sack in which it belongs. This gives you a record of how children sorted, and provides children practice writing words that include the patterns they are learning.

5.11 *Fly-Away*

Skill: Reading words spelled with the patterns children are learning.

Children read words on make-believe flies, bees, or mosquitoes and, as quickly as possible, read words and smack the insects with a swatter. Books like *The Giant Jam Sandwich* (Lord, 1972) and *Why Mosquitoes Buzz in People's Ears* (Aardema, 1975) are examples of stories that feature insects. The activity is appropriate for small groups.

Things You'll Need: Two fly swatters; tape; construction paper cut into flies, bees, or mosquitoes with words on them. Or you could use index cards and pretend they are flying away.

Directions: Tape the fly-away words to the board, spacing them fairly far apart, as shown in Figure 5-10. Divide players into two teams. Call one player from each team up to the board; give each a swatter. Say a word that is spelled with one of the patterns children are learning in your classroom. Each player finds and swats the word as fast as possible. If the player is correct, the swatted word is taken off the board—it "flies away"—and the team gets a point. The team with the most fly-away words wins. At the end of the game, hold up fly-away words and ask children to read them in chorus.

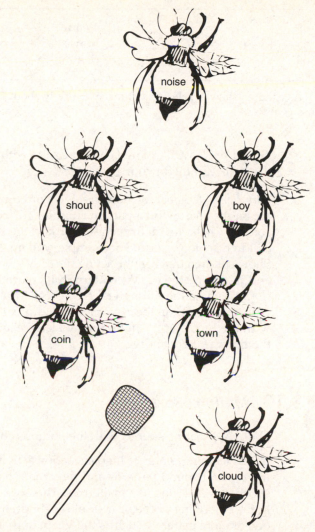

Figure 5-10 An example of fly-away where children "swat" words that contain the letter-sound patterns they are learning.

5.12 *Puzzles*

Skill: Reading words spelled with the patterns children are learning.

Children working with a partner, individually, or in a learning center or literacy station solve puzzles with a clue word (like *steam*) and a set of instructions (*– ea + or =*) that transform the clue into a solution word (*storm*), as shown in Figure 5-11.

coin	–	oi	+	or	=	_____	steam	–	ea	+	or	=	_____
sheet	–	ee	+	ir	=	_____	house	–	ou	+	or	=	_____
coat	–	oa	+	ar	=	_____	dealing	–	ea	+	ar	=	_____

Figure 5-11   As children solve puzzles, they think analytically about the sounds that the letters in patterns represent in words.

Things You'll Need: Colored chalk; puzzles with the letter-sound patterns children are learning in your classroom.

Directions: Demonstrate how to solve word puzzles. Do this by writing a puzzle on the board with a pattern children are learning in your classroom. Use colored chalk (or a dry erase marker) to highlight the transformations children are to perform. For example, you might write *steam - ea + or = ____*. Show children that in subtracting the *ea* (VV vowel team) long-vowel pattern and in adding the *or* (Vr) pattern in its place, children transform *steam* into *storm*. Remind the children to cross-check to verify solutions by sharing them with a classmate. In the examples in Figure 5-11, children solve word puzzles with the Vr pattern. Children may also create their own puzzles and share them with other children.

5.13 *Mailbox Sort*

Skill: Associating sounds with the patterns children are learning.

In this learning center or literacy station activity, children sort words according to letter-sound patterns and then mail the words by slipping them into shoeboxes that look like mailboxes. This sort is appropriate for first-graders at the beginning of the year or older children who are learning words with one or more patterns, such as the VC pattern in *cat* and VV pattern in *coat*.

Things You'll Need: Two or more shoeboxes with tightly fitting lids for mailboxes; mock postcards with words that are spelled with the patterns children are learning in your classroom; a few postcards with an extra line under the word for writing the name of a child in the class to whom the postcard might be sent. Cut a slit in the lid of the shoeboxes; cover each lid with construction paper or shelf paper. Above each slit, glue a picture of a word to represent a certain sound, such as a *boat* to represent a long *o* sound, or write a description of the patterns children are learning, such as long vowel and short vowel, as shown in Figure 5-12.

Directions: Place mailboxes and postcards in a center or literacy station. Children sort the postcard words according to their letter-sound patterns by

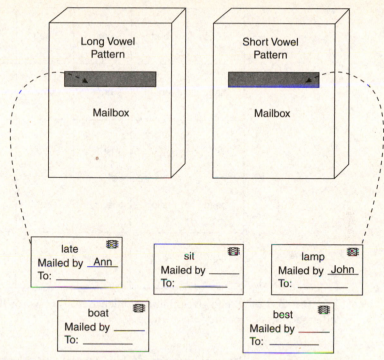

Figure 5-12   In this learning center activity, children sort "postcards" according to the letter-sound patterns in spelling and mail the postcards by slipping them into shoebox mailboxes.

slipping each postcard word through the proper shoebox slot. Tell children to be on the lookout for postcards sent from their classmates. Children write the name of a classmate to whom they would like to send a special word. Discuss the words children receive; talk about the letter-sound pattern.

5.14 *Bingo*

Skill: Reading words spelled with the patterns children are learning.

An oldie but goodie for children of any age, bingo is a favorite activity that can be used with any pattern children are learning. This version of bingo gives children practice reading words with the patterns they are learning in your classroom.

Things You'll Need: Bingo cards; pencils. Make a model and duplicate it. Write words in squares, or write a word list on the board and ask children to select words from the list and write them in squares. The words in Figure 5-13 feature the short- and long-vowel patterns (VV vowel team and VCe).

same	bed	coat	seed	play
ham	cute	boat	time	slim
got	they	Free	mine	why
bead	slip	train	cut	bat
cap	tree	ship	Sam	cat

Figure 5-13   Bingo gives children practice reading words that are spelled with the letter-sound patterns they are learning.

Directions: Pass out bingo cards. Say a word and ask children to locate the word on their bingo cards, and cover it with a token. Traditional rules hold that a child with any five consecutively covered squares lined up diagonally, horizontally, or vertically wins. Four corners or postage stamps (four squares in any corner) are fun to play, too. Coveralls are always challenging, but they take more time, so save them for days when there is plenty of flexibility in the schedule.

5.15 *Scrapbooks*

Skill: Associating sounds with the patterns you are teaching.

Children working in a learning center or literacy station make scrapbooks of words that are spelled with the patterns they are learning. Scrapbooks are not only a record of the words and patterns children are learning, but also a resource for writing and phonics activities.

Things You'll Need: Magazines; markers; large pieces of light-colored construction paper with a letter-sound pattern or a word with an underlined pattern at the top; glue; a stapler.

Directions: Place construction paper pages with a pattern (*th*) and a word with the underlined pattern at the top (<u>thump</u>), scissors, glue, magazines, and other consumable print in a learning center or literacy station. Children look for words in magazines and other print that have a specific letter-sound pattern, cut the words out, and glue them onto a large page that has the targeted letter pattern and word. As children learn new letter-sound patterns, have them make a scrapbook page for each one. Staple pages together to make a large scrapbook. Use the words in scrapbooks when reviewing the patterns and as resources for letter-sound activities.

5.16 *Wheels*

Skill: Reading words spelled with the patterns children are learning.

Wheels are two circles, each with one or more letter-sound patterns. Working with wheels makes a good center or literacy station activity for children working in pairs.

Things You'll Need: Two oak tag circles, one larger than the other; a brad; a marker. Make one circle about nine inches in diameter, the other about six inches. On the outermost portion of the large circle, write patterns that come at the beginning of words. On the outermost portion of the small circle, write vowel patterns that come at the end of words. Poke a hole in the center of each and fasten them together with a brad.

Directions: Children turn the circles to align letter patterns (see Figure 5-14). Children then read the word to a partner who cross-checks to make sure that the combination forams real word. Have one of the children write down the words they make.

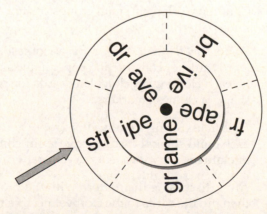

Figure 5-14   Children think about the sounds the letters in patterns represent and then turn wheels to form real words.

5.17   *Phonics Cloze*

Skills: Using letter-sound patterns and context clues to read words.

A typical cloze sentence has a word deleted and replaced with a blank (*The ball rolled into the _____.*). Only part of a word is deleted in phonics cloze sentences (*The ball rolled into the str_____t.*). Children use sentence structure, meaning, and letter-sound cues to figure out the identity of the partially missing words and to write in the missing letters.

Things You'll Need: Modified cloze sentences. To make modified cloze sentences, delete portions of words so as to focus readers' attention on certain patterns.

Directions: Children read the sentences; consider sentence structure, meaning, and letter-sound patterns; and then write the missing letter patterns in the blanks. For example, modified cloze sentences for practice using sentence structure, meaning, and the *oy* and *oi* diphthong patterns would look like this:

> *John got a t_____car for his birthday. (toy)*
> *Nancy planted the seeds deep down in the wet s_____l. (soil)*
> *Glenda wanted to j_____n the club. (join)*
> *The b_____s like to play marbles during recess. (boys)*

5.18   *Clothesline*

Skill: Associating sounds with the patterns children are learning.

Children working in small groups create a clothesline of words that share the same pattern.

Things You'll Need: A rope for a clothesline; an assortment of clothespins; word cards (or construction paper in the shape of clothes with words written on each clothing article); blank cards (or pieces of construction paper in the shape of clothes); markers.

Directions: String a clothesline (rope) across a corner of the room and give each child several cards (or pieces of construction paper cut in the shape of clothes).

After discussing the pattern with the group, children read the words and then pin the cards to the clothesline, like the "clothes" in Figure 5-15. Children also may add their own words to the clothesline by writing words on blank cards. When finished, everyone reads the words in chorus.

Figure 5-15   Pinning words that are spelled with the same letter-sound pattern to a clothesline gives readers opportunities to analyze the letter-sound patterns inside words and to draw conclusions about how the letter-sound patterns represent sound.

5.19   *Chalkboard Sort*

Skill: Associating sounds with the patterns you are teaching.

In this activity, children in a small group work together to sort words on cards according to the letter-sound patterns they are learning and then tape words to a chalkboard or whiteboard, thereby making long chalkboard lists. This type of group sorting is especially useful to help children recognize patterns that are easily confused, such as the VC and VCe patterns in *mad* and *made,* or the VC and r-controlled patterns in *bun* and *burn.*

Things You'll Need: Word cards with masking tape loops on the back.

Directions: Write several letter-sound patterns on the board, such as the long *a* in *stay* (a vowel team pattern), *time* (VCe), and *train* (vowel team). Give children word cards with masking tape loops on the back. Children sort the words by putting them under the words on the board (*stay, time,* and *train,* in this example) that share the same pattern. When finished, read the words in chorus, point out the patterns, and ask children to explain why they pronounce each word as they do. If, on reading the lists, children find a few mistakes, simply move the words to the proper columns.

5.20   *Movies with a Flip Camera or a DIY Projector*

Skill: Spelling words with the patterns children are learning; writing short stories or movie scripts.

Children working in small groups use their prior knowledge, understanding of story structure, and knowledge of words spelled with important letter-sound patterns to produce "homemade" movies.

Things You'll Need: A flip camera. If you do not have one, you can make your own projector with the following materials: a cardboard box; two dowels; a knife; tape; butcher paper. Cut butcher paper into strips, one strip for each group. Partition each long piece of butcher paper into movie frames by drawing horizontal lines at equal distances. Make two extra frames, one at the beginning and one at the end of the movie. These extra frames are later wound around and fastened to dowels, as described next.

To make a movie projector, cut a rectangle in the bottom of a cardboard box to serve as a viewing screen. Cut two sets of holes on either side of the box. Cut one set toward the top of the box (one above the "screen"), the other toward the bottom (one below the "screen"). Make the holes large enough for a dowel to fit through. Slide each dowel through one set of holes. Now, working through the back of the box, tape the movie (which is written on the butcher paper) to the dowels. Wind the entire movie around one dowel; wind only the lead (the blank butcher paper that precedes the movie frames) around the other dowel. Turn the dowels to simulate a movie as the paper film moves from one dowel to another, as illustrated in Figure 5-16. Adjust the tension by turning either the top or bottom dowel. Advise children to make the pictures and text a little smaller than the actual frame. This way, there is some leeway in case the frames drawn on butcher paper are not positioned quite right on the movie screen.

Directions: Pairs or groups of three or four children write and edit a short story. If using a flip camera, have children make a storyboard that shows the scenes they plan to film that will accompany their text. Have children practice reading

Figure 5-16   Children produce homemade movies and, in the process, get experience writing and reading words with the letter-sound patterns they are learning.

their script. Once children are confident, have them film their movie, showing action while reading their script. If you are using a DIY projector, have children divide their story into episodes and then write one episode in each frame, draw an appropriate picture, and underline words with the special patterns they are learning. Fasten the butcher paper to dowels and insert it in the home-made projector. As the dowels are turned, different frames appear on the screen and children read their stories frame by frame. Have children talk about the movies, the story structure, and some of the words with the movies that contain letter-sound patterns they are learning.

5.21 *Vowel Pattern Sort*

Skill: Associating sounds with the vowel patterns children are learning.

This small group activity is beneficial for any age reader who needs more practice identifying, comparing, and contrasting long, short, and r-controlled vowel patterns.

Things You'll Need: A grid with spaces for long-, short-, and r-controlled vowel pattern words, as shown in Figure 5-17; pencils; cards with a variety of words with long-, short-, and r-controlled vowel patterns.

Directions: Ask children to work with a partner. Give each set of partners a piece of paper with a grid that has different patterns and a stack of word cards. Partners sort the words according to the vowel letter patterns—long

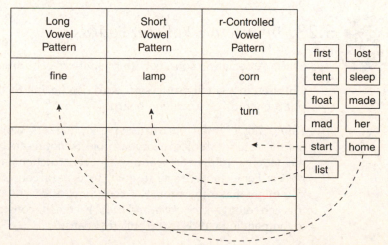

Figure 5-17 Sorting words by their vowel letter-sound pattern gives children opportunities to compare and contrast the sounds the letters in patterns represent.

vowel, short vowel, or r-controlled—and then fill out the grid by writing each word in the appropriate square. Use the completed sort to compare and contrast the different vowel patterns and how they represent sound. Ask children to find or think of other examples of familiar words that include the vowel patterns. Make this activity easier by asking children to sort for only two letter-sound patterns.

5.22   *Baggie Books*

Skill: Spelling words with the patterns children are learning.

Children use their knowledge of patterns when writing stories, which are then edited and slipped inside plastic bags to make durable books. The Baggie Books activity is appropriate for first-graders.

Things You'll Need: Gallon-size plastic bags that lock at the top; a hole punch; ribbon; paper and pencils; colored highlighters.

Directions: Children write and edit stories on paper. Put two pages of the story back to back. Slip them into a gallon-size plastic bag and seal the bag. When all the pages are inside bags, use a paper punch to make three holes on the far left of the bags, as shown in Figure 5-18. Thread colorful ribbon through holes and tie the ribbon in a bow. This fastens the pages of the book together and adds a cheerful splash of color, too. Share baggie books with the class, and, when you do this, talk about story sequence, meaning, and the letter-sound patterns in words.

5.23   *Interactive Bulletin Boards*

Skill: Associating sounds with the patterns children are learning.

Children in a small group sort words according to shared patterns and then put the words on a bulletin board.

Things You'll Need: Construction paper; markers; word cards. Before introducing this activity, think of everyday objects (nouns are best) that are spelled with the patterns children are learning. Cut construction paper into the shapes of the objects. For instance, if you are going to focus on consonant blends and digraphs, you might make a *shoe* for *sh*, a *cloud* for *cl*, and a *truck* for *tr*. Make a word card for each cutout—*shoe, cloud,* and *truck*. Fasten the construction paper cutouts and accompanying words to the bulletin board.

Directions: Read the words on the bulletin board, drawing attention to the patterns children are learning. Give children word cards. You may wish to

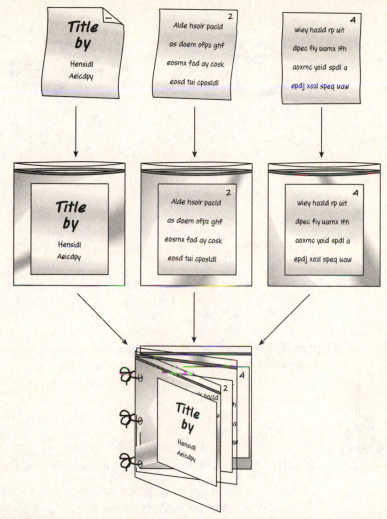

Figure 5-18 Writing stories that are then made into baggie books gives children opportunities to use their knowledge of letter-sound patterns when writing.

give children some cards with words that have the letter patterns on the bulletin board and some cards with words that do not include the targeted patterns. If a word has the same letter-sound pattern as one of the bulletin board words (*shoe*, *cloud*, or *truck* in this example), children add it to the bulletin board, as illustrated in Figure 5-19. You may wish to leave a few blank cards for children to add their own words and words they find on the word wall, on charts, and in the books they are reading in your classroom.

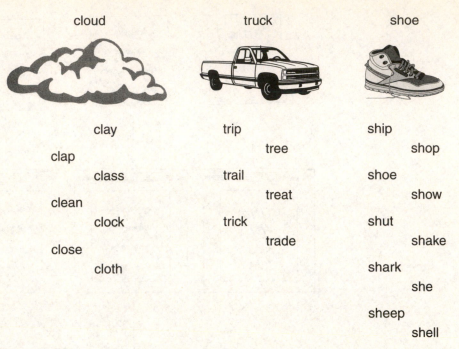

cloud   truck   shoe

clay   trip   ship

clap   tree   shop

class   trail   shoe

clean   treat   show

clock   trick   shut

close   trade   shake

cloth   shark

she

sheep

shell

Figure 5-19   An interactive bulletin board. Children make colorful bulletin boards by sorting words according to their letter-sound patterns.

5.24 *Blocks*

Skill: Spelling words with the patterns children are learning.

Children working in small groups or in learning centers or literacy station use blocks with letter patterns on them to build words.

Things You'll Need: Blocks with a letter-sound pattern on each side; markers. Purchase blocks at a craft store or make your own out of square tissue boxes covered with shelf paper. Each block has six sides, so you will want to think of three patterns for each block and write each pattern twice per block. For instance, to build words with the VV vowel team pattern, children would use three blocks, each with the same pattern written twice: One block might have *tr*, *gr*, and *th*; the second, *ai*, *ee*, and *oa*; the third, *t*, *n*, and *p*. Block-building is more challenging when blocks have six different letter patterns, one pattern on each of the six sides.

Directions: Place blocks in a literacy station or distribute them to children in a small group. Using the blocks you provide, children build as many words as possible and then write the words they build, as shown in Figure 5-20.

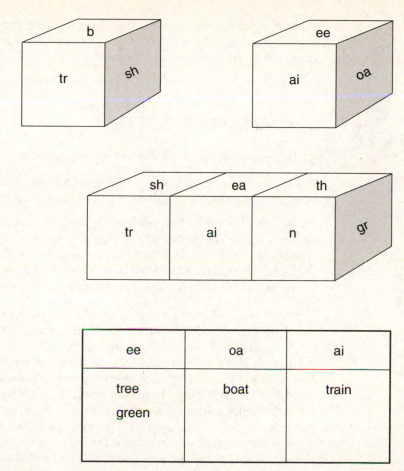

Figure 5-20   An example of blocks. Children apply their knowledge of letter-sound patterns when building words with blocks that have letter-sound patterns on them and then writing the words they build.

5.25 *Catch-a-Word*

Skill: Reading words spelled with patterns the children are learning.

Children get practice reading words with letter-sound patterns they are learning when they "catch" words projected onto a wall or whiteboard. Catch-a-Word is appropriate for large or small groups.

Things You'll Need: Overhead projector; acetate for writing words with patterns the children are learning; gardening gloves.

Directions: Turn the lights down. Have children take turns wearing the garden gloves. Move the overhead fairly close to a white board or blank wall.

Write a word on the acetate. The child wearing the gloves "catches" the word by putting the glove in front of the projected word. The child then reads the word he or she caught and passes the glove to another child.

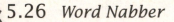

5.26   *Word Nabber*

Skill: Spelling words with the letter patterns children are learning.

In this competitive word game, children in a small group use letter cards to build words, write the words, and cross-check for accuracy.

Things You'll Need: Letter cards with multiple copies of each vowel, two copies of often-used consonants (*b, c, f, g, l, m, n, p, r, s,* and *t*), one copy of the remaining consonants (*h, j, k, qu, v, w, x, y,* and *z*), and one copy of consonant digraphs (*sh, th, ch,* and *ph*). Make the vowel cards in a different color from the consonant cards. Each child needs a paper and a pencil.

Directions: Deal six cards to each player. Have players place their cards face-down on the table. Make sure each child has at least one vowel card. Set a timer or track the second hand on your watch. Give children two or more minutes to make as many words with the six letters as possible. The round begins when you say "go." Players turn over their cards and begin word building. The letters may be used to make as many words as possible within the time limit. Children write the words they build on a piece of paper. After two minutes, call "time's up." Players put their pencils down. Players who were in the midst of writing a word may finish that word. Each player then shows the group the list of words built and reads the words aloud. Other players watch for misspellings. If a player notices a misspelling, that player calls out "nabber." The nabber gets an extra point and the player with the misspelling loses the points for the word. In scoring the round, award one point for each correctly used letter. For instance, if a child spelled five words with a total 21 letters, the player would earn 21 points. Play from three to six rounds.

5.27   *Colorful Vowel Patterns*

Skill: Associating sounds with the vowel patterns children are learning.

Children underline or write vowel patterns in words in color. Writing vowel patterns in color draws children's attention to the patterns. This activity is appropriate for large groups, small groups, or learning centers or literacy stations.

Things You'll Need: Words spelled with the vowel patterns children are learning or texts children are reading or a word list; colored pencils, markers, or crayons.

Directions: Focus on one or two vowel patterns, depending on children's needs. Give children colored pencils, crayons, or markers, and a short word list of words spelled with the patterns they are learning. Alternatively, you might give children text they are reading in your classroom. If using a word list, have children rewrite the words using a different color for each vowel pattern. If using text children are reading, have them look for words in text that are spelled with the vowel patterns you are focusing on. For example, children might write the VCe long-vowel patterns in *home* in red; the VV vowel team pattern in *rain* in orange; the short-vowel pattern in *hat* and *chin* in green. If children are learning r-controlled vowels, have them write the Vr pattern in red. In this example, the *ar* in *star* and *ur* in *hurt* would be written in a color, say blue. Read the words together in chorus; talk about the patterns children wrote in color.

SPARE-MINUTE ACTIVITIES FOR TEACHING LETTER-SOUND PHONICS

5.28   *Silent Letter Cross-Out*

Skills: Recognizing silent letters; reading words with these letters.

Write several words with silent consonants on the chalkboard. Ask a child to pronounce one of the words and then to come to the chalkboard and draw a line through the "silent" consonant. For example, the second *b* in *rabbit* and the second *t* in *mitten* would be crossed off. You also might want to have individual children cross out silent letters on duplicate copies of grade-appropriate text.

5.29   *Dictation*

Skills: Writing and reading words spelled with the patterns children are learning.

Slowly spell a word letter-sound pattern by letter-sound pattern. Children write each pattern and, when finished, read the word aloud. For example, you might say /fl/ as children write *fl*; /ow/ as children write *ow*; /er/ as children write *er*. Children then read the word—*flower*. Letter-sound dictation helps children focus on the patterns that form words and helps children use their letter pattern knowledge to read words.

5.30 *Change-a-Letter*

Skill: Spelling words with the letter-sound patterns children are learning.

Write a word on the chalkboard, such as *team*. Children take turns changing one letter to make a new word, such as changing *pine* into *pin*, *pin* into *pen*, *pen* into *ten*, *ten* into *men*, *men* into *mean*, *mean* into *man*, *man* into *main*.

TEACHING LETTER-SOUND PHONICS TO ENGLISH LANGUAGE LEARNERS

Juana (Figure 5-21) speaks Spanish at home. In writing, Juana combines her knowledge of English with a rich knowledge of Spanish. Notice that Juana replaces *of* with *de*, the Spanish word that would ordinarily be used in this syntactic structure. Notice, too, that Juana writes *ticher* for *teacher*. The letter *i* in Spanish represents the sound heard in *routine*, not *line*, so Juana's spelling is consistent with her first language heritage. Juana is aware of how the English alphabet represents sound, as we see in her spelling of *tois* for *toys*. English language learners, like Juana and

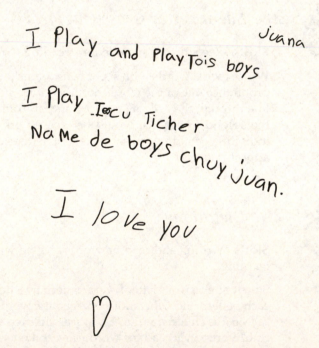

Figure 5-21   The written messages of children who speak languages other than English at home, such as Juana, whose family speaks Spanish, may reflect a combination of children's home language and English.

English-only children learn phonics in a similar sequence. You can therefore teach the same sequence of letter-sound patterns to Juana and the English-only children in your classroom (Chiappe, Siegel, & Wade-Woolley, 2002; Rupley, Blair, & Nichols, 2009). This said, some English language learners may learn phonics at a slower pace (Denton, Anthony, Parker, & Hasbrouck, 2004), depending on how well children speak English and their previous educational experiences. Some English language learners may also have more difficulty associating sounds with letters when the sounds are not in their native language. Therefore, you will want to be aware of the English sounds that are new to English learners and be ready to set aside more time to teach these sounds and the letters that represent them.

Teach English language learners and English-only children together in small groups according to their shared needs, and model how to use phonics. Say the sounds aloud when you model decoding, and have English learners say the sounds aloud as they decode. Phonics has a large oral language component. English language learners develop a better understanding of phonics when you explicitly say the sounds aloud as you show them how to decode. Similarly, English language learners need to see, hear, and say sounds as they decode. Having children say sounds as they decode not only gives them practice pronouncing English sounds and blending, but also gives you valuable insight into how much they know about the patterns and how well they are able to apply the information.

The reading ability of English learners like Juana improves when they receive supplemental instruction over an extended period of time (Gunn, Smolkowski, Biglan, & Black, 2002). In fact, by the end of second grade, English learners who struggle with phonics and who also receive supplemental instruction read as well as the average achieving English-only children (Lesaux & Siegel, 2003). Insofar as your own classroom reading program is concerned, your program will be more effective when you monitor the progress of English learners and target instruction to their specific needs. Progress monitoring is assessing children's abilities on a periodic basis so that you, the teacher, are aware of how children's reading is developing. The results of progress monitoring indicate what children need to learn and what you need to teach. With this information, you are in a position to target instruction to meet children's specific needs. Targeted, direct small-group instruction with continuous progress monitoring significantly improves the reading ability of English learners in first and second grade (Kamps et al., 2007).

Developing children's ability to speak English is an integral part of classroom reading programs for children like Juana. Vocabulary is important for learning phonics and for comprehending text later in school (Hemphill & Tivnan, 2008). Encourage children to talk in your classroom, in the cafeteria, and at play. Create opportunities for English learners to use English in a variety of settings. Ask English learners to decode English words that are already in their English speaking vocabularies. When English learners do not know the meaning of the words they decode, decoding is merely changing an unrecognized written word into an unfamiliar spoken word. Children cannot cross-check for meaning (Chapter 1) because they do not bring enough word knowledge to text. We know that it is important to show children how phonics helps them support comprehension through reading and spelling new words (Lapp, 2010). Decoding does not support comprehension when English learners do not have the words they are decoding in their English vocabularies. In developing English learners' English vocabulary, you (a) help children develop the word knowledge base that helps support comprehension of text, (b) give children a language base for decoding and spelling, and, of course, (c) enhance their ability to form thoughts in English as they write.

Taken together, if you teach children like Juana who are learning to speak English while they are also learning to read English, your classroom program will be more effective when it includes direct instruction in phonics and in phonemic awareness appropriate to Juana's needs. Juana's teacher plans activities and experiences that make it possible for Juana to add more words to her English speaking vocabulary. Supplementary instruction is available in Juana's school, so she has the opportunity to receive extra help beyond that provided by her classroom teacher. Her classroom teacher provides targeted instruction in reading, spelling, and writing in accordance with Juana's developing literacy. Juana has ample opportunities to read, write, spell, talk, and engage in creative activities like role playing, puppet theater, and art. She has a wide variety of books in her classroom that feature familiar cultural topics, as well as children from different cultures and countries. Juana's teacher welcomes Juana's family into the classroom and sets aside time for parents and other adults to share their culture. The classroom reading program includes English learners' culture, language, and heritage in literacy experiences. In so doing, the classroom reading program supports Juana as she makes connections from her home culture to reading and writing, and, in the process, the classroom program helps Juana's English-only classmates make connections to Juana's culture and language.

TEACHING LETTER-SOUND PHONICS TO CHILDREN AT RISK

Children who struggle with phonics read fewer words than their classmates of average progress, they guess at words they do not instantly recognize, and they misspell many words. Noah (Figure 5-22) is a second-grader at risk. He wrote this story after his class read books about fall and talked about autumn. Noah copied *crunchy*, *leaves*, and *calm* from the classroom word wall. Notice that he does not consistently begin sentences with a capital letter, though he does place a period at the end of sentences. Noah knows the short vowel (VC) pattern, but often does not use this knowledge to decode words he does not instantly recognize. Noah struggles with the phonemic awareness skills of segmenting and with blending. If you teach children at risk like Noah, you will be a more successful teacher when you directly teach phonemic awareness, teach phonemic awareness along with phonics, and make segmenting and blending as easy as possible when you first begin to develop phonemic awareness skills (see Chapter 2).

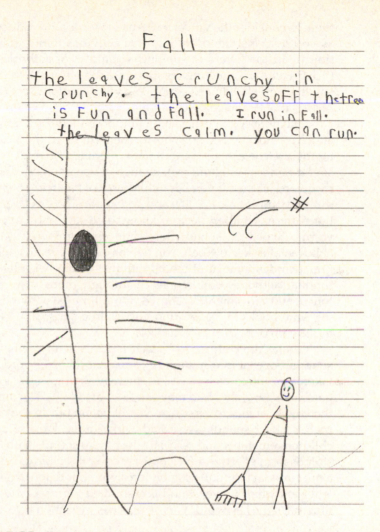

Fall

the leaves crunchy in crunchy. the leavesoFF thetree is Fun and Fall. I run in Fall. the leaves calm. you can run.

Figure 5-22   Noah has difficulty segmenting and blending, and his knowledge of letter-sound patterns lags behind that of his second-grade classmates. He will benefit from direct, targeted instruction in phonemic awareness and phonics.

Noah does not look at all the letters in the words he tries to decode. Rather than analyzing words from left to right, he looks at the beginning and ending letters, and then makes a guess based on these partial clues. Sometime Noah glances at letters and then pronounces a word with similar letter patterns. For example, children at risk like Noah might read *strong* for *string* or *house* for *horse*. It is important for readers like Noah and others at risk to learn to analyze unfamiliar words from left to right. Show children how to begin with the first letter and move all the way through the word, ending with the last letter. This helps them to consider the vowel patterns in words, and reduces guessing. Think aloud as you demonstrate decoding. Use activities that require children to pay attention to all the letters in spelling. Examples of activities include word building (5.3, 5.4 and 5.5), spelling for sounds (5.2), pattern sorts (5.10), mailbox sort (5.13), small group chalkboard sort (5.19), vowel pattern sort (5.21), interactive bulletin boards (5.23), and change-a-letter (5.30).

Noah needs to learn all the important letter patterns of phonics in Table 5–1 and Appendix A. For now, his teacher will teach the VCe pattern (*came*) followed by the VV vowel team pattern (*boat*). Because Noah does not know enough letter-sound patterns or blend well enough to use phonics effectively, he is not an effective word learner. If you have children like Noah in your classroom, teach phonics directly (Rupley et al., 2009) and systematically (de Graaf et al., 2009), and teach all the patterns children need to know to be successful at reading and spelling new words. Expect to spend more time and provide extra phonics instruction to children at risk like Noah. You will be a more effective teacher when your instruction includes some multimodal activities (Campbell, Helf, & Cooke, 2008). In multimodal activities children learn through more than one sense—sight, sound, touch, and movement. Examples of multimodal activities in this chapter are making scrapbooks (5.15), writing vowels in color (5.27), catching words (5.25), and building words with blocks (5.24).

Some the children we teach have difficulty remembering the short vowel sounds. For example, in sounding out a short vowel word, such as *bet*, the child mistakenly pronounces a short /i/, thereby saying /bit/. When asked "What sound goes with /e/," the child may say "/i/" or "/a/". The difficulty lies not so much in the child's ability to recognize vowel letters but in the child's ability to recall the precise short sounds associated with letters. We use *cued vowel sounds* to help children remember and associate the proper sounds with short vowels. Cued vowel sounds is an effective, efficient way to remind children of short vowel sounds. It is a multimodal technique combining sight, sound, touch and movement. Each vowel letter and short vowel sound is associated with a key word and a movement that illustrates the key word. We use the cues explained below:

- *Aa* – short /a/: Key word /apple/. Hold you had near your mouth as though you are going to take a bit out of an apple and say "/a/ /a/ /apple/."
- *Ee* – short /e/. Key word /edge/. Run your hand over the edge of a table saying, "/e/ /e/ /edge/."
- *Ii* – short /i/: Key word /itch/. Pretend to itch your arm while saying "/i/ /i/ /itch/."
- *Oo* – short /o/: Key word /octopus/. Turn your hand palm side down and move your fingers to simulate an octopus as you say "/o/ /o/ /octopus/.
- *Uu* – short /u/: Key word /up/. Point your thumb up and say "/u/ /u/ /up/.'

These key words and movements help children at risk remember the short vowel sounds. In remembering sounds, children are more successful in associating the correct sounds with vowel letters. This, in turn, improves children's ability to decode and spell VC short vowel words.

Explain and model how to use phonics; give children opportunities to practice using phonics under your guidance, and provide immediate feedback on children's efforts to decode and spell new words. Use decodable books that feature the patterns children are learning. Do not ask children to read decodable books that feature patterns they have learned or patterns you have not yet taught. These books are useful tools to give children extra practice in applying letter-sound knowledge while reading. Even though decodable books can be helpful tools for targeted practice in reading words with particular patterns, they should not supplant reading text that is engaging. Children at risk need to use phonics in meaningful contexts through reading mind-engaging books and writing. Reading interesting, well-written books and writing for personally meaningful purposes gives children practice decoding and spelling new words that, in turn, contributes to strengthening their knowledge of why, how, and when to use phonics patterns.

E-RESOURCES FOR TEACHING LETTER-SOUND PHONICS

Graphic Media

Wordle™ Word Clouds (*http://www.wordle.net/*):

Use this activity as a follow up for Colorful Sound Clouds (activity 5.6), which is a chalkboard or whiteboard activity. Have children make lists of words spelled with letter patterns they are learning. Ask children to write their favorite words several times. After children type the lists, paste lists on the Wordle website. Select the font, color and direction for the display. The more often a word appears on the list, the larger the word appear on the finished display.

Websites with Activities or Lessons for Computers or Interactive Whiteboards (IWBs)

Professor Garfield (*http://www.professorgarfield.com/pgf_home.html*):

Click on Transport to Reading, then click on Garfield's Island to find two interactive phonics games: Fishing with Phonics, which is a click-and-drag game for identifying beginning or ending sounds; and Match of Mystery, which includes memory games where the player matches words with the same short-vowel, long-vowel, vowel team, VCe, or diphthong sounds. Click on Knowledge Box for long vowel games where children identify pictures that match long vowel words. Although most words are presented as onsets and rimes in these games, the focus is on identifying and reading words with long vowel patterns. Look in Brain Busters for Match Attack, a memory game where the player matches an English word with a Spanish word. Words change daily, so players will get practice with different words on different days. Examples of games children play for fun are (1) Word Soup, a game where children unscramble words, (2) Cross

Words, a crossword puzzle game, (3) Word Search, and (4) Code Busters, an cryptogram game.

Scholastic™ (*http://teacher.scholastic.com/whiteboards/languagearts.htm*) and (*http://www2 .scholastic.com/browse/collection.jsp?id=615*):

In the Clifford the Big Red Dog™ Make a Word game, children click on letters to spell VC short-vowel words. This is an IWB-ready activity. This site also has IWB lessons for long *o*, long *a*, Vr, digraphs, and soft and hard consonant sounds (see Appendix A for an explanation of soft and hard sounds). The second address features IWB phonics activities for (1) long *a*, (2) long *o*, (3) Vr, (4) consonant digraphs, and (5) hard and soft *c* and *g*.

Progressive Phonics™ (*http://www.progressivephonics.com/~suzettew*):

Progressive Phonics is a website for teaching phonics through reading short books that have words spelled with specific letters and sounds, such as the digraphs *th*, *ch*, and *sh*. Books are categorized by their teaching and learning focus. Look for beginning phonics books to teach short vowel sounds, intermediate phonics for teaching phonics patterns such as digraphs, blends, long vowels, r-controlled (*Vr*) vowels, and advanced phonics for teaching *y* as a vowel, hard and soft *g* and *c*, and exceptions to vowel and consonant patterns. Some books have activity sheets in a zip file that include (1) trace-read-write worksheets, (2) flash cards, (3) high-frequency words, and (4) a word search game.

Sadlier-Oxford (*http://www.sadlier-oxford.com/phonics/student.cfm*):

Phonics games are categorized by grade level on this site. Grade 1 includes games for matching pictures and words that have long vowels or short vowels. Grade 2 includes games for matching pictures and words with Vr r-controlled vowels, the diphthongs *ou* and *ow*, and *oy*, *oi*, and also *ew*. Other second-grade games call for indicating the beginning and ending consonant digraphs, vowel pairs, or consonant blends in words. Two games for third and fourth grades indicate words with *oo* in sentence contexts. Circus Builder calls for identifying words with the same vowel sound, including words in which the same sound is represented by different letters. Phonics and word study systems can be purchased by grade level and include a teacher's edition, student edition, phonics cards and other materials.

PBS Kids™ (*http://pbskids.org/*; *http://pbskids.org/whiteboard* and *http://pbskids.org/ electriccompany/#/Games*):

Examples of IWB-ready games that ask children to apply letter and sound knowledge include (1) Super Why! Princess Presto's Golden Crown Spelling Bee; (2) WordWorld: Dog's Letter Pit; (3) Between the Lions: Alphabet Soup; (4) Between the Lions: Chicken Stacker; (5) Between the Lions: Fuzzy Lion Ears; and (6) Super Why! Super Reader Challenge. Make Way for Noddy is a spelling game where children pop balloons with the correct letters. Super Why! Create-Your-Own Super Hero gives children practice associating sounds with letters. Electric Company's Word Transformer features (1) Word Party for application of the bossy *r* (Vr r-controlled); (2) Prime Time Change for recognizing words with the VCe pattern; and (3) Changing the Shape of Things for practice with consonant digraphs. Look, too, for the Chain Game, where children spell words by substituting short *u*, *a*, and *e*, the diphthong *ou*, and consonant blends.

Smart Exchange™ (*http://exchange.smarttech.com*):

Smart Exchange has a variety of phonics activities that feature question sets focused on specific letter-sound associations. Also available on this site are activities created by teachers.

ReadWriteThink (*http://www.readwritethink.org*):

This website, co-sponsored by the International Reading Association and the National Council of Teachers of English, offers lesson plans for teaching phonics linked to language arts standards.

Fun4theBrain (*http://www.fun4thebrain.com/English/magice.html*):

This game is a quest to change a frog into a prince by reading VCe words and completing sentences. The word reading practice and theme make it appealing and appropriate for girls in late first grade, second, and third graders who need extra practice.

Arcademic™ **Skill Builders** (*http://www.arcademicskillbuilders.com/*):

Click on Language Arts then on Coconut Vowels for a game where the player selects the vowel patterns that complete words, and on Turtle Dash for a multi-player game where players select vowel patterns to make words. Spelling Bees is a multiplayer game where up to four children compete to build bee hives by correctly spelling words. This site also has games for antonyms and synonyms which would be helpful for children who need to increase their vocabulary.

Game Goo™ (*http://www.earobics.com/gamegoo/gooeyhome.html*):

Sponsored by Earobics®, this site features several interactive phonics games, among them (1) Fearless Freida: Skillful Skateboarding, where children spell short vowel words, (2) Fearless Freida: The Big Kahuna, which calls for application of the VCe pattern and consonant blends, and (3) Alien Scavenger Hunt, which calls for spelling words by identifying letters and letter-sound correspondences. Both games are linked to standards, which can be accessed from the homepage. Other games are listed in the inventory accessed through the address above. Look for new games posted on this website.

Roy the Zebra (*http://www.roythezebra.com/reading-games-long-vowel-phonemes.html*):

This site has a variety of downloadable phonics games that can be used on IWBs. Look for over 30 games for spelling words with long vowels, diphthongs, and r-control (Vr). Children click and drag the vowel combinations to spell words.

ict Games (*http://www.ictgames.com/literacy.html*):

Phoneme Pop Letters and Sounds, CVC Pop, Blending Bingo, Sound Bingo, and Letters and Sounds Bingo are interactive games for associating letters with sounds. The pop games call for clicking on balloons with designated letters. The bingo games feature wheels that turn to make words, complete with sound effects for drama. In projecting bingo games on an IWB, children can see the words as they are generated. Numerous, downloadable bingo cards are available to use with the bingo games. The word generator on the bingo games has a feature that indicates words that have already been played, which is useful for checking the bingo cards at the end of the game. Another game, Ladybug Lander, gives children practice spelling words and hearing the sounds the letters represent. This would be a good activity for an IWB. Blending Dragon features phonics letter-sound patterns in real and nonsense words. Players must decide which letter combinations make real words and which do not. DJ Cow's Spelling Patterns creates word searches for words with the letter-sound pattern you select.

Starfall™ (*http://starfall.com*):

This site has free interactive games for making words with the VCe and vowel team patterns, r-control (Vr), as well as *y* and long *e*. Also available for various patterns are matching games, books read aloud, and sorting activities. Movies and short video clips highlight letter-sound patterns. Books for letter-sound patterns highlight each word as the child clicks on it while a voice pronounces the word letter-sound by letter-sound, and then the voice pronounces the whole word. Also available are printable pages for practice reading and writing short-vowel words. Printables include (1) classification, which is categorizing short-vowel words, such as animal words and thing words; (2) silly stories, which entails filling in blanks to write stories that include short-vowel words; (3) word searches; and (4) label the puzzle, which consists of pictures with blanks where children write in short-vowel words. While these printables are intended for use with the phonics puzzles available for purchase on the site, the printables can be used as intact activities to practice and reinforce learning.

foniks (*http://www.foniks.org/*):

This has a large grid with a letter or letter pattern in each square. Children click inside the boxes to hear and see a letter, and words spelled with the letter. The site encourages children to hear, say, trace, write and read patterns. Click on the printer icon at the top of the page to print a copy. Printable activities are organized into books that can be downloaded and used for extra practice. Also look for a list of common foreign words, and explanations of the use of apostrophes and common punctuation.

BBC (*http://www.bbc.co.uk/schools/wordsandpictures/index.shtml*):

This site has a variety of activities. Click Phonics Year 2 to find Sandcastle Quiz, a spelling game, and Write a Postcard, where children click-and-drag letters to complete words. This game is especially useful for helping children understand that the same sound can be spelled with different letter combinations. Printable worksheets and games are also available. Look in VC Words for a Whirlybird Machine game; Consonant Clusters has a word blending game where the player listens to a word and then selects the beginning and ending letter groups to spell the word. Click Long Vowel Sounds to find Poem Pack which has 10 poems featuring words spelled with *ee, ei, ea, oa, ay, ae, oo, y, igh,* or *ie.* Children can hear poems, read poems, find words with the featured sound, and add words to complete sentences. Poems are printable. Poems are read with a British accent on this United Kingdom website. Under Long Sounds are Snap and Click 'n' Spell. Snap is similar to the card game. To play Snap, a player clicks when a vowel pattern and the letters on a card make a word. Drag 'n' Spell is a game where the player drags vowel patterns to spell words.

Brown Bear (*http://www.bigbrownbear.co.uk*):

On the Brown Bear homepage click on Magnetic Letter Resource to access a Magnetic Letters game. This IWB-ready word building game has colorful facsimiles of magnetic letters. As many as 21 letters can be on the magnetic board at one time. Look in Phoneme Frames for Phoneme Jigsaws, a word building game. In Phoneme Blender, also accessed from the homepage, children decide if the letters aligned by spinning wheels result in real or nonsense words. There are six lists of letter and sound patterns for the Phoneme Blender game.

Fast Phonics (*http://www.abcfastphonics.com*):

This site has tutorials that explain basic phonics letter sound patterns. Children click on speakers to hear explanations. It is a useful resource for children who need more exposure to the letter sound patterns and explanations of the patterns.

Kids Spell (*http://www.kidsspell.com*):

This free website has over 800 spelling lists and nine spelling games that range from easy to difficult. Teachers have the option of creating and saving their own spelling lists.

Reading Rockets® (*http://www.readingrockets.org*):

The Reading Rockets® website has resources for teachers and parents. Among the features of this site are web casts for teacher development, research, tips for effective teaching and working with parents, teacher guides to accompany Reading Rockets® PBS television shows for teaching reading, and interviews with children's authors.

Phonics Play (*http://www.phonicsplay.co.uk*):

This website features free games as well as resources that are available through subscription. Click on Free Phonics Play, then Phase 2 for two free games (1) Buried Treasure and (2) Dragon's Den. In playing these games, children decide whether words are real or nonsense. Look in Phase 3 for (1) Picnic on Pluto and (2) Pick a Picture. Picnic on Pluto is similar to the Buried Treasure and Dragon's Den games. Pick a Picture calls for clicking on one of four pictures that represents the picture. Teachers select the letter patterns for Buried Treasure, Dragon's Den and Picnic on Pluto games.

NGfL Cymru (*http://www.ngfl-cymru.org.uk*):

Look for (1) Word Maker Long Vowels 1, (2) Word Maker Long Vowels 2, and (3) Word Maker Long Vowels 3. These games ask children to click and drag letters to make words. To access the games, (1) click on English on the homepage, (2) then click on Keystage1, (3) click on English again, and (4) last click on phonics.

Printable Materials

Word Way (*http://www.wordway.us.com*):

This website offers downloadable materials organized around word families. The word families feature rimes spelled with long vowel patterns, the r-controlled (Vr) pattern, digraphs, and diphthongs. Use the rimes to call attention to phonics patterns and the sounds patterns represent. Materials include books and games for patterns.

Scholastic™ (*http://printables.scholastic.com/printables/home/?ESP=PRT/ib/20100104/ acq/merch_none///IWB/txtl////*):

This site offers a plethora of printable phonics materials. Search the site for downloads that are appropriate for your classroom program. Additional downloads are available through a subscription.

Reading Target (*http://readingtarget.com/*):

This site is a parent resource that has short assessments for estimating children's phonics knowledge and printable sheets that show pictures and words with a single phonics pattern. There are many printable sheets that could be used to introduce or review patterns.

The websites sited above offer *some* resources or all resources on their sites free of charge, with the exception of Wordle™ which is a subscription only site. Many sites make resources available only with a subscription. Examples of subscription sites are (1) Reading a-z (*http://www.readinga-z.com*), (2) ClickN Kids® (*http://www.clicknkids .com/Phonics.php*), and (3) Reading Eggs (*http://readingeggs.com/?gclid=CIPIlcnX3a QCFYpa2godfFzbdw*).

Smart Phone and Tablet Apps

Scholastic: Spelling VC words (*http://www.scholastic.com/iphoneapps/index.htm*):

Clifford the Big Red Dog Be Big with Words is a click-and-drag game for spelling VC pattern words. Also look for Word Girl for exploring word meaning.

Word Magic: Associating sounds with letters (*http://www.anusen.com/*):

iPhone app that is appropriate for kindergartners or other children who need practice associating letters and sounds. Children select a letter to complete words; three levels include missing beginning, middle, or ending letters.

REFERENCES

Aardema, V. (1975). *Why mosquitoes buzz in people's ears*. New York: Dial Books for Young Readers.

Armbruster, B. B., Lehr, F., & Osborn, J. (2001). *Put reading first: The research building blocks for teaching children to read*. Washington, DC: National Institute for Literacy.

Bailey, M. H. (1967). The utility of phonic generalizations in grades one through six. *The Reading Teacher*, *20*, 413–418.

Bear, D. R., Invernizzi, M., Templeton, S., & Johnston, F. (2007). *Words their way: Word study for phonics, vocabulary, and spelling instruction* (3rd ed.). Upper Saddle River, NJ: Pearson Education.

Blachman, B. A., Schatschneider, C., Fletcher, J. M., Francis, D. J., Clonan, S. M., Shaywitz, B. A., & Shaywitz, S. E. (2004). Effects of intensive reading remediation for second and third graders and a 1-year follow-up study. *Journal of Educational Psychology*, *96*, 444–461.

Campbell, M. L., Helf, S., & Cooke, N. L. (2008). Effect of adding multisensory components to a supplemental reading program on the decoding skills of treatment resisters. *Education and Treatment of Children*, *31*(3), 267–295.

Chiappe, P., Siegel, L. S., & Wade-Woolley, L. (2002). Linguistic diversity and the development of reading skills: A longitudinal study. *Scientific Studies of Reading*, *5*, 369–400.

Christensen, C. A., & Bowey, J. A. (2005). The efficacy of orthographic rime, grapheme-phoneme correspondences, and implicit phonics approaches to teaching decoding skills. *Scientific Studies of Reading*, *9*, 327–340.

Clymer, T. (1963). The utility of phonic generalizations in the primary grades. *The Reading Teacher*, *16*, 252–258.

Conrad, N. J. (2008). From reading to spelling to reading: Transfer goes both ways. *Journal of Educational Psychology*, *100*(4), 869–878,

de Graaff, S., Bosman, A. M. T., Hasselman, F., & Verhoeven, L. (2009). Benefits of systematic phonics instruction. *Scientific Studies of Reading*, *13*(4), 318–383.

Denton, C. A., Anthony, J. L., Parker, R., & Hasbrouck, J. E. (2004). Effects of two tutoring programs on the English reading development of Spanish-English bilingual students. *The Elementary School Journal*, *104*, 289–305.

Ehri, L. C. (2005). Learning to read words: Theory, findings, and issues. *Scientific Studies of Reading*, *9*, 167–188.

Ehri, L. C. (2006). More about phonics: Findings and reflections. In K. A. D. Stahl & M. C. McKenna (Eds.), *Reading research at work: Foundations of effective practice* (pp. 155–165). New York: Guilford Press.

Emans, R. (1967). The usefulness of phonic generalizations above the primary grades. *The Reading Teacher*, *20*, 419–425.

Foorman, B. R., Schatschneider, C., Eakin, M. N., Fletcher, J. M., Moates, L. C., & Francis, D. J. (2006). The impact of instructional practices in grades 1 and 2 on reading and spelling achievement in high poverty schools. *Contemporary Educational Psychology, 31*, 1–29.

Gunn, B., Smolkowski, K., Biglan, A., & Black, C. (2002). Supplemental instruction in decoding skill for Hispanic and non-Hispanic students in early elementary school: A follow-up. *Journal of Special Education, 36*, 69–79.

Hemphill, L., & Tivnan, T. (2008). The importance of early vocabulary for literacy achievement in high-poverty schools. *Journal of Education for Students Placed at Risk, 13*, 426–451.

Juel, C., & Roper-Schneider, D. (1985). The influence of basal readers on first grade reading. *Reading Research Quarterly, 20*, 134–152.

Kamps, D., Abbott, M., Greenwood, C., Arrega-Mayer, C., Wills, H., Longstaff, J., Culpepper, M., & Walton, C. (2007). Use of evidence-based, small group reading instruction for English language learners in elementary grades: Secondary-tier intervention. *Learning Disability Quarterly, 30*, 253–168.

Lapp, S. I. (2010). Literacy and the English language learner. In E. N. Whelan Aziza (Eds.), *Not for ESOL teachers: What every classroom teacher needs to know about the linguistically, culturally, and ethnically diverse student* (2nd ed.) (pp. 71–77). Boston: Allyn & Bacon.

Lesaux, N. K., & Siegel, L. S. (2003). The development of reading in children who speak English as a second language. *Developmental Psychology, 39*, 1005–1019.

Lord, J. V. (1972). *The giant jam sandwich*. Boston: Houghton Mifflin.

National Reading Panel. (2000). *Teaching children to read: An evidence-based assessment of the scientific research literature on reading and its implications for reading instruction: Reports of the subgroups* (NIH Publication No. 00-4754). Washington, DC: U.S. Government Printing Office.

Rupley, W. H., Blair, T. R., & Nichols, W. D. (2009). Effective reading instruction for struggling readers: The role of direct/explicit teaching. *Reading & Writing Quarterly, 25*(2), 125–138.

Shanahan, T. (2005). *The national reading panel report: Practical advice for teachers*. Naperville, IL: Learning Point Associates.

Shankweiler, D., & Fowler, A. E. (2004). Questions people ask about the role of phonological processes in learning to read. *Reading and Writing: An Interdisciplinary Journal, 17*, 483–515.

CHAPTER 6

Analyzing the Structure of Long Words in Third Grade and Above

The Strategy of Using Multiletter Word Parts to Read and Learn Complex Words

This chapter describes how readers use the multiletter groups in word structure to read and spell long words. You will learn about multiletter groups or chunks from parts of long words that represent prefixes and suffixes, and about how syllables represent sound. In reading this chapter, you will learn the best practices for teaching prefixes, suffixes, and syllables; how to support readers as they strategically analyze word structure; and activities for teaching the structure of long words. Here you will also find suggestions for teaching word structure to English language learners and children at risk of struggling with reading, as well as e-resources to support teaching word structure in your classroom reading program.

KEY IDEAS

▶ Readers automatically recognize and pronounce large, intact letter groups in long words.

▶ Many word parts indicate meaning—for example, the prefix *un-* in *unhappy*, the suffix *-ly* in *friendly*, and the root word *sign* in *signal* and *signature*.

▶ Syllables are units of pronunciation, such as the syllables *dis*, *trib*, and *ute* in *distribute*.

▶ The strategy of analyzing long words to find useful multiletter groups is more efficient than other word identification strategies.

▶ The strategy of using large, multiletter groups in the structure of long words is the last word identification strategy to develop before readers automatically recognize the words they see in text.

KEY VOCABULARY

Accented syllable

Affix

Automatic word recognition

Base word

Bound morpheme

Chunk

Cognates

Compound word

Consolidated word learner

Contraction

At a mere glance, you know how to pronounce *astroport*, as used in Figure 6-1, and you know it is a noun. You recognize that it is most likely an interstellar station for the space traveling public and, if asked, could use *astroport* in a sentence. All this is quite interesting since *astroport* is not a real word—at least, not yet.

The way to unlock this word's pronunciation and get insight into its meaning is to divide *astroport* into the two large, meaningful multiletter chunks: *astro* and *port*. A **chunk** is a group of letters that represents meaning and sound (the *re-* in *redo*) or sound only (the two syllables in *na/tion*). Each word part is spelled the way it sounds and contributes to the word's definition, provided you know that *astro* means "star" and *port* means "to carry." With this knowledge, you might logically infer that an *astroport* is a site to which space travelers are transported, just as an *airport* is a site to which airline passengers are transported.

After reading and writing the same letter sequences time and time again, readers perceive these groups as large, intact units. In so doing,

Derivational suffix

Free morpheme

Greek and Latin word parts

Inflectional suffix

Morpheme

Prefix

Structural analysis

Suffix

Syllable

Syllable and affix spellers

Unaccented syllable

Astroport

Figure 6-1   Meaningful letter groups give insight into pronunciation and word meaning. The student who drew this picture used knowledge of *astro* and *port* to show what they might mean if put together.

readers chunk, or join together, groups of letters mentally. Multiletter groups or chunks significantly reduce the energy readers put into word identification and, when readers know the meaning of letter groups, they have some insight into the definition of words as well. Readers who use multiletter groups do not recall analogous onsets and rimes in known words to identify unknown words as do users of analogy-based phonics, nor do they sound out and blend letter-sound patterns as do users of letter-sound-based phonics. Instead, readers recognize and pronounce all at once entire groups of letters in words (*complete = com + plete; unworkable = un + work + able*). Identifying multiletter groups as whole chunks in long words is more efficient than associating sounds with either word family rimes or letter-sound patterns.

When you, the teacher, help readers use multiletter groups to read new words, you are teaching **structural analysis.**[1] Rather than focus on the sound level, which is the scope of phonics-based instruction, structural analysis focuses on teaching the

---

[1]Analysis of meaningful units in words is part of morphology, a specialized study in linguistics that concentrates on word forms and their connections to meaning. Prefixes, suffixes, contractions, compound words, base words, and root words are more accurately described as morphemic analysis because each deals with meaning. Syllables, accents, and other pronunciation units, such as rimes, represent sound and therefore are associated with phonics analysis. Combining meaningful and nonmeaningful chunks under the umbrella of structural analysis makes sense for the purpose of teaching inasmuch as readers recognize these letter groups as single, intact units.

large structural units that make up complex words. When you demonstrate how the meaning of *effort* changes when you add *-less* to make *effortless*, you are teaching structural analysis. You also teach structural analysis when you help readers understand how *isn't* consists of *is* and *not*. When you help a fifth-grader use a hyphen to divide the word *government* into syllables so as to write part of the word on one line (*govern-*) and part on another (*ment*), you are teaching structural analysis.

THE STRUCTURE OF LONG WORDS

In analyzing the structure of long words, children pay attention to the following seven multiletter groups:

1. *Prefixes.* Prefixes are added to the beginning of words to change meaning (the *un-* in *unpleasant*) or to make meaning more specific (the *mid-* in *midweek*).
2. *Suffixes.* Suffixes are added to the end of words to clarify meaning (the *-s* in *cats*) or to change grammatical function (the *-able* in *drinkable*). We use the term **affix** when referring to word parts that are attached or fastened together. For the purposes of this book, we will use affix to refer collectively to prefixes and suffixes.
3. *Base Words.* Base words (also called morphemes) are the smallest meaningful units, or words, in English that can stand alone (*play, go, come, here, father*).
4. *Greek and Latin Root Word Parts.* Greek and Latin word parts are borrowed from these two languages (*astro* borrowed from Greek and *port* from Latin) to form English words.
5. *Compound Words.* Compound words are two base words that, when combined, make an entirely new word (*cow + boy = cowboy*).
6. *Contractions.* Contractions are shortcuts for writing two words together (*isn't, we're*).
7. *Syllables.* Syllables are the basic units of pronunciation in our English language (the *ta* and *ble* in *table*). All words have one or more syllables, and each syllable has one vowel sound.

Free and Bound Morphemes

Shady consists of two meaningful parts or morphemes—*shade* (the base word) and *-y* (the suffix meaning "full of or having"). **Morphemes** are the basic meaning units in language. They can be free or bound.

Free morphemes represent meaning in and of themselves; they can stand alone. *Lady* is an example of a free morpheme. We do not need to add any other morpheme to associate meaning with *lady*. Furthermore, we cannot reduce *lady* to a smaller word. *Lady* is a complete, meaningful word all by itself.

Bound morphemes have meaning only when they are attached to another morpheme. *Shady* consists of two morphemes: one free morpheme (*shade*) and one bound morpheme (the suffix -*y*). For the -*y* to be meaningful, we need to add it to another morpheme, such as *baggy*, *chewy*, or *foamy*. Bound morphemes have meaning, but that meaning is expressed only when these morphemes are attached to another morpheme. Bound morphemes include prefixes, suffixes, and word parts borrowed from other languages to form English words. Examples of bound morphemes include the *pre-* in *prepay*, the *-ing* in *laughing*, and the Greek word part *phon* in *phonics*.

Combining morphemes is a common way to form multisyllable words. It follows, then, that one way to identify an unfamiliar long word is to identify free and bound morphemes in the word. For example, on seeing *laughable*, readers would find the bound morpheme *-able* and the free morpheme *laugh*. Having disaggregated the word into morphemic parts, readers now know how to pronounce this word and have insight into word meaning. You may see the term *morphemic analysis* in reference sources or teachers' manuals. Morphemic analysis is identifying the meaningful parts—free and bound morphemes—in words. For instance, in using morphemic analysis to read a word like *reapplied*, readers would note the prefix *re-*, the suffix *-ed*, and the base word *apply*. Readers would know how *re-* and *-ed* affect the meaning of *apply* and, therefore, not only identify *reapplied* but also understand the meaning of *reapplied* within the context of the reading selection.

TEACHING WORD STRUCTURE IN YOUR CLASSROOM READING PROGRAM

First and Second Grades

If you are a first- or second-grade teacher, you will teach the word parts that children need to know to be successful readers and spellers in these early grades. As a first-grade teacher, you will introduce common suffixes like *-s/es*, *-ly*, *-ing*, *-ed*, *-er*, and *-est*; a few common prefixes such as *un-* and *re-*; compound words; contractions; and, perhaps, a few syllable patterns such as VC (*cap*), VCe (*cape*), CV (*he*), or C + *le* (*table*). In the second grade, children review the word parts taught in the first grade. As a second-grade teacher, you will introduce compound words and contractions that were not taught in first grade and a few more common prefixes and suffixes, such as *mis-* (*mistook*) and *-less* (*useless*). Additionally, you might introduce easy-to-recognize and consistently pronounced syllables like the *-tion* in *nation*. While word structure is taught in first and second grades, phonics is the main focus of first- and second-grade classroom reading programs.

Third, Fourth, and Fifth Grades

Classroom reading programs emphasize word structure in the third, fourth, and fifth grades because the children in these grades have a reasonable grasp of phonics. They do not need focused phonics instruction. The classroom reading programs in these grades focus instead on the multiletter units or chunks in word structure, reflecting the fact that third- through fifth-graders read and spell long, complex words. This said, we acknowledge that third grade is a transition year. The third-grade classroom reading program may review or reteach some phonics letter-sound patterns and will most certainly devote a good amount of time teaching patterns to third-graders who have low phonics knowledge. By and large, however, the third-grade program shifts throughout the year from reviewing or reteaching phonics patterns to teaching the structure of long, multisyllable words. Refer to Chapter 5 for a more in-depth explanation of phonics patterns.

Third-, fourth-, and fifth-grade teachers usually spend about 15 minutes a day on word work (or word study). If you teach third grade, your classroom reading program may use several approaches to teaching word structure. You may use direct instruction, practice reading text with long words, and spelling words that include the word parts children are learning. If you teach fourth or fifth grade, you will teach word structure through spelling. Spelling long words that contain the word parts children are learning is beneficial because it helps to develop in-depth knowledge of how adding affixes affects base word spelling, how affixes affect word meaning, and how syllables are spelled in long words. Teachers might, for example, challenge children to learn to spell words like *supernatural* (five syllables) or *illogical* (four syllables).

The classroom program may include a review of prefixes and suffixes taught in previous grades such as *un-* and *-ly*. You will teach new prefixes and suffixes such as *over-* (*overdue*) or *-ive* (*creative*), homophones (words that sound alike but are spelled differently, such as *wait-weight*), and words that look alike but do not sound alike (*present-present*). Greek and Latin word parts usually enter the curriculum in the fourth grade. Fourth-grade teachers introduce frequently used word parts like *phon-* in *telephone* or *-port* in *transport*. Fifth-grade classroom reading programs usually include teaching Greek and Latin word parts like *aud-* in *auditory* or *-logy* in *biology*. At the end of elementary school, the average reader recognizes a variety of prefixes and suffixes, knows how affixes affect word meaning, reads and spells multisyllable words, and infers the meaning of new words by analyzing Greek and Latin word parts. The average reader is fully independent, confident, and skilled at learning new words in content areas and enjoys reading for pleasure.

How Children Read New Words by Analyzing Word Structure

Analyzing the intact letter groups in the structure of long words takes less mental attention than sounding out words with the letter-sound strategy and requires less time away from comprehending text. Readers realize that spoken and written words can be divided into a variety of units, some small and some large. Readers decode long words by breaking them into chunks. In this strategy, children identify known word chunks first and then use these chunks to read the whole word. These readers know that the same letter groups are part of many different words, such as the *-ter* in *butter* and *terrific* or the *-ous* in *famous* and *dangerous*. They recognize word parts that indicate pronunciation only (the *-ter* in *butter*), as well as those that indicate meaning and pronunciation (the *-ing* in *playing*). The more reading and writing experiences children have in school, the more they learn about the structure of words, and the more accomplished they become at using structural analysis to read long words.

The strategy of analyzing the structure of long words hinges on identifying the intact letter groups that make up word structure. Let's look at an example. Peter comes across the new word *antiseptic* in this sentence from his science book: "Perhaps you recall getting a cut on your knee. Someone may have disinfected the cut with an antiseptic" (Hackett, Moyer, & Adams, 1989, p. 27). Peter's science class has already discussed *antiseptics* and their function, so this word is in his speaking and listening vocabularies. Peter also knows that *anti* means "against or preventing" when it is in common words like *antismoking* and *antitheft*. All things considered, Peter brings a good deal of prior knowledge to word identification. He knows what the spoken word *antiseptic* means, how *anti* contributes to a word's definition, and how to recognize many different types of intact, multiletter chunks in the words he reads. Here is how Peter goes about using this streamlined strategy:

1. Peter recognizes *anti* and, in so doing, instantly recalls its pronunciation and meaning.
2. He identifies two additional word parts: *sep* and *tic*. Peter now has divided *antiseptic* into three pronounceable groups: /anti/ + /sep/ + /tic/.
3. Peter blends /anti/ + /sep/ + /tic/ into /antiseptic/.
4. Last, he cross-checks to make sure that he pronounces and understands the word in the context in which it is used in his science book. He asks himself: "Does *antiseptic* sound and look right? Does *antiseptic* make sense in the passage?" If *antiseptic* makes sense, Peter continues reading.

In the way Peter separated them, the first group of letters is *anti*; the second, *sep*; and the third, *tic*. However, there are other ways Peter might have chosen to group letters. Though the *septic* in *antiseptic* is a meaningful word part, Peter is not familiar with it. Had he known the meaning of *septic*, Peter might have divided *antiseptic* into these two meaningful chunks: *anti* + *septic*. Or he could have divided *antiseptic* into *an* + *ti* + *septic*. Though the specific multiletter groups individual readers use will vary depending on each reader's background knowledge, all readers who use this strategy are sensitive to which letters form intact chunks and which do not.

Take *ing* as an example. Readers know that *ing* represents meaning and sound in *playing* and only signals pronunciation (a rime) in *swing*. They also know that *ing* is not a viable word part in *hinge*. When identifying multiletter groups, readers bring to bear their knowledge of the letter-sound patterns in a word. Peter and readers like him use their knowledge of letter-sound patterns to determine the letters in new words that are most likely to belong in the same groups. This explains why Peter did not identify the *ise* as an intact unit in *antiseptic*. This kind of in-depth knowledge is not an overnight phenomenon. Rather, it develops gradually as readers strategically use the multiletter groups in word structure to read and write long words.

Correcting Misidentifications

Readers who do not successfully identify words on the first try may choose from among the following four alternatives:

1. Reanalyze long words (divide words into different multiletter groups and then blend).
2. Fall back on either the letter-sound or analogy strategy.
3. Look up words in the dictionary.
4. Ask expert readers for help.

The strategy of analyzing word structure does not come into its own until after readers have had experience using the analogy and letter-sound strategies. Readers like Peter who look for multiletter chunks in word structure are in the *consolidated stage of word learning* and the *syllables and affixes stage of spelling*, as you will learn in the next section.

CONSOLIDATED WORD LEARNERS AND SYLLABLES AND AFFIXES SPELLERS

Readers in the **consolidated word learning** stage have insight into the letter-sound patterns of phonics and have consolidated, or grouped, letter sequences in memory (Ehri, 2005). Readers at the consolidated stage recognize meaningful parts in long words, such as the *un-* and *-ed* in <u>*unfinished*</u>, as well as nonmeaningful syllables, such as the *cir* and *cle* in *circle*. While the transition into the consolidated stage comes toward the end of second grade for most readers, some will move into this stage during the third grade. Average third-grade readers quickly recognize multiletter groups in words. Because these readers automatically associate sounds with whole groups of letters, they read words faster and with greater accuracy than their classmates who try to decode long words letter-sound by letter-sound (Neuhaus, Roldan, Boulware-Gooden, & Swank, 2006).

Readers at the consolidated stage use the reading context to help them identify words and use cross-checking to determine whether words make sense in the passages they read. These readers know when to self-correct and, because their focus is on meaning, know when it is necessary to fix a word identification miscue. They do not sound out words letter-sound by letter-sound, nor do they think about analogous rimes to read word family words. Instead, these readers instantly recognize large intact letter groups in words. They recognize syllables, such as the *-tion* in *nation*, and they also automatically recognize prefixes (the *pre-* in *preheat*), suffixes (the *-er* in *smaller*), base words (the *clean* in *cleaning*), compound words (*snowman*), and contractions (*she'd*).

Readers at the consolidated stage are at the **syllables and affixes spelling** stage (Bear, Invernizzi, Templeton, & Johnston, 2007; Henderson, 1990). These spellers have insight into the structure of words and use this understanding when spelling. When you look at the writing of syllables and affixes spellers, you will notice that they conventionally spell most one-syllable words. Children are learning to spell (1) common word endings (such as -s, -ed, -ing, and -ly), (2) common prefixes (such as re- and un-), (3) syllable patterns in long words, and (4) base words that require a spelling change when adding certain suffixes. Understanding how to spell affixes and syllable patterns makes it possible for children to use long and more complex words in writing. And, of course, there is a complementary relationship between recognizing the multiletter groups in the long words in reading and using these letter groups to spell complex words. The more children learn about multiletter chunks through reading, the greater their insight into spelling. The more insight children have into the spelling of multiletter groups, the greater the probability that they will use this knowledge when reading long and complex words.

By late spring of second grade, Shania correctly spells common word endings (*lives*, *fishing*, and *lunches*, for instance), uses the VV team long-vowel pattern (*street* and *each*), and puts a vowel in every syllable, as you can see in Figure 6-2. She writes a vowel before the letter *r* (*together* and *over*), though she sometimes writes letters in the wrong sequence (*evrey*). And, of course, she conventionally spells most of the words in her reading vocabulary. When Shania misspells, she writes

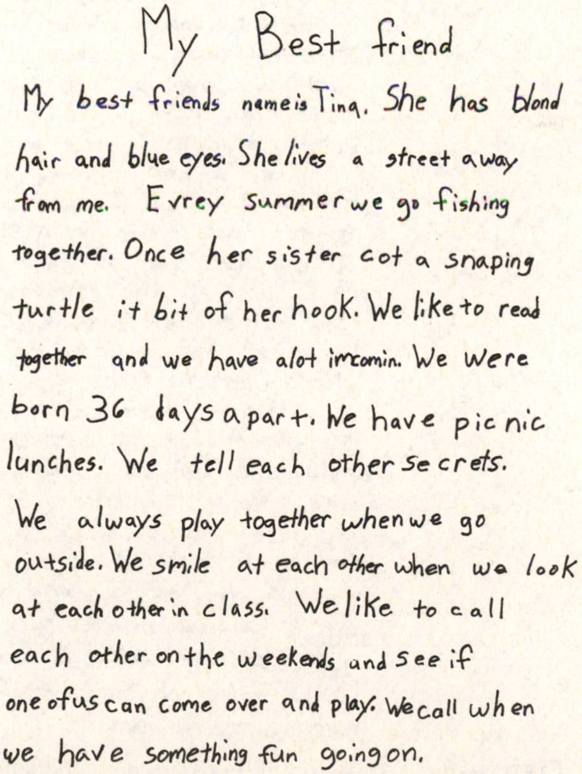

My Best friend
My best friends name is Tina. She has blond
hair and blue eyes. She lives a street away
from me. Evrey summer we go fishing
together. Once her sister cot a snaping
turtle it bit of her hook. We like to read
together and we have alot imcomin. We were
born 36 days apart. We have picnic
lunches. We tell each other secrets.
We always play together when we go
outside. We smile at each other when wa look
at each other in class. We like to call
each other on the weekends and see if
one of us can come over and play. We call when
we have something fun going on.

Figure 6-2   Shania is learning to recognize the multiletter chunks in word structure and uses this knowledge when she reads and spells.

words the way she believes they sound (*comin* for *common*). From her misspelling of *snaping* for *snapping*, we can infer that Shania is still learning how to add endings to words that require doubling the last consonant. As a third-grader, Shania will be ready to make the transition from learning and using letter-sound phonics to learning more about the word parts that make up the structure of long words. The more literacy experiences she has, the more sensitive she will become to the structure of long words, and the more effectively she will use this knowledge when she reads and spells.

Fifth-grader Kristen spells all words conventionally, with the exception of *restaurant*, which she spells *restarant* (see Figure 6-3). She has a large reading

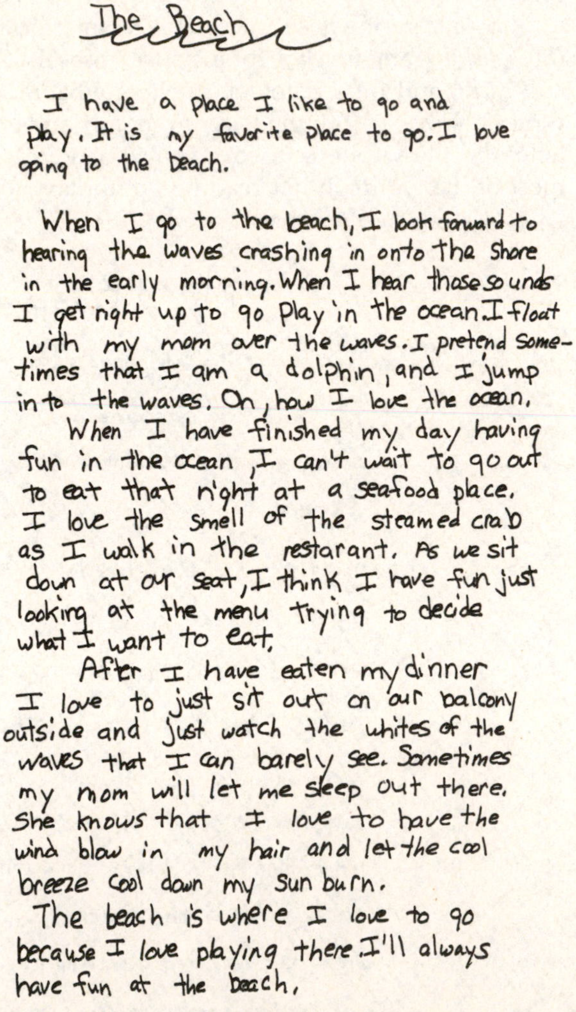

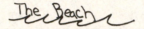

> The Beach
>
> I have a place I like to go and play. It is my favorite place to go. I love oping to the beach.
>
> When I go to the beach, I look forward to hearing the waves crashing in onto the shore in the early morning. When I hear those sounds I get right up to go play in the ocean. I float with my mom over the waves. I pretend sometimes that I am a dolphin, and I jump into the waves. Oh, how I love the ocean.
>
> When I have finished my day having fun in the ocean, I can't wait to go out to eat that night at a seafood place. I love the smell of the steamed crab as I walk in the restarant. As we sit down at our seat, I think I have fun just looking at the menu trying to decide what I want to eat.
>
> After I have eaten my dinner I love to just sit out on our balcony outside and just watch the whites of the waves that I can barely see. Sometimes my mom will let me sleep out there. She knows that I love to have the wind blow in my hair and let the cool breeze cool down my sun burn.
>
> The beach is where I love to go because I love playing there I'll always have fun at the beach.

Figure 6-3　Kristen, a fifth-grader, conventionally spells the words in her fluent reading vocabulary. When reading, she looks for pronounceable multiletter groups or chunks in the words she does not instantly recognize.

vocabulary and automatically identifies many words. When she does not instantly recognize a word, she is most likely to analyze word structure to find intact multi-letter groups. Kristen's knowledge of word structure will continue to grow in middle and high school. This is important because she will rely on the strategy of reading mutliletter groups as whole chunks when she is challenged to learn the long, complex technical terms in high school textbooks.

In due time, children's reading vocabularies become so enormous that they include all the words children typically see in text. Readers who automatically recognize all the words they read are at the fifth and final stage: **automatic word recognition.** Now word recognition is completely automatic, with the exception, of course, of unusual words and some content subject words. These children spell known words conventionally, including irregular words; they know when words are not spelled right and fix their own misspellings. Accomplished high school readers use many effective comprehension strategies and, because they automatically recognize words, they concentrate on comprehending and learning from their textbooks. When these readers encounter new words, they use the strategy of analyzing word structure, calling on their extensive knowledge of multiletter chunks to learn words in subjects like geometry, physics, geography, and American literature.

PREFIXES, SUFFIXES, AND BASE WORDS

Prefixes, suffixes, and base words are meaningful chunks or morphemes. **Prefixes** are added to the beginning of words (*prepay*); **suffixes** are added to the end of words (*movement*). Prefixes and suffixes cannot stand alone; they are bound morphemes and must be attached to words. For example, the word *like* can stand alone, but the prefix *un-* and the suffix *-ly* cannot. When *un-* and *-ly* are added to *like*, we create a word with a different meaning and grammatical function, *unlikely*. **Affixes** make words longer, as we see in *unlikely*, *reworked*, and *returnable*. Unlike prefixes and suffixes, base words stand alone. **Base words** are free morphemes and are the smallest real words in English. We add affixes to base words. For example, we might add *-ing* to *learn* to make *learning*, *-able* to *train* to spell *trainable*, and *in-* and *-ive* to *act* to write *inactive*.

Prefixes, suffixes, and Greek and Latin word parts tell readers something about word meaning, which in turn supports the understanding of text. Therefore, knowing the meaning of these structural units makes it possible for readers to infer word meaning. As children have experiences reading and writing, and as they learn about the structure of words from their teachers, children come to understand that some words consist of two or more meaningful units. Eventually, children become so familiar with the meaningful parts in words they read words with more than one chunk, such as the suffix and base word *shady*, faster than words with only one meaningful chunk, as in *lady* (Carlisle & Stone, 2005).

Prefixes

Prefixes either change word meaning completely, as in *non + fat = nonfat*, or make meaning more specific, as in *re + write = rewrite*. A mere smattering of prefixes, four to be exact, account for 58 percent of the words with prefixes that third-through ninth-graders are likely to read (White, Sowell, & Yanagihara, 1989). The four most frequently occurring prefixes are *un-* (*unhappy*), *re-* (*rewrite*), *in-* (meaning "not," as in *inaccurate*), and *dis-* (*dislike*). *Un-* accounts for the lion's share: A full 26 percent of words with prefixes begin with *un-* (White, Sowell, et al., 1989). While *un-*, *re-*, *in-*, and *dis-* are certainly useful, older readers benefit from knowing more difficult prefixes, because these prefixes offer considerable insight into word meaning. The 20 prefixes in Table 6–1 are the most important prefixes to teach children in grades three through nine. When the prefixes in Table 6–1 have more than one meaning, the meaning listed is that given by White, Sowell, et al., 1989.

TABLE 6–1   *The 20 Most Common Prefixes*

Prefix	Meaning	Examples
anti	against	anti-trust, anti-knock, anti-crime, anti-glare, anti-theft
de	from, away	debug, defog, decaf, defrost, deplane, derail
dis	apart from, not	disarm, disbar, disown, disuse, disable, dislike
en, em	in	enact, enclose, enable, embark, embody, embattle
fore	in front of, before	foresee, forego, forewarn, foreground, foretell
in, im, ir, il	not	invisible, improbable, irresponsible, illogical
in, im	in or into	inborn, inflow, inward, immigrant, immoral
inter	between, among	interact, intermix, interlace, interlock, interplay
mid	middle	midair, midday, midway, midweek, midnight
mis	wrong, bad, not	misfit, misplace, mislay, misuse, misdeed
non	not	nonfat, nonskid, nonprofit, nonstick, nonstop
over	too much	overage, overdue, overeat, overlap, overlook
pre	in front of, before	precut, premix, prepay, predate, precook
re	back, again	rearm, retell, redo, renew, repay, rerun
semi	half, partly	semicircle, semisoft, semifinal, semisweet
sub	under, inferior	subplot, subzero, subset, submarine, substandard
super	above, in addition	superman, superfine, superhero, superheat, superstar
trans	across, through	transact, transport, transplant, transform, transpolar
un	not	uncut, unfit, unlit, untie, unzip, unhappy, unsure
under	too little	underage, underfed, underpay, underdone

Suffixes

Suffixes either clarify word meaning or change grammatical function. There are two types of suffixes: **inflectional suffixes** and **derivational suffixes.** Inflectional endings consist of -*s(es)*, -*ed*, -*ing*, -*er*, and -*est*. These suffixes change the number (*dog-dogs*), affect verb tense (*walk-walked*), or indicate comparison (*big, bigger, biggest*). Inflectional endings are the most frequently occurring of all the suffixes (White, Sowell, et al., 1989). Table 6–2 has generalizations about adding suffixes to base words.

TABLE 6–2 *Generalizations for Adding Suffixes*

-*s* and -*es*

Add -*s* to one-syllable VC and VCe words: *win-wins, make-makes*. Add -*es* to words that end in *s, ss, ch, sh, x,* and *z*: *bus-buses, wish-wishes*. When a word ends in *f* or *fe*, and the plural includes a /v/, change the *f* or *fe* to a *v* before adding -*es*: *leaf-leaves, shelf-shelves*.

Words Ending in a Consonant

The spelling of base words that end in a consonant often does not change when adding a suffix: *short-shorter, alarm-alarming*.

VC Short-vowel Words

We often double the last consonant before adding a suffix that begins with a vowel: *big-biggest*. Doubling the last consonant indicates the vowel is short (*hop-hopped*). When the final consonant is not doubled, the vowel in the base word is usually long: *ride-rider, hope-hoped*.

VCC Short-vowel Words

Simply add suffixes to one-syllable words ending in a VCC short-vowel pattern. The final consonant is not doubled because there is no chance of confusing these short-vowel words with long-vowel VCe words: *talk-talking, soft-softer*.

VCe Long-vowel Words

Drop the final *e* before adding a suffix that begins with a vowel or -*y*: *dine-dining, large-largest, ease-easy*. We do not need the final *e* because the suffix begins with a vowel. Keep the final *e* when adding a suffix that begins with a consonant: *move-movement, like-likely*.

Words Ending in Y, y

Simply add a suffix to words ending in *ay, oy,* and *ey*: *play-plays, obey-obeyed*. Generally change the *y* to an *i* before adding a suffix when a word ends in a *y* preceded by a consonant: *carry-carries, busy-busiest*. Generally keep the *y* when adding a suffix that begins with an *i*: *try-trying, boy-boyish*.

Words Ending in ce or ge

Do not drop the *e* when adding suffixes that begin with a vowel: *notice-noticeable, manage-management*. Drop the *e* before adding a suffix that begins with an *e*: *change-changed, admire-admired*.

Two- or More Syllable Words Ending in a VC Syllable

Double the final consonant when the last syllable represents a VC pattern and is accented: *begin-beginner, occur-occurrence*. Do not double the final consonant when the final VC syllable is *unaccented*: *open-opener, cover-covered*.

Derivational suffixes affect meaning and grammatical usage, such as changing *dirt* (noun) to *dirty* (adjective), *history* (noun) to *historic* (adjective), and *agree* (verb) to *agreeable* (adjective). Children's knowledge of derivational suffixes increases from the third to the fifth grade (Mahony, Singson, & Mann, 2000; Singson, Mahoney, & Mann, 2000). You can expect older readers to more readily recognize and understand derivational suffixes like *-ment*, *-able*, and *-ic* than younger, less experienced readers. Table 6–3 is a list of the 20 most common suffixes (White, Power, & White, 1989).

Ross's story in Figure 6-4 illustrates how a precocious first-grader uses common suffixes. Ross conventionally spells words with *-ed*, *-ing*, and *-s/es* and correctly forms contractions. Ross has learned these multiletter groups so well that they are second nature when he reads and writes. For example, he drops the final *y* in *try* and writes an *i* before adding *-ed* to spell *tried*. Notice the word *cutted*, which

TABLE 6–3 *The 20 Most Common Suffixes*

Suffix	Meaning	Examples
al, ial	relating to	bridal, global, rental, burial, memorial, personal
ed	past tense	played, jumped, painted, hopped, kicked
en	relating to	liken, ripen, olden, frozen, waken, wooden
er, or	one who	painter, player, reader, worker, visitor, actor, sailor
er	comparative	quicker, higher, fatter, uglier, faster, slower
est	most (comparative)	biggest, slowest, highest, largest, fastest, nicest
ful	quality of	artful, joyful, beautiful, plentiful, careful, fearful
ible, able	able to, quality of	readable, eatable, fixable, defensible, divisible
ic	like, pertaining to	historic, scenic, acidic, atomic, poetic
ing	ongoing	reading, listening, running, jumping, helping
ion, ation, ition, tion	act or state of	action, addition, adoption, construction, donation
ity, ty	state or quality of	dirty, dusty, nutty, salty, fruity, oddity, activity
ive, ative, itive	tending to, relating to	creative, active, massive, formative, additive
less	without	joyless, aimless, fearless, endless, jobless, useless
ly	every, in the manner of	friendly, badly, kindly, dimly, boldly, calmly
ment	result or state of	payment, argument, judgment, excitement, shipment
ness	quality of	fitness, illness, happiness, madness, goodness
ous, eous, ious	full of, state of	studious, joyous, envious, furious, gaseous
s, es	plural	dogs, houses, boys, girls, ashes, boxes, teachers
y	quality, full of	ability, muddy, baggy, bossy, bumpy, chewy, jumpy

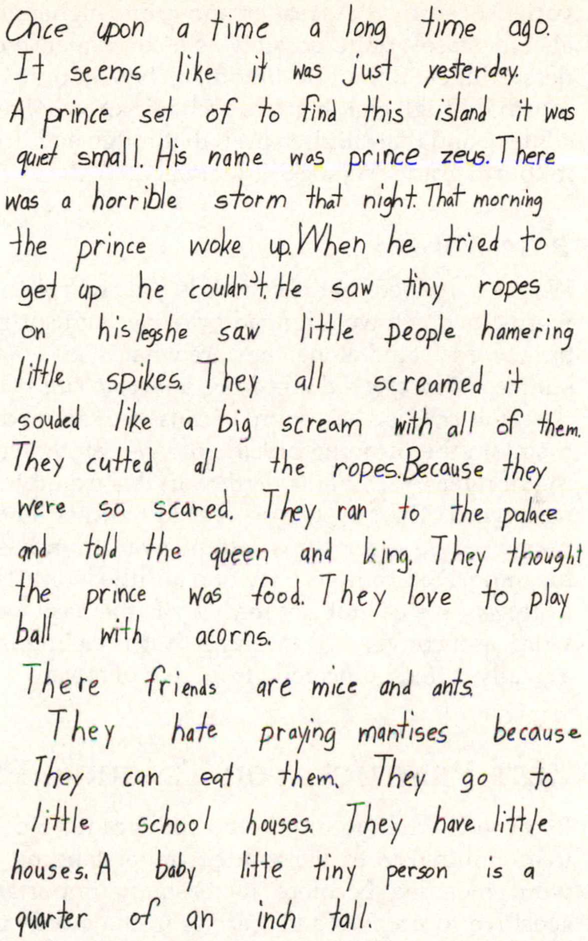

> Once upon a time a long time ago.
> It seems like it was just yesterday.
> A prince set of to find this island it was
> quiet small. His name was prince zeus. There
> was a horrible storm that night. That morning
> the prince woke up. When he tried to
> get up he couldn't. He saw tiny ropes
> on his legshe saw little people hamering
> little spikes. They all screamed it
> souded like a big scream with all of them.
> They cutted all the ropes. Because they
> were so scared. They ran to the palace
> and told the queen and king. They thought
> the prince was food. They love to play
> ball with acorns.
> There friends are mice and ants.
> They hate praying mantises because
> They can eat them. They go to
> little school houses. They have little
> houses. A baby litte tiny person is a
> quarter of an inch tall.

Figure 6-4 Through his writing, Ross demonstrates that he knows how to correctly use and conventionally spell common suffixes and how to form contractions.

does not need an -*ed* to signal past tense. Ross writes the way he talks, and he sometimes says *cutted* when he means *cut*. Though Ross does not use *cut* conventionally, he shows us that he understands the convention of doubling the last consonant, the letter *t*, before adding the -*ed*. Ross's teacher thinks he will benefit from learning more about writing in complete sentences and using periods and capitals, so she has formed a small, flexible skill group to give Ross and a handful of his classmates extra help with punctuation.

The number of words with affixes doubles from fourth to fifth grade and doubles again by the seventh grade (White, Power, et al., 1989). It is estimated that fifth-graders may meet an average of 1,325 words a year that include the prefixes *in-*, *im-*, *ir-*, *il-* (meaning "not"), *un-*, *re-*, and *dis-*. Seventh-graders may identify 3,000 words, and perhaps as many as 9,000 words, with these prefixes as well as a variety of suffixes. As readers move into higher grades, their knowledge of suffixes also increases, quite possibly as a consequence of increased grammatical awareness (Nunes, Bryant, & Bindman, 1997). So, it is not surprising that children in fourth through eighth grade use their knowledge of suffixes to read new words in context, and that children in sixth through eighth grade are better at this than those in fourth grade (Wysocki & Jenkins, 1987).

Base Words

We have learned that base words (free morphemes) are the smallest real English words to which we might add prefixes and suffixes. Unlike prefixes and suffixes, base words stand alone; they are what is left when we take away the prefixes and suffixes (*drinkable – able = drink; unhappy – un = happy*).

Butterfly is a base word because we cannot divide it into *butter* and *fly* and still maintain the meaning of *butterfly*. We can, however, add a suffix to *butterfly*. We might refer to several *butterflies*. In this example, the *-es* ending is not part of the base word. The purpose of *-es* is to indicate that there is more than one *butterfly*. Likewise, we cannot take letters away from base words and still preserve their meaning. For example, if we find a "little word," such as *wag*, in a "big word," such as *wagon*, we cannot say that *wag* is the base word for *wagon*. *Wagon* is the base word, as it conveys the meaning. *Wag* is an English word, to be sure, but it conveys a totally different meaning from that of *wagon*.

BEST PRACTICES FOR TEACHING PREFIXES AND SUFFIXES

Because children in fourth and fifth grade read longer and more complex words than children in earlier grades, understanding how prefixes and suffixes affect word meaning becomes increasingly important. Children in fifth grade are sensitive to prefixes and suffixes in the words they read (McCutchen, Logan, & Biangardi-Orpe, 2009). Fourth- and fifth-graders who understand how prefixes and suffixes affect base word meaning have larger reading vocabularies and better comprehension than their classmates with less knowledge (Carlisle, 2000; Deacon & Kirby, 2004; Nagy, Berninger, & Abbot, 2006). In using the following best practices, you will effectively teach children how to recognize, read, and write words with prefixes and suffixes.

1. *Break words into meaningful parts, talk about the parts, and put the words back together again.*   In following this teaching sequence, you show children how affixes combine with base words. This makes children more aware of affixes and teaches them something about word meaning. For example, you might begin with *unfairly*, break it into parts—*un, fair, ly*—and talk about the meaning of each part, and then show children how the parts work together to make *unfairly*.

2. *Teach the peel-off strategy.*   Peeling prefixes and suffixes away from long words is helpful because this reveals base words that are already part of

readers' reading vocabulary. We will use the word *unfriendly* as an illustration. Show readers the following steps:

    a. *Do I see a prefix?* Look for a prefix. If you see a prefix, peel it off. Peeling *un-* away from *unfriendly* (*unfriendly* − *un* = *friendly*) reveals *friendly*.

    b. *Do I see a suffix?* Look for a suffix. If you see a suffix, peel it off too. Peeling *-ly* away from *friendly* (*friendly* − *ly* = *friend*) reveals the base word *friend*.

    c. *Do I know this base word?* If you see a familiar base word, read it to yourself.

    d. *Put the word back together.* The word is *unfriendly*. Now I can read this word.

3. *Teach inflectional suffixes (-s/es, -ed, -ing, -er, -est) in the first and second grades.* Begin to explore meaningful word parts early, and suffixes are a better investment in learning than prefixes. Authors who write for young readers frequently use words that end with *-es*, *-ing*, and *-ed*, which makes these suffixes extremely important. The comparative suffixes *-er* and *-est* are useful because they are important for understanding comparisons such as *quick*, *quicker*, and *quickest* or *large*, *larger*, and *largest*.

4. *Give children practice reading and writing many different words with the same prefixes and suffixes.*   As children's reading ability increases, you can expect their knowledge of multiletter chunks to expand as well. In reading and writing words with the same prefixes and suffixes, children learn how these affixes contribute to word meaning. Prefixes and suffixes are significant features of syntax and therefore contribute to the strength of sentence structure cues. This is especially true for the inflectional endings. When children read and write in your classroom, take naturally occurring opportunities to ask them to find base words with affixes and to explain in their own words how the affixes affect word meaning.

5. *Teach base word meaning.*   Children need to know the meaning of the base words to which the affixes are added. Once children understand base word meaning and recognize base words in text, then it is appropriate to teach them how affixes affect base word meaning.

6. *Directly teach affixes in meaningful reading and writing contexts.*   Teaching words in context helps children develop an appreciation of how affixes change the meaning of base words. Demonstrate how to divide unfamiliar long words into base words and affixes when readers meet these words in context. Explain, too, how the meaning of base words with affixes is consistent with the reading context. Give children opportunities, under your guidance, to read and write base words with affixes and to discuss the meanings of these words in the books they read in your classroom and at home in their leisure time.

GREEK AND LATIN WORD PARTS

Greek and Latin word parts are borrowed from both languages. When the scholars, philosophers, and authors of the Renaissance became interested in writing in their own language, English, they borrowed liberally from ancient Greek and Latin

(Ayers, 1980). Just as the great thinkers and writers of the Renaissance used Greek and Latin words to make lots of new words, so too do we continue this tradition today. When we ventured into space in the middle of the 20th century, a new word was needed for space explorers. Rather than devising a whole new word from scratch, the term *astronaut* was coined by combining the Greek root *astro*, meaning "star," with *naut*, meaning "sailor." Considering the Greek origin, modern-day *astronauts* are *star sailors*, a term that suggests all sorts of engaging images.

Words that share the same Greek or Latin word parts, such as the *aud* (meaning "to hear") in *auditory*, *audible*, and *audience*, form meaning families (Henderson, 1990). By organizing words into meaning families, readers have a platform for figuring out the meaning of unfamiliar words with the same Greek or Latin root. For example, *aqua* (of Latin origin) means "water," and therefore words with *aqua* also have something to do with water, as in *aquarium*, *aquatic*, *aqueduct*, and *aquaplane*. Likewise, *magni* (from Latin) means "great or large." Consequently, *magnify*, *magnificent*, *magnanimous*, and *magnitude* all pertain to conditions in which an object or action is great or large. From a practical standpoint, you can expect readers who recognize and appreciate Greek and Latin word parts to learn a great many technical terms with relative ease, and to do so with less guidance from you than their classmates who do not understand the contribution Greek and Latin word parts make to English words.

Generally speaking, fourth- and fifth-graders learn Greek and Latin word parts. Teachers introduce the word parts and their meaning and then show how the word parts give readers some insight into meaning. For example, the root word *phon* in *phonics* and *telephone* tells readers that these words pertain to "sound"; *microchip* and *microprocessor* refer to "small" because each includes the root *micro* from the Greek language. Readers are not likely to figure out the meaning of borrowed word parts from normal reading experiences. In part, the reason is that Greek and Latin word parts are semihidden in words, and in part because each English word that includes them has a slightly different meaning. A*quarium* and *aquaplane* both pertain to water, but the meaning of the individual words is quite different. Consequently, to develop the ability to strategically use Greek and Latin word parts, readers need explicit explanations of them and modeling of how to use them to unlock word meaning, as well as many opportunities to read and write words with them. Look at Table 6–4 for Greek and Latin word parts.

COMPOUND WORDS

Compound words are formed when two words—for example, *finger* and *print*—are glued together to create a third word—in this case, *fingerprint*. Compounds differ depending on how far a field meaning wanders from the definitions of the individual words that are put together. In the case of *fingerprint*, the general definition of each word is unchanged. A second sort of compound is made of words whose meanings are somewhat different than that of the combined form, such as *basketball*, *driveway*, *skyscraper*, and *spotlight*. In a third category, the meaning of the

TABLE 6–4 *Greek and Latin Word Parts*

Root	Meaning	Example	Root	Meaning	Example
aqua	water	aquarium	ast(er)	star	asterisk
aud	hear	audience	bio	life	biography
cycl	circle, wheel	bicycle	dict	speak	dictionary
duct	lead	conduct	fin	end, limit	final
geo	earth	geography	graph	write	biography
hydr	water	dehydrate	ject	throw	project
loc	place	location	logy	study of	psychology
magn	great	magnify	meter	measure	thermometer
micro	small	microscope	nov	new	novel
numer	number	numeral	pend	hand	pendulum
phon	sound	symphony	port	carry	airport
quest	seek, ask	question	rupt	break	interrupt
sci	know	science	scribe	write	subscribe
semi	half	semicircle	serv	keep	preserve
spect	see	spectator	scop	see	telescope
sphere	ball	stratosphere	sub	under, less	submarine
tele	far	telescope	terr	land	territory
therm	heat	thermometer	vid	see	video
vis	see	visual	voc	voice	vocal
Numerals					
bi	two	bicycle	dec	ten	decade
hex	six	hexagon	kilo	thousand	kilometer
oct(a) (o)	eight	octopus	pent(a)	five	pentagon
quad(r) (ri)	four	quadrant	sept(i)	seven	septet
sex	six	sextet	tetra	four	tetrapod
tri	three	triangle	uni	one	unison

compound has practically nothing to do with the meaning of the individual words. Examples include *butterfly*, *hardware*, *turtleneck*, and *peppermint*.

The first-, second-, and third-grade readers we teach find compound words to be relatively easy to learn. Perhaps this is because compounds are made of two whole words and thus are not overly challenging to identify. When the words that make up compounds are already in children's reading vocabularies, pronunciation is merely a question of saying the words together. As for the meaning of compounds, we find that readers are intrigued by the changes in meaning that occur when words are glued together. First-graders enjoy finding words that are glued together in compounds. Older readers, on the other hand, have so much experience that the compounds they see in everyday text usually pose no challenge whatsoever. This said, some teachers may continue to introduce a few new compound words through the fifth grade, depending on the reading program. When compound words are part of fourth- and fifth-grade programs, they are usually taught through spelling.

CONTRACTIONS

Contractions are formed when one or more letters (and sounds) are deleted from words. Missing letters are replaced by an apostrophe, which is a visual clue telling readers that a word is abbreviated, as in *hasn't*, *he's*, *she'll*, and *let's*. Words mean exactly the same thing whether they are written as a contraction or individually. First- and second-graders meet contractions in everyday reading material, so it is important that these readers learn to recognize the contractions they see in storybooks. Older children may occasionally review how to form contractions and the words that contractions represent.

All children encounter contractions in reading and use them in writing, so teaching contractions is a good large group activity. Use a set of magnetic letters and a magnetic apostrophe (or an IWB) to illustrate how contractions are formed. Ask first- and second-graders to change words like *she* and *will* into *she'll* as well as to reverse the process by changing contractions (*she'll*) into two words (*she* and *will*). Then you write pairs of sentences. In the first sentence, you underline two words that can be combined to form a contraction. In the second sentence, you leave a blank where the contraction should be:

1. The dog <u>did not</u> find the bone.
2. The dog _____ find the bone.

Children then read the first sentence, form a contraction from the two underlined words (*did* and *not*), and write the contraction (*didn't*) in the blank in the second sentence. Everyone then reads both sentences together in chorus while you sweep your hand under the words as they are read.

SYLLABLES

The **syllable** is the basic unit of pronunciation. Each syllable has one vowel sound, so the number of syllables in a word equals the number of vowels heard. Try saying *lilac*. How many vowels do you hear? /li/-/lac/ has two vowel sounds and hence two syllables. Now try *table*. When you pronounce the last syllable, *ble*, you do not notice a distinct vowel. You hear instead a vowel-like sound—/bul/. So when we divide words into syllables, we listen for vowel and vowel-like sounds. One vowel or vowel-like sound equals one syllable.

Readers can identify the syllables in unfamiliar written words by counting the vowel patterns. Just as a spoken word has as many syllables as vowel sounds, so too is a written word divided into as many syllables as vowel patterns. Words with one vowel pattern have one syllable: the VC short-vowel pattern in *got*; CV in *go*; VV vowel team in *goat*; VCe in *gave*. Words with two vowel patterns have two syllables: *ba-con* and *be-gin* each with a CV and VC pattern, for example. Those with three vowel patterns have three syllables (*in-ter-nal*), four patterns have four syllables (*in-ter-nal-ize*), and so on.

Let us review what we know about the syllable: (1) Each syllable has one vowel sound, though a syllable may have more than one vowel letter. (2) A syllable may be a single word (*be*) or part of a long word (*be-tween*). (3) A syllable may be just one letter when that letter is a vowel, as in the word *a* or the *e* in *ego* (*e-go*).

Syllable Patterns

When we say words aloud, it is sometimes hard to decide where one syllable ends and another begins. When consulting the dictionary, we occasionally find that syllable division does not reflect pronunciation. Our goal is to help children read new long words by dividing them into pronounceable syllables, not to have readers memorize dictionary-style syllabication. It is more important for readers to recognize syllables in long words than to memorize the different syllable patterns. Table 6–5 shows the major syllable patterns readers will see in long words. The syllable patterns are intended to help you, the teacher, organize and focus instruction. Use the clues to syllable division to help children.

The children you teach may be perplexed as to when to double the final consonant when adding a suffix. In looking at the syllable patterns in Table 6–5, we see that the VC short-vowel syllable pattern has one vowel letter followed by at least one consonant letter. Therefore, doubling the consonant when adding a suffix to a word with a VC pattern (*hop*) keeps the vowel in its closed syllable pattern (*hopped*, *hop-ped*). When the final consonant is not doubled, this indicates a long-vowel pattern, as in *hoped*. Therefore, doubling (*pinned*) or not doubling the final consonant (*pined*) helps readers identify the proper vowel pattern: *The rabbit hopped across the road as she hoped to find a nice, juicy carrot in the farmer's garden.* It takes a lot of reading and writing experience for children to learn when to double (or not to double) the last consonant. Anticipate spending extra time helping children edit their writing and, perhaps, form a flexible skill group to give special practice to those who need it.

Clues to Syllable Division

1. *Single consonant between two vowels VCV (V-CV).*   When there is a single consonant between two vowels, as in *bagel*, we often divide the word right *after* the first vowel (*ba-gel*). The second consonant frequently begins the

	TABLE 6–5 *Syllable Patterns*	

Syllable Pattern	Description	Examples
Open *CV*	An open syllable ends in a long-vowel sound. Many *CV* syllables have one vowel (*be*), though some have two vowel letters that represent one long-vowel sound (*bee*).	she <u>ta</u>-ble <u>clo</u>-ver <u>ba</u>-con <u>fi</u>-nal
Closed *VC*	A closed syllable ends in a consonant and the vowel represents a short-vowel sound.	nap-<u>kin</u> pen-<u>cil</u> rep-tile
VCe	The first vowel is long and the *e* is silent in an accented syllable.	lo-<u>cate</u> stam-<u>pede</u> pro-<u>vide</u>
Vowel Pair	A syllable with two adjacent vowels. Vowel pairs consist of *ai, ay, ea, ee, ey, oa, ow* (pronounced long *o*), *oi, oy, ou, ow* (pronounced as a diphthong), *au, aw, ew, ue,* and *oo*.	<u>rai</u>-sin mon-<u>key</u> ap-<u>proach</u> <u>trou</u>-ser <u>loy</u>-al <u>laun</u>-dry <u>law</u>-yer <u>jew</u>-el ar-<u>gue</u> car-<u>toon</u>
Vr	A syllable with a vowel followed by the letter *r*. The *Vr* syllable often includes surrounding consonants.	bar-<u>ber</u> <u>mar</u>-ket but-<u>ter</u>
C-le	A final syllable that consists of a consonant followed by *le*.	cra-<u>dle</u> stum-<u>ble</u> ex-am-<u>ple</u>
Affix	Prefixes and suffixes usually form syllables, save for the -*s* (*cats*) and -*ed* when pronounced /t/ (*jumped*). Some prefixes (Table 6–1) consist of more than one syllable. In this case, divide the prefixes into as many syllables as there are vowel sounds.	<u>un</u>-like-<u>ly</u> <u>re</u>-wrote seem-<u>ing</u>-<u>ly</u> sem-<u>i</u>-sweet

second syllable. The consonant-vowel sequence for *bagel* is CV-CVC, where the first syllable is a CV open syllable. There are exceptions to the single consonant between two vowels guideline, however. In some words with a VCV pattern, the first vowel is short, as in *river* (*riv-er*) and *magic* (*mag-ic*). Advise readers to first try dividing a word with a VCV pattern *before* the consonant to form an open, long-vowel CV syllable (*ba-gel*); if this does not result in a contextually meaningful word, try dividing the word *after* the consonant to form a short-vowel pattern (*lim-it*). The Vr pattern is a logical exception to this syllable division because the vowel is not separated from the *r* in the Vr pattern (*car-ol*, not *ca-rol*; *mer-it*, not *me-rit*; and *chor-us*, not *cho-rus*).

2. *Two adjacent consonants VCCV (VC-CV).*   When there are two consonant between two vowels, divide the syllable between the two consonants (*sig-nal*; *rab-bit*). The first syllable is a closed syllable. We represent the consonant-vowel sequence in *signal* and *rabbit* as CVC-CVC.

3. *Consonant digraphs and consonant blends.*   In general, divide a word into syllables before or after consonant digraphs (*fa-ther*, *fa-shi*on) and consonant blends (*se-cret*). There are exceptions, however, as in *whis-tle* and *mis-ter*. Sometimes whether the syllable divides between the letters in a digraph or blend is more important for the precision of dictionary word division than for reading. Children will figure out the pronunciation of words like *mister* whether they divide the syllable between (*mis-ter*) or after the blend (*mist-er*).

4. *C-le final syllable.*   In words that end in a C-*le* syllable—*ble*, *cle*, *dle*, *fle*, *gle*, *kle*, *ple*, *sle*, and *zle*—the consonant usually begins the last syllable and the vowel is a soft sound: /bul/, /cul/, /dul/, /ful/, /gul/, /kul/, /pul/, /sul/, and /zul/.

5. *Compound words.*   Divide compounds between the two "words," as in *tea-cup* and *pop-corn*.

The goal is for readers to divide long words into pronounceable chunks that can be blended together to produce meaningful words. It is important for readers to recognize these patterns in long words. Recognizing syllable patterns and understanding clues to syllable division is far more useful than memorizing the names of the patterns or syllable division rules. Therefore, you will want to emphasize teaching the patterns in the context of real words and determine success by how well children recognize the patterns in the long words they read. Bear in mind that it is not necessary to always divide words in precisely the same manner as the dictionary. Let's take *oyster* as an example. In the dictionary, *oyster* is divided as *oys-ter*. But *oy-ster* also yields two pronounceable chunks. Either of these is acceptable for word recognition. At the end of the day, you want the children in your classroom to be able to tackle long words independently, without support from you or other accomplished readers. Since syllables are by their nature pronounceable chunks, learning to find letter groups that form syllables is a helpful strategy. If children's syllable division is not as precise as the dictionary but still yields contextually meaningful words, then the purpose of finding pronounceable chunks is fulfilled.

Accent Patterns

The syllables in long words are given different stress. **Accent,** the stress given to syllables, is very important because it affects vowel pronunciation. There are three levels of stress: primary, secondary, and reduced (or unaccented). For simplicity, we will call the syllable with the most stress the primary accent. The vowels in accented syllables tend to follow the pronunciation we would expect from their placement in letter-sound patterns. Most vowels in **unaccented syllables** have a soft, or short, sound. We will therefore focus on the accented syllable and will put a (') after the syllable to indicate primary stress.

When we shift the primary accent, we also shift pronunciation. Try saying these words by placing the primary accent on the first or second syllable, as indicated: *con'-tent* and *con-tent'*; *ob'-ject* and *ob-ject'*; *con'-vict* and *con-vict'*. In these examples, shifting the primary accent from the first to the last syllable also changes word meaning. Reread *con'-tent*, *ob'-ject*, and *con'-vict*. What do you notice about these words? If you conclude that they are nouns, you are right. The primary accent tends to fall on the first syllable of a noun. In an accented syllable, the accent, or force of the voice, makes the vowel pattern represent the vowel sound we expect. In unaccented syllables, the vowel sound may be a short /uh/ or a short *i*. Here are five guidelines to indicate where to place the primary accent:

1. All one-syllable words are accented syllables.
2. The primary accent most often falls on the first syllable of a two-syllable word (*ma'-ple* and *tal'-ent*), unless the last syllable includes two vowels (*con-ceal'* and *ap-proach'*) and then that syllable is often stressed, with some exceptions.
3. Prefixes and suffixes are ordinarily not accented. The base word receives the primary accent, as in *name'-less* and *ex-chang'-ing*.
4. The primary accent usually falls on the first word of compounds, such as *snow'-man* and *base'-ball*.
5. When a word has two like consonants, the primary accent generally falls on the syllable that closes with the first letter, as in *rab'-bit* and *ham'-mer*.
6. In multisyllable words ending with the suffix *-tion*, *-sion*, or *-ic*, the primary accent usually falls on the syllable preceding the suffix (*na'-tion*, *re-vi'-sion*, *his-tor'-ic*).

Two additional tips help with certain spellings: First, C-*le* (consonant-*le*) syllables are generally not accented, as in *tram'-ple* and *tur'-tle*. Second, syllables ending in *ck* are often accented, such as *buck'-et* and *at-tack'*. When teaching readers about the manner in which dictionaries represent syllables and pronunciation, point out that the way we divide words in writing does not always correspond to the way we group sounds together when speaking. The boldface type in the dictionary indicates how we divide a word when writing; the type in parentheses shows how we pronounce words when speaking. It is the type in parentheses that shows where to place the accent.

BEST PRACTICES FOR TEACHING SYLLABLE PATTERNS AND ACCENT

1. *Teach syllables and accent patterns after children have a good understanding of phonics letter-sound patterns.*   Because syllables are multiletter chunks that include phonics letter-sound patterns, readers first need to know how letter-sound patterns, particularly vowel patterns, represent sound. Therefore, understanding the letter-sound patterns of phonics forms the basis for understanding syllable patterns and for deciding which letters form syllables and which do not.

2. *Give children opportunities to apply their syllable knowledge when reading and writing.*   Asking children to engage in activities that are far removed from real reading and writing, such as memorizing syllable or accent patterns, is pointless because readers are unlikely to use the memorized information.

3. *When introducing syllables, use words children already know how to read.* When you first teach children about syllables, select two-syllable words children already know. Demonstrate how to find the syllable patterns and explain how accent affects the vowel sounds. Once children begin to understand the patterns, give children practice using their knowledge to identify multisyllable words they have not read before.

After children have had a great deal of practice reading and writing long words, they automatically apply syllable and accent patterns. In fact, as an expert reader, you can read, with the proper accent, nonsense words that conform to English spelling, even though you may not be able to "say" the rules. To prove this, read and divide into syllables these two nonsense words: *quimlar* and *plygus*. Did you divide them into the syllables of *quim-lar* and *ply-gus*? Did you pronounce them with the accent on the first syllable—*quim'-lar* and *ply'-gus*? If so, you are doing what other good readers do, using your in-depth knowledge of our writing system, including syllable and accent patterns, to read and pronounce new words.

CLASSROOM ACTIVITIES FOR TEACHING THE STRUCTURE OF LONG WORDS

The following activities help readers learn and use the multiletter groups in word structure. The more readers know about the multiletter chunks in word structure, the more effective and efficient they will be at reading and spelling long words. Select the activities that will be most beneficial for the children you teach and adapt activities to suit your own special classroom environment and teaching style. Look, too, in e-resources for activities and lessons to teach and review multiletter groups.

6.1 *Fold-Over Contractions*

Skill: Reading contractions.

This easy activity graphically demonstrates how we form contractions. It is manipulative and appropriate for working with children in large or small groups. Fold-over contractions look like accordions with deleted letters simply folded out of sight and replaced by a piece of masking tape with an apostrophe on it. The tape holds the fold-over contraction in place, as shown in Figure 6-5.

Things You'll Need: Construction paper strips about two inches wide and six inches long; markers; masking tape.

Directions: Give each child a paper strip and a small piece of masking tape. Children decide on the contraction they wish to make or follow your lead in making the contraction you designate. Have children count the letters in the two separate words and fold a paper strip accordion style to make as many boxes as there are letters in the two words. For example, in turning *are not* into a fold-over contraction, children would make six boxes on the paper strip. Then children write the two words one after the other, putting one letter in each box. In this example, children write six letters: *a, r, e, n, o,* and *t.* Children then write an apostrophe on the small piece of masking tape. Turn the accordion into a contraction by folding the square with the letter to be deleted (*o*) under the square with the preceding letter on it (*n*), and putting the masking tape apostrophe at the top to hold the contraction together, thus forming *aren't.* Encourage children to describe in their own words the purpose and placement of the apostrophe. Look in e-resources for IWB-ready activities to teach or review contractions.

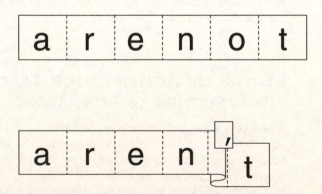

Figure 6-5 Fold-over contractions is a hands-on activity in which children fold deleted letters in contractions out of sight and replace them with an apostrophe.

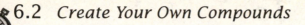

6.2   *Create Your Own Compounds*

Skill: Reading compound words.

In this small or large group activity, first- through third-graders put everyday words together to create their own unique compounds.

Things You'll Need: Pencils; crayons or colored markers.

Directions: Readers think of two words they use every day and then put those words together to make a brand-new compound word. Have children illustrate their own compound words, as in Figure 6-6. Then have children look for compound words in text. Make a list of the words children find. Divide the list into two groups—one for compounds with meaning that can be inferred from the individual words and one for compounds with meaning that is removed from the meaning of the individual words.

6.3   *Prefix Binders*

Skill: Reading and writing words with prefixes.

Children collect words with the prefixes they are learning, put the words in binders, and then use the words as references when writing and participating in other classroom activities.

Things You'll Need: Each child needs a binder with tabs that have prefixes on them; notebook paper for the binder.

Directions: Children write one prefix on each tab and put the tabs in the binder to separate pages with different prefixes. Then have children write one prefix at the top of each page of notebook paper followed by words to which the prefix is added. For instance, one page may have the prefix *un-* at the top and words like *unhappy*, *unkind*, and *unplugged* underneath. Ask children to be on the lookout for words with prefixes in everyday reading and to add these words to their prefix binder. Use the prefixes and base words as a ready resource for other word study activities.

6.4   *Affix Graffiti*

Skill: Reading words with prefixes and suffixes.

Here's a quick and easy opportunity for children to spontaneously express themselves while using prefixes and suffixes. This activity is appropriate for end-of-year second-graders and above.

TooThCoat

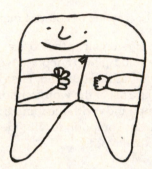

A tooth coat is a coat for your teeth

Seahouse

A seahouse is a house under the water

Figure 6-6   Coining new compounds gives children opportunities to creatively use their knowledge of word meaning and to write definitions for the unusual compounds they create.

Things You'll Need: A large piece of newsprint; colorful markers.

Directions: Fasten a large piece of newsprint to a bulletin board or put it on the floor. Write one or two affixes at the top of the paper. Over the course of several days, children write words on the newsprint that contain one or more of the affixes. Children may write in any color marker and may write words in any script, so long as the words are legible. At the end of several days, ask the whole class to read the words in chorus and to find graffiti words with certain affixes. Add some of the words to the word wall, or, if children are keeping personal binders for words with prefixes, add some of the words to the binders.

6.5   *Prefix Chalkboard Sort*

Skill: Reading words with prefixes.

This activity, which allows children to move around as they compare base words with prefixes, is appropriate for second- through fifth-graders.

Things You'll Need: Two, three, or four cards with prefixes; cards with base words only; masking tape loops.

Directions: Tape on the board two, three, or four cards with prefixes the children are learning (such as *un-, re-,* and *dis-*). Discuss how the prefixes affect word meaning. Then give each child one or more base word cards, each with a masking tape loop on the back. Children read the base words, find prefixes on the board to which their word might be added, and then tape the base words underneath the prefixes, thereby creating columns of words, as shown in Figure 6-7. Children then analyze the chalkboard lists to answer the questions: Does every combination make a real word? Are there base words that might be combined with more than one prefix? Rearrange cards, when appropriate. Now give children blank cards; ask them to write their own base words on the cards and to add them to the chalkboard lists.

6.6   *Affix Cloze*

Skill: Reading and writing words with prefixes and suffixes.

In this activity, readers use context and their knowledge of word structure to fill in the missing words in sentences. This activity is suitable for readers working in small groups. It is also suitable as a learning or literacy center activity.

Things You'll Need: Three or four cloze sentences on a transparency or written on the board for showing students how to fill in the missing words; enough copies of practice sheets with modified cloze sentences for every child in the group; cloze sentences children are to complete.

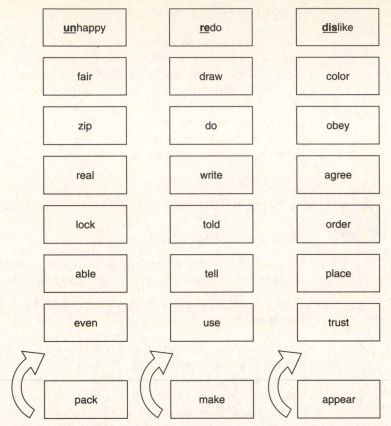

unhappy	**re**do	**dis**like
fair	draw	color
zip	do	obey
real	write	agree
lock	told	order
able	tell	place
even	use	trust
pack	make	appear

Figure 6-7 In this sorting activity, children pay attention to prefixes and base words, talk about how prefixes affect word meaning, and cross-check for accuracy and meaning.

Directions: Make an overhead with several cloze sentences like the ones below. Model how to use context and suffixes (or prefixes) to decide which word belongs in each blank. If using paper and pencil, have children circle the correct word or write it on the blank. Examples of the types of cloze sentences you might use to give children practice reading and understanding common prefixes and suffixes are:

1. The man _____ his house bright red.
   (*painted, painting, painter*)
2. After John threw a ball through the window, Mrs. Jones had to
   _____ the broken glass.
   (*replace, displace, placed*)
3. Tom _____ the door and peeked into the room.
   (*opening, opens, opened*)

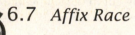 **6.7** *Affix Race*

Skill: Reading and writing words with prefixes and suffixes.

This gamelike activity gives children valuable practice thinking of affixed words and remembering how to spell them.

Things You'll Need: Nothing special.

Directions: Have children line up in two teams. Write a base word on the board. The teams talk among themselves and write the base word with different prefix and suffix combinations on scratch paper. Alternating teams, ask a child from a team to go to the board and add a prefix or suffix to the base word. Have a child from each team add different prefixes and suffixes to the base word. For example, for the base word *limit*, a child from team A might write *limited*; team B, *limitless*; team A, *unlimited*; and so forth. Remember to start with a different team each time you write a base word on the board. Depending on children's needs, you may want to ask them to add only prefixes or only suffixes. Every correct answer earns one point. Writing must be legible for the team to earn a point. The team with the most points wins.

 6.8 *Affix Hunt*

Skill: Reading words with prefixes and suffixes.

Hunting for words with prefixes and suffixes is a good small group or center activity that is appropriate for children from late second through fifth grade.

Things You'll Need: Print that is appropriate for children's reading level, including a variety of magazines, coupons, and newspapers; a highlighter for each child.

Directions: Give children a variety of age-appropriate print, such as old magazines, coupons, and newspapers. Children use a highlighter to flag words with the prefixes or suffixes you specify. Write the words on the board; use them when making affix wall charts.

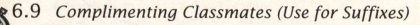 **6.9** *Complimenting Classmates (Use for Suffixes)*

Skill: Reading and writing words with suffixes.

Children in fourth and fifth grade use their knowledge of suffixes to write compliments for their classmates.

Things You'll Need: One piece of oak tag cut in the shape of a shield for every child in your class; several thesauruses.

Directions: Review adjectives like the compliments *cheerful* and *artistic.* Discuss also how suffixes can change a noun (*friend*) or a verb (*imagine*) into an adjective (*friendly* or *imaginative*), and how *-er* and *-est* show comparative relationships, such as *kind, kinder,* and *kindest.* Give each child an oak tag shield. Have each child write his or her name in pencil at the top of the paper, above the shield. Have each child write one compliment in pencil—a positive character trait—on the shield of every classmate. When writing, children cannot use worn-out adjectives or use the same compliment twice. For example, if Tom uses *imaginative* to describe a classmate, then no one else can write *imaginative* on that child's shield. Make sure that each child has written one compliment on each shield. Return the shields to their owners. Have the shield's owner trace over the penciled compliments in ink. Any mistakes children accidentally make when writing the original compliments are easily erased, making the finished shields smudge-free and error-free. Laminate shields and put them on the bulletin board. Fourth-graders made the shield in Figure 6-8.

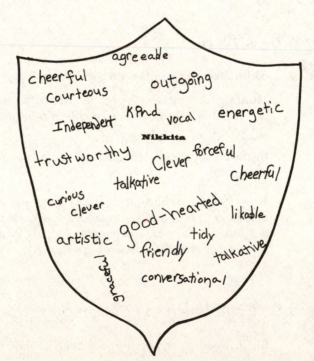

Figure 6-8 Making shields to compliment classmates gives children opportunities to better understand adjectives and to consider how suffixes affect word meaning.

6.10   *Affix Roundup (Card Game)*

Skill: Reading words with prefixes or suffixes.

This card game fits nicely in centers and is appropriate for two to four players. Players take turns reading a face-up affix and deciding if they hold a base word card in their hand that combines with the affix to make a real word. The player who makes a real word gets to keep the affix. The player with the most affix cards—who rounds up the most affixes—wins.

Things You'll Need: Index cards with prefixes, suffixes, and base words on them. Use base words children know how to read. Make six base word cards for each player and multiple cards with the suffixes and prefixes children are learning in your classroom. We find it helpful to use colored index cards. We write base words on one color and prefixes and/or suffixes on another color.

Directions: Shuffle the base word cards and deal six cards to each player. Affix cards are shuffled and placed face-down on the table. Players take turns drawing an affix card, placing the card face-up, and then examining the base words in their hand to see if the affix can combine with a base word. If so, the player rounds up the affix by placing the base word card beside the affix, reading the word, and telling its meaning. For instance, *dis + like* makes *dislike*, which means "not to like" or "does not like." Players place affixes that match base words in a "roundup" pile. Each affix is worth one point. The player with the most points wins. This game gets easier when affix cards consist of suffixes only and gets more challenging when affix cards contain both prefixes and suffixes.

6.11   *Comic Strips (Use with Prefixes and Suffixes)*

Skill: Reading and writing words with suffixes.

Children create their own comic strips using dramatic illustrations, dialogue balloons, and words with the prefixes and suffixes they are learning in your classroom.

Things You'll Need: Large pieces of construction paper or oak tag; colored markers or cartoon-making tools in e-resources.

Directions: Have children divide a large piece of oak tag into boxes. Each box will be used for one scene in the comic strips children are to write. After deciding on a story line, children divide the story into four scenes, create fictional characters, write dialogue that uses a smattering of designated prefixes and suffixes, and illustrate their work, as shown in the comic strip in Figure 6-9. Give writers opportunities to share their comic strips with their classmates.

Figure 6-9 Writing cartoons is a natural opportunity to use suffixes and to explore the contribution that suffixes make to word and passage meaning.

When children share their comic strips, have them point out base words with affixes. Talk about how the affixes affect word meaning and, if your classroom reading program is currently focusing on derivational suffixes, discuss how these suffixes sometimes change a word's grammatical function. Look in the e-resources section for websites children can use to create comic strips.

6.12 *Suffix Draw*

Skill: Reading and writing words with suffixes.

In this gamelike activity, two teams draw suffix cards out of a bag (or other container), select a base word from a chalkboard list, and then write the base word–suffix combination. In so doing, children get practice reading and writing words with suffixes and you, the teacher, have an opportunity to target nettlesome base word–suffix combinations, such as correctly spelling VC (*mopped*) and VCe (*moped*) words when adding suffixes.

Things You'll Need: A bag; cards with base words.

Directions: Put several suffix cards in a bag, such as *-ed*, *-ing*, *-ly*, *-s/es*, *-er*, *-est*, and *-ly*. Write several base words on the board such as *talk*, *hop*, *slow*, *hope*, *try*, *jump*, *please*, *short*, *fast*, *large*, *drive*, *simple*, and *happy*. Divide the class (or group) into two teams. Alternating from team to team, a child draws a suffix card from the shoebox, goes to the board, selects one of the base words (*hop*, for example), writes the word, and adds the suffix (*hopping*). If the base word–suffix combination is a meaningful, correctly spelled word, the team gets a point, and that base word is erased. Continue playing until all the words are erased. Take the opportunity to discuss examples of nettlesome base word–suffix combinations, such as when and when not to double the final consonant or change the *y* to *i* before adding a suffix to a base word.

6.13 *Pin-Up Suffixes*

Skill: Reading words with suffixes.

This activity can be used for practice with the suffixes the children are learning. It is appropriate for large and small groups of first- and second-graders.

Things You'll Need: One lightweight rope several yards long; construction paper cut into either rectangles or objects that are consistent with the theme of a book children are reading; clothespins; a shoebox; 3×5 inch cards with base words. Put the word cards in a sack.

Directions: Write a suffix on the board, such as *-ed*, and a few base words, perhaps *jump*, *hop*, *help*, and *hope*. Demonstrate how to add *-ed* to the base words to make *jumped*, *hopped*, *helped*, and *hoped*. Explain that there are lots of words in the sack, but that *-ed* (or any other suffix the children are learning) cannot be added to every one of them. Children pick a word from the sack and then decide if *-ed* can be added to it. If so, children write the word with the *-ed* suffix on a piece of construction paper (or a shape consistent with a theme in a book children are reading), and use a clothespin to put the word on the line, as shown in Figure 6-10. Children put words that cannot have an *-ed* added to the side of the sack. After all the words with *-ed* are pinned up, read them in chorus and have children practice writing them on the board. Reinforce the concept of adding suffixes to base words. In this example, you would want to reinforce the idea of doubling the final consonant when adding *-ed* toVC words by asking children to write words like *hopped* and *hoped* on the board. Then you would want to talk about why the consonant

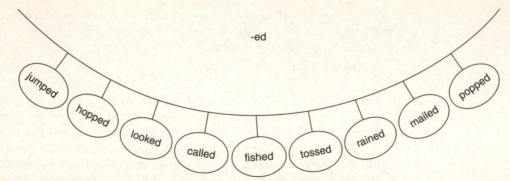

Figure 6-10 In this example, children pin up words to which the suffix *-ed* can be added. Later, words are taken down and children write them on the board with the suffix.

(p) in *hop* is doubled when adding *-ed* and why the *p* is not doubled when adding *-ed* to *hope*. End by asking children to find words with doubled consonants on the pin-up line.

6.14 *Affix Memory Match*

Skill: Reading words with prefixes or suffixes.

This is another version of the memory game in which players remember which two facedown cards of 20 (or fewer) match. Children remember which pairs of base words and prefixes or suffixes make a match, such as *tall-taller* or *happy-unhappy*.

Things You'll Need: Cards with pairs of base word and base word prefix or suffix combinations, such as *joy-joyous*, *happy-happier*, *happy-unhappy*, and *like-dislike*.

Directions: Put cards face down in rows. Players flip up two cards, one at a time. If the base word card and the base word affix card match (*joy-joyous*), the player keeps the two cards. If not, the cards are flipped face down again, and the next player takes a turn flipping cards face up. The player with the most cards wins.

6.15 *Roots and Branches (Use with Prefixes, Suffixes, or Greek and Latin Roots)*

Skill: Reading and writing words with prefixes, suffixes, or Greek and Latin word parts.

This activity uses a tree to illustrate how many different words are built by adding prefixes and suffixes or contain Greek and Latin word parts. It is appropriate for third-graders and above who are learning prefixes and suffixes and for fourth-graders and above who are learning Greek and Latin word parts. This activity is suitable for children working individually, in learning or literacy centers, or with a learning partner.

Things You'll Need: Pencils; dictionaries; copies of base words and branches; paper with several drawings of different trees, as shown in Figure 6-11.

Directions: Review base words, prefixes, and suffixes, or Greek and Latin word parts. Give children the base words and branches paper (see Figure 6-11). Explain that each tree shows the many different "branches" that may be created by adding prefixes and suffixes to a single base word or that contain Greek and Latin word parts. Children think about the word at the base of each tree, decide which prefixes and suffixes can be added to that base word, and then write those words on the branches. Or children look for words that belong to the same meaning family—share the same Greek or Latin root. Children may consult dictionaries. Children share the base words with affixes that grew from the base word tree or words in a meaning family with a shared Greek or Latin root.

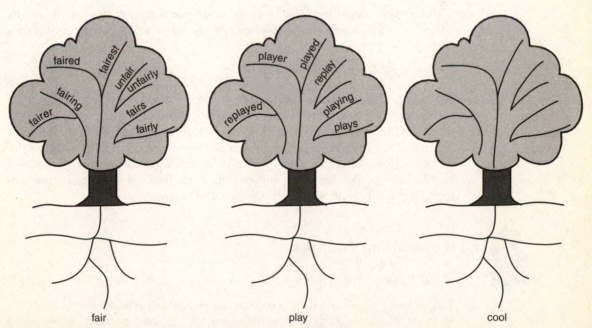

Figure 6-11   Writing words on branches that grow from the same base word helps children develop more in-depth knowledge of the relationship among prefixes, suffixes, and base words.

6.16 *Root Roundup*

Skill: Reading and writing words with Greek and Latin word parts.

Teams compete for three days to find words with the Greek and Latin word parts they are learning in your classroom.

Things You'll Need: Nothing special.

Directions: Create groups of four to six readers. Ask the groups to find as many words as possible in three days that include the Greek and Latin word parts they are learning in your classroom. Teams write the words on a sheet of paper and indicate where the words were found. Teams earn one point for each word they find. At the end of the third day, teams share the words and, if appropriate, get a prize for finding different types of words, such as (a) the most words, (b) the most unusual word, (c) the longest word, or (d) the word with the most syllables.

6.17 *Coin-a-Word*

Skill: Reading words with Greek and Latin word parts.

Children use common Greek or Latin word parts to coin their own words. (*Astroport*, the word at the beginning of this chapter, is the invention of a fifth-grader.)

Things You'll Need: Nothing special.

Directions: Children work individually or in pairs to coin words by combining Greek and Latin word parts, write a definition for the coined words, and illustrate their new words. Put the coined words and illustrations on bulletin boards, along the chalk tray, or anywhere they are in plain view. Discuss the coined words. Children then decide in which meaning family the coined words belong. For instance, the coined word *bioforce* belongs in the *bio-* meaning family with words like *biology* and *biography*.

6.18 *Meaning Families*

Skill: Reading and writing words with the same Greek or Latin word parts.

This activity illustrates how common Greek and Latin word parts are found in many English words. It is suitable for mid- to end-of-year fifth-graders who are reading words with Greek and Latin word parts in content area textbooks.

Things You'll Need: Oak tag sentence strips cut in half; markers; masking-tape loops; dictionaries.

Directions: Select two or three common Greek or Latin word parts that usually come at the beginning of words. Write on the board several long words that begin with the Greek or Latin word parts, such as *geography*, *biology*, and *microscope*. Talk about how common Greek and Latin word parts contribute to word meaning. Discuss how *bio* means "life," *geo* means "earth," and *micro* means "small." Write the Greek or Latin word parts on sentence strips. Tape the strips fairly far apart on the board. Distribute dictionaries, blank oak tag strips, markers, and tape to small groups. Assign, or ask groups to choose, one of the Greek or Latin word parts on the oak tag strips. Each group then finds words in dictionaries and context area textbooks that include the word parts. Groups write the words they find on oak tag strips and tape the strips under the designated word parts on the board, as shown in Figure 6-12. Conclude by inviting a volunteer from each group to explain how their Greek or Latin root contributes to word meaning.

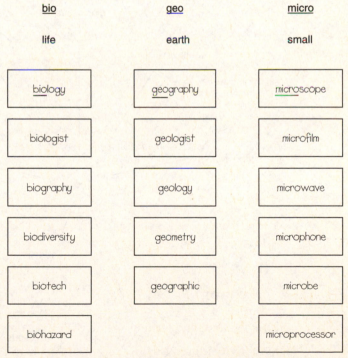

Figure 6-12   Creating words. In writing words with often-used Greek and Latin word parts, children learn how the word parts contribute to the meaning of many different words.

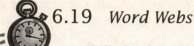 6.19 *Word Webs*

Skill: Reading words with Greek and Latin word parts, or words with affixes.

Word webs begin with a single, often-used prefix, suffix, or Green or Latin root and then spin off into many different examples, as shown in Figure 6-13. Webs with prefixes and suffixes are appropriate for third- through fifth-graders, while webs with common Greek and Latin word parts are best suited for fifth-graders. This activity is most successful when readers work cooperatively in groups.

Things You'll Need: Dictionaries; a large piece of chart paper for each cooperative group; colored construction paper; colorful markers.

Directions: Write an often-used prefix, suffix, or Greek or Latin root in the center of the board and draw a bubble around it. Write a word with the prefix, suffix, or Greek or Latin root to the upper right of the first bubble; draw a

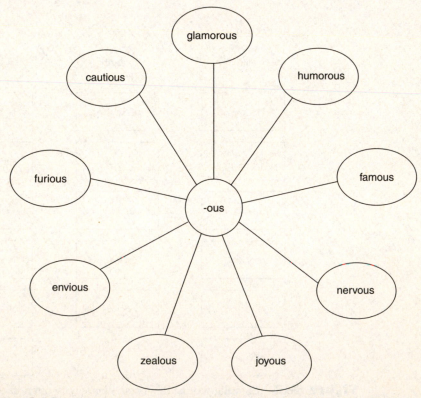

Figure 6-13 Word web for suffix *-ous*. Creating word webs helps children draw the conclusion that many words share the same prefix, suffix, or Greek or Latin word part.

bubble around it; and draw a straight line from this word to the prefix, suffix, or Greek or Latin root, as shown in Figure 6-13. Challenge readers to think of another word that includes the same prefix, suffix, or Greek or Latin root. Add suggested words to the web, drawing bubbles around them, and drawing a line from each word (called a web strand) to the prefix, suffix, or Greek or Latin root in the center. Children now are ready to work together in small groups to make their own word webs, using words found in materials they study throughout the day as well as words they find in dictionaries, wall charts, signs, and posters. After webs are perfected to the satisfaction of group members, invite the groups to share their webs with the entire class, and to explain the connections among words, telling why and how each word is a member of the meaning family. Figure 6-13 shows a word web for the suffix -*ous*.

6.20 *Syllable Word Building*

Skill: Identifying and combining syllables to spell words.

Children combine syllables into words and cross-check to make sure that the combined syllables make real words. This activity is appropriate for children working individually, with a learning partner, or in a center.

Things You'll Need: Cards with syllables on them.

Directions: After discussing syllable patterns, give each child or set of learning partners a few syllable cards. Children put the syllable cards together to build words, cross-check for meaning, and then write the words they build. When finished, discuss the words the children built. Talk about how syllables help us read new words. Discuss, too, the importance of cross-checking to be sure that the words are real, not nonsense. Table 6–6 shows an example of separate syllables and words that might be built from the syllables.

6.21 *Syllable Scoop*

Skill: Identifying the syllables in long words.

Children analyze long words into syllables by drawing semicircles under each syllable (scooping) and then pronounce the long words.

What You'll Need: Long words children read and write.

Directions: Model scooping by writing a long word, pronouncing the word, talking about the syllables, and then scooping each syllable. Then pronounce the scooped syllables, blending them together to say the entire word. Once children understand syllable scooping, ask them to scoop—draw a semicircle—under

TABLE 6–6 *Syllable World Building*	
Syllables	
car	par
ty	pet
son	per
ter	bat
Words	
party	
carpet	
person	
petty	
carpenter	
Carter	
batty	
batter	
car	
pet	
son	
Bart	

each syllable in long words. Have children pronounce the syllables and then blend the syllables to say the complete word. Give children feedback on the syllables they scoop; help children correct misidentified syllables by erasing the mistaken scoop and drawing another scoop in its place. For example, handle would look like *handle*; circumstance would look like *circumstance*. Ask children to explain in their own words why they scooped the syllables the way they did.

SPARE-MINUTE ACTIVITIES FOR ANALYZING THE STRUCTURE OF LONG WORDS

6.22 *Syllable-by-Syllable Decoding*

Skill: Reading long words with several syllables.

Write a long word on a sentence strip, such as *retirement*. Gently fold the strip so that only the first syllable, *re*, shows. Ask children to read the first syllable.

Reveal the second syllable, *tire*, and ask children to read it. Then ask the children to read the two syllables together. Unfold the strip to reveal the last syllable, *ment*. Have children read the whole word, *retirement*.

6.23   *One-, Two-, and Three-Syllable Sort*

Skill: Identifying the syllables in long words.

Put masking tape loops on cards with one-, two-, and three-syllable words. Children take turns sticking the cards to the board. One-syllable words go under the numeral 1; two-syllable words, under 2; three-syllable words, under 3. Use this activity with third- and fourth-graders.

6.24   *Long Word Charts*

Skill: Reading words with prefixes and suffixes or Greek and Latin word parts.

Make large wall chart lists of words with prefixes, suffixes, or Greek and Latin word parts. In making large wall charts, readers think about words that include the multiletter chunks they are learning in your classroom, read the words, and then refer to them when participating in many different classroom reading and writing activities.

6.25   *Prefix-Suffix Circle*

Skill: Reading words with prefixes and suffixes.

This is another variation of the peel-off strategy. Here, children (1) circle prefixes and suffixes, (2) underline the base word, (3) pronounce each part, and (4) blend the parts together.

6.26   *Affix Definitions*

Skill: Reading words with prefixes and suffixes.

Tape cards with prefixes and suffixes to the board. Move over a few feet and tape cards with prefix-suffix definitions to the board. Children match the definitions to the prefixes and suffixes by moving the cards to line up definitions with the correct prefix or suffix.

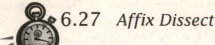

6.27 *Affix Dissect*

Skill: Reading and writing words with prefixes and suffixes.

Have children write on the board or write on a blank piece of paper. Children draw three columns. Have them label the first column *Prefix*, the second *Base Word*, and the third *Suffix*. You pronounce words and children write the base words, the prefixes, and the suffixes.

6.28 *Add the Right Suffix*

Skill: Reading and writing words with suffixes.

Working in pairs or individually, children read base words, two- or three-suffix choices, and then write the base words with the appropriate suffix (see Table 6–7).

TEACHING WORD STRUCTURE TO ENGLISH LANGUAGE LEARNERS

Chan, a fifth-grader whose story is shown in Figure 6-14, speaks Vietnamese at home. Sometimes Chan's home language crosses over into written and spoken English. For instance, when Chan writes, he does not always include all function words such as prepositions and conjunctions. When Chan reads aloud, he pronounces *mother* as /muder/ and leaves out many plurals, possessives, and other word endings, thus reading *wanted* as /want/. While Chan reads words like *large* and *snake*, he sometimes forgets to add the silent *e* when spelling, as we see in his written retelling of *The Great Kapok Tree* (Cherry, 1990). Although Chan learns many common words through everyday interactions, he is unlikely to learn words like

TABLE 6–7 *Add the Right Suffix*		
Base Word	**Suffix**	**Base Word + Suffix**
long	er/ment/ly	longer
joy	ment/ing/ful	joyful
hand	er/ tion/ y	handy
move	ly/able/tion	moveable
happy	ness/ed/able	happiness

The great kapot tree

The great kapot tree are The raini forest.
The great kapot tree is larg.
The great kapot tree is where the
animals live. The butterfly and
The easur live in The top
loge. The monkey, the sloth live
in The umbrella or canpy. The
tree frog and the snak live in the
understory. The Last
is all the amimalscan live There.

Figure 6-14   The transfer of home language to written English suggests that children are interacting with English text in meaningful ways.

canopy and *understory* without explicit instruction accompanied by experiences reading, writing, and talking in his classroom.

Knowledge of word structure is a good predictor of comprehension for English language learners in the fifth grade (Kiefer & Lesaux, 2008). Therefore, you will be a more effective teacher when you teach the meaning of affixes explicitly, and in the context of the real words children like Chan read and write. In introducing an affix for the first time, use base words in which the affix meaning is the most obvious. For instance, in introducing the prefix *un-*, words like *unhappy* and *unfair* are wiser choices than words like *unaware* and *unjust*. Also use base words English learners already have in their English speaking and reading vocabularies. If English learners do not know the base words to which affixes are attached, then teach base word meaning *before* asking children to read base words with affixes. Demonstrate and teach the peel-off strategy described earlier in this chapter, and use prefix-suffix circle (6.25) to give children extra practice identifying affixes and base words. Use wall charts (6.24) as ready resources for the word parts English learners need to recognize in long words. Activities like affix cloze (6.6), affix graffiti (6.4), prefix sort (6.5), and affix definitions (6.26), as well as other activities described earlier, give children many opportunities to identify, read, and understand long words with affixes.

Give English language learners positive feedback, use ample teacher modeling, and give children opportunities to practice reading long words under your supervision before children use their newfound skill independently. Syllable-by-syllable decoding (6.22), syllable word building (6.20), scoop syllables (6.21), and syllable sorting (6.23) are good choices. Show English learners how to use a slash to indicate the syllables in long words. First write several long words on the board. Read the words with the children in chorus, and then have the children place a slash between syllables. *Saddle* would look like *sad/dle*; *temperature* like *tem/per/a/ture*. Take the opportunity to point out syllable patterns in the words children read and write, and have children explain in their own words why they placed the slashes as they did.

Cognates

Cognates are words with a common origin across two languages. True cognates have the greatest overlap. These cognates are spelled the same in both languages. *Patio* is an example of a true cognate in English and Spanish. Semi-true cognates are spelled almost the same. *Azure* in English and *azur* in Spanish is an example of a semi-true cognate. The more English overlaps with children's home languages, the greater the probability of finding cognates. There are many cognates in Spanish, French, and German that are useful for developing English vocabulary. Examples of Spanish cognates are *exit* (*éxito* in Spanish), *family* (*familia*), *tourist* (*turista*), *salad* (*ensalada*), and *bicycle* (*bicicleta*). French cognates include *pastel* (*pastel* in French), *garage* (*garage*), and *November* (*novembre*). *Mother* (*mutter* in German), *hamburger* (*hamburger*), and *October* (*Oktober*) are German cognates. Children who recognize a cognate in their home language have some insight into the meaning of that same word in English. Because cognates look quite similar, children who are literate in their home language are likely to recognize cognates when written in English.

False Cognates

False friends or *false cognates* look and sound similar but have different meanings in two languages. For example, the French word *brave* means "nice," not "courageous"; a *librairie* is a bookstore, not a lending library; a *crayon* is a pencil, a *raisin* is a grape. *Embarazada* in Spanish means "pregnant," not "embarrassed"; *delito* refers to a minor "crime," not to something that is "delightful." It is important make sure that words are cognates before teaching them. True or semi-true cognates can be powerful tools for affirming English learners' home languages, and for extending the vocabulary of English learners and English-only children alike. Capitalize on cognates by making a list of cognates to display in your classroom, have children make a cognate dictionary, or create a cognate bulletin board that shows the many cognates from different languages. Encourage children to make PowerPoint presentations showing cognates, use a flip camera to make presentations of cognates by showing objects or actions while children pronounce the cognates in English and in their home language, or use an interactive white board (IWB) lesson where children touch-and-drag or write cognates. The main point is that cognates, if one is careful to identify true and semi-true cognates from false friends, are an effective avenue for teaching word meaning and word structure, and for connecting with English learners through shared vocabulary.

TEACHING WORD STRUCTURE TO CHILDREN AT RISK

Many children who struggle with reading have difficulty recognizing familiar words when these words are clad in affixes. If you teach children who instantly read a word like *danger* but misread *dangerous*, show them how to use the peel-off strategy as described earlier in this chapter. Teaching children at risk how to spell words with suffixes (Table 6–2) increases the ability to read and spell new words (Kirk & Gillon, 2009). Bear in mind that children at risk may have more difficulty with base words that change spelling when certain suffixes are added (*love-lovable*, *empty-emptiness*) as compared to base words whose spelling does not change (*climb-climbable*, *weak-weakness*). Even when children identify the suffixes, the change in base word spelling may confuse them (*empty-emptiness*).

Have children develop their own prefix binders (6.3), and encourage them to refer to these binders when reading and writing. Use activities that call for active learner involvement when teaching affixes, such as sorting words (6.5) and hunting for prefixes (6.8). Use affix close (6.6) to develop knowledge of words with affixes in sentences. Activities like affix race (6.7), affix roundup (6.10), suffix draw (6.12), and affix dissect (6.27) give children practice with base words and affixes in gamelike formats. Children will also enjoy using their knowledge of affixes to write graffiti (6.4) on charts in your classroom. Because most prefixes and suffixes are usually syllables, children will be able to use these units to help them pronounce complex words (*un-use-able*; *il-logic-al*).

One reason children at risk may struggle to read long words is that they lack the tools to divide long words into pronounceable syllables. Show these children the syllable patterns in the long words they read in your classroom (Table 6–5). Support children as they build words with syllables (6.20), scoop syllables (6.21), and decode syllable-by-syllable (6.22). Scooping syllables and syllable-by-syllable decoding demonstrate how to read three- or more syllable words and give children practice blending the syllables. When you teach syllable scooping, ask children find the vowel pattern and then ask them to scoop the syllables that contain the vowel patterns. Combine scooping and syllable-by-syllable decoding with slashing syllables (explained in the previous section). When you ask children to slash syllables, point out the *C-le* syllable at the end of words and have children use slashes to identify *C-le* syllables. Explain that *C+le* syllables are pronounced with a consonant and a short vowel sound.[2] For example, *ble* in *bram/ble* is pronounced /bul/, the *tle* in *rat/tle* is pronounced /tul/, and the *kle* in *ankle* as /kul/. If children have difficulty understanding that a syllable has one vowel sound but may have more than one vowel letter, use a chinny-chin-chin activity to demonstrate the syllables. To use this activity, write several two- or more syllable words. Ask children to lightly touch their chin with the back of their hand. You say each word and the children repeat it. In saying a word, children will notice that their chins drop as they pronounce a vowel sound. Since each syllable has one vowel sound, each chin movement represents one syllable. Count the syllables in each word. Count the vowels in each word. Then use slashes to divide each word into syllables, as described in the previous section. Ask children to explain in their own language how to find the syllables in long words. Explaining how to find syllables helps children put their learning into language they understand and develop better metacognitive awareness (see Chapter 1 for a discussion of metacognition).

Understanding Greek and Latin word parts gives children at risk a measure of insight into word meaning, and makes long words that consist of one or more of these parts less daunting. In teaching Greek and Latin word parts, remember that these parts are semiburied in English words. Consequently, you will need to explicitly teach the word parts, and the meaning families of English words that include them. If you do not have a curriculum guide to specify which Greek and Latin word parts to teach, begin by teaching the word parts that are present in the words in content subject classes. For example, *bio-* in content vocabulary in science (*biology*, *biologist*) and language arts (*biography*, *biographer*). Preteach some of the new words with Greek and Latin word parts in the text children read, and the meaning of all the Greek and Latin word parts contained in them. If children are familiar with a Greek or Latin word part contained in a new word, ask them to think of what they already know about the Greek and Latin word part and the English words that contain the word part. Help children realize that when they see words in their textbooks or hear words in classroom discussions that contain the same Greek and Latin word parts, the English words have some similarity in meaning (*telephone*, *television*). Use words with Greek and Latin word parts in discussion and encourage children to use them in discussions, too. Point out the words in text, and encourage children to use these words in writing. When children can recognize the meaningful (affixes, Greek and Latin word parts) and pronounceable chunks (syllables) in long words, use context clues and bring their background knowledge to bear when reading, children have the tools they need to learn long and complex words while reading in school and at home.

---

[2]The short vowel is a lax vowel called a schwa (∂). The schwa is pronounced in many unaccented syllables rather than the sound we normally associate with the vowel letter. For the purposes of teaching children at risk to pronounce the C-*le* syllable, the important point is the consistency with which this syllable pattern is pronounced, not the term we use for this lax vowel.

e-Resources for Teaching Word Structure

Websites with Activities or Lessons for Computers or Interactive Whiteboards (IWBs)

Harcourt (*http://www.harcourtschool.com/activity/book_buddy/arthur/skill.html*):

In this game, the player selects a prefix or suffix to add to a base word, then reads sentences with blanks where the new word might be added and decides which sentence makes sense with the new word.

Smart Exchange™ (*http://exchange.smarttech.com/#tab=0,*
http://exchange.smarttech.com/search.html?q=prefix&sbj=eland,
http://exchange.smarttech.com/search.html?q=suffix&sbj=ela
http://exchange.smarttech.com/search.html?q=contractions&sbj=ela, and
http://exchange.smarttech.com/search.html?q=syllable&sbj=ela, and
http://exchange.smarttech.com/search.html?q=compound+words&sbj=ela):

Smart Exchange offers a free, downloadable SMART Notebook lesson on different syllable patterns and words that illustrate the patterns. Look IWB many lessons developed by teachers and the staff at Smart Exchange that focus on learning, reviewing, and identifying prefixes, suffixes, contractions, syllables, and compound words.

BBC (*http://www.bbc.co.uk/schools/teachers/ks2bitesize/english/spelling.shtml* and *http://www.bbc.co.uk/skillswise/*):

Click Spelling in the first address to find a lesson on prefixes that features *de-, dis-. non-, pro-,* and *sub-.* Included are objectives, a lesson plan, a whiteboard-ready activity that is also downloadable to your own website or blog, along with a worksheet and online quiz.

Click Spelling on Skillwise homepage for five activities that focus on affixes or syllables. Each activity includes a printable fact sheet, worksheet and quiz. Click on Spelling Plurals for a fact sheet, a worksheet, a quiz, and a game that calls for selecting correctly spelled plurals. Click on Syllables for a fact sheet, worksheet, quiz, and a game called Syllables Factory. Players hear and read words from one to four syllables and determine the number of syllables in each. After the syllable count is determined, the syllable division is shown. The visual and audio combination in a game format is useful for readers who need extra practice. Players view their performance after each round.

Brown Bear (*http://www.bigbrownbear.co.uk/*):

This site features several games with affixes. On the homepage click on Pairs for a memory game where children match words with the same prefix. At the end of the game there is a list of the words matched. Other examples of games on this website are (1) Prefixes, a game where children click and drag a prefix and base word to make a new word; children then check their work to see if they have successfully built a real word and (2) Suffixes, which asks children to combine base words with suffixes. These games are IWB ready. The click-and-drag word building format and the built-in check make the prefix and suffix games especially useful for engaging small or large groups.

NGfL Cymru (*http://www.ngfl-cymru.org.uk*):

This is a website for teachers who work in Wales. The site has several whiteboard-ready activities for contractions. Click English and then click on Keystage 2. On the KS2—Stage 2—page click on English again, then click on Writing, and click on Functional Skills – Punctuation to bring up activities. Look in apostrophes for contraction and possession to find four options (1) starter activity part 1, (2) starter activity part 2, (3) main session part 1, and (4) main session part 2. The first option, starter activity part 1, is a three-part lesson. The third part has an interactive game that uses animation to illustrate the formation of contractions. Main session part 1 asks children to click on two words to make contraction. A dragon is released from a cage when all the word pairs are identified. Click on apostrophes for contraction to find a IWB-ready activity.

Fun4theBrain (*http://www.fun4thebrain.com/english.html*):

This site features several games, three of which are appropriate for reinforcing knowledge of word structure. In Syllable Split, the player selects one of three words that is correctly divided into VC/CV syllables. Base Word Baseball asks the player to select the correct suffix for a base word. Some base word spellings change when suffixes are added, which makes this game a useful tool for review and reinforcement. The suffixes in this game are appropriate for children in the first and second grade. My Reading Tools includes an activity to give the player practice selecting a word with the correct syllable division.

Cricket Web (*http://www.crickweb.co.uk*):

Click on Links on the homepage to find the apostrophes game on the NGfL site. Children learn how to use an apostrophe to show contractions and possession. The cricket web site also includes a compound word activity with a downloadable worksheet and notes to guide the teacher in using the activity.

Sadlier-Oxford (*http://www.sadlier-oxford.com/phonics/student.cfm*):

This site has a number of word games. Under Grade 2, you will find a Fly-by-Contractions game, where the player types a word that matches a definition, and a Suffixes game, where the player uses knowledge of suffix meaning to select a word that matches a definition. Grades 3-4 has the game Flamingo for adding *-y* or *-ly* to base words, and the game Crystal Castles for adding *in-* or *im-* to base words. In Grades 5–6, you will find the syllable game Space Station, and Fish Tanks 1 for identifying prefixes, suffixes, and base words. Other materials are available for purchase.

ReadWriteThink (*http://www.readwritethink.org*) and *http://www.readwritethink.org/classroom-resources/student-interactives/flip-chip-30031.html*):

Look for a Flip-a-Chip lesson plan and accompanying interactive game where the reader selects words with endings that fit the context of short sentences in a paragraph. This site also offers lesson plans and a printable card game called Make a Word that features Greek and Latin word parts. Use this game with advanced fifth-graders, or make your own game by writing the word parts on playing cards (affixes as well as Greek and Latin word parts) that children are learning in your classroom.

Primary Games (*http://www.primarygames.com/*):

Look for See 'N Spell activities. In one activity, children add *-s* or *-es* to words. This would make a good IWB activity for a small or large group.

Manattee District Schools, Florida (*http://www.manatee.k12.fl.us/sites/elementary/ samoset/Resources/contractions.htm*):

This site offers a good set of activities for choosing contractions that fit a sentence context. The activities would be useful for large or small groups when presented on an IWB. Also look for printable contractions cards for learning or literacy centers or small group work.

Websites for Creating Comic Strips

ToonDoo (*http://www.toondoo.com*):

This website offers children many choices for creating comic strips. Comic strips can be saved, published, and printed. Characters are appropriate for elementary children. Children select characters, background, props, and clip art for the comic strips.

The Super Hero Show™ (*http://superherosquad.marvel.com/create_your_own_comic*):

This is a free resource, supported by Marvel Entertainment, Inc. and part of the *MarvelKids.com*™ website, for creating comic strips that feature words with the mul-tiletter chunks children are learning. Children may select the layout, background, a male or female superhero, dialog balloons, fonts for dialog, objects, and back-grounds. Comic strips can be created in languages other than English. In light of the super hero theme, be sure to preview this site to judge the appropriateness of the characters for the children whom you teach.

Make Beliefs™ **Comix** (*http://www.makebeliefscomix.com*):

Children can make their own comic strips with options to choose the characters, dialog or thought balloon, the background color for frames, and characters. Features allow children to rotate and scale objects in frames. Comic strips can be created in several languages. Preview this site to judge whether the characters are appropriate for the children in your classroom.

Artisan Cam (*http://www.artisancam.org.uk*):

Click on Activities on the homepage. Then click on Super Action Comic Maker to bring up the comic maker page. Children create six-frame comic strips by selecting characters, background, and dialog boxes. Comic strips can be created in languages other than English. This site is primarily for sharing and exploring the arts. Artists who work in different mediums are featured, there is a section for teachers, and there are opportunities to create art online.

Printable Materials

First School Years (*http://www.firstschoolyears.com/literacy/word/other/prefixes/ prefixes.htm*):

This United Kingdom–based site offers a variety of materials for teachers, including numerous printable worksheets for classroom use. Keep in mind that some of the spelling is consistent with British conventions. Use games and printables to reinforce learning.

FreeReading™ (*http://www.freereading.net/index.php?title=Main_Page http://www .freereading.net/index.php?title=Prefixes_and_Suffixes_Activities*):

Click on Find Literacy Activities on the main page. This no-cost, open-source website includes a kindergarten and first–grade intervention program as well as a section for teaching prefixes and suffixes that includes lesson plans and graphic organizers to accompany the lessons.

Family Education (*http://www.fekids.com/kln/index.html*):

Click on Go to Games Plus and find an icon with an Egyptian pharaoh for the Race to Ramses game. This game is scalable for grades two through three or four through six. This quest game calls for making words with prefixes and suffixes to reach the tomb of Ramses before grave robbers claim the treasure. Three parts to the game and good graphics give players practice building and reading words with affixes.

Super Teacher (*http://www.superteacherworksheets.com/syllables.html*):

This site features a number of printable worksheets to give readers practice identifying syllables and dividing multisyllable words into syllables.

Adrian Bruce (*http://www.adrianbruce.com/reading/room4/gofish/GoFishsyllrule1vccv. pdf*):

Here you will find a colorful, printable Go Fish card game with VC-CV syllable words where one syllable is in color.

Scholastic (*http://teacher.scholastic.com/products/instructor/mar05_prefixessuffixes .htm*):

The web address links to a page with explanations of classroom activities for base words, prefixes and suffixes. Look for the Spin-a-Word Game and a downloadable game board. In playing this race-and-chase game, players add suffixes to words to move around the board. Good for two players and suitable for a learning center.

REFERENCES

Ayers, D. M. (1980). *English words from Greek and Latin elements*. Tucson: University of Arizona Press.

Bear, D. R., Invernizzi, M., Templeton, S., & Johnston, F. (2007). *Words their way: Word study for phonics, vocabulary, and spelling instruction* (3rd ed.). Upper Saddle River, NJ: Pearson Education.

Carlisle, J. F. (2000). Awareness of the structure and meaning of morphologically complex words: Impact on reading. *Reading and Writing: An Interdisciplinary Journal, 12,* 169–190.

Carlisle, J. F., & Stone, C. A. (2005). Exploring the role of morphemes in word reading. *Reading Research Quarterly, 40,* 428–449.

Cherry, L. (1990). *The great kapok tree*. New York: Harcourt Brace.

Deacon, S. H., & Kirby, J. R. (2004). Morphological awareness: Just "more phonological"? The roles of morphological and phonological awareness in reading development. *Applied Psycholinguistics, 25,* 223–238.

Ehri, L. C. (2005). Learning to read words: Theory, findings, and issues. *Scientific Studies of Reading, 9,* 167–188.

Hackett, J. K., Moyer, R. H., & Adams, D. K. (1989). *Merrill Science*. Upper Saddle River, NJ: Merrill/Prentice Hall.

Henderson, E. H. (1990). *Teaching spelling* (2nd ed.). Boston: Houghton Mifflin.

Kiefer, M. J., & Lesaux, N. K. (2008). The role of derivational morphology in the reading comprehension of Spanish-speaking English language learners. *Reading and Writing, 21,* 783–804.

Kirk, C., & Gillon, G. T. (2009). Integrated morphological awareness intervention as a tool for improving literacy. *Language, Speech, and Hearing Services in Schools, 40,* 341–351.

Mahoney, D., Singson, M., & Mann, V. (2000). Reading ability and sensitivity to morphological relations. *Reading and Writing: An Interdisciplinary Journal, 12,* 191–218.

McCutchen, D., Logan, B., & Biangardi-Orpe, U. (2009). Making meaning: Children's sensitivity to morphological information during word reading. *Reading Research Quarterly, 44*(4), 360–376.

Nagy, W., Berninger, V. W., & Abbot, R. D. (2006). Contributions of morphology beyond phonology to literacy outcomes of upper elementary and middle-school students. *Journal of Educational Psychology, 98,* 134–147.

Neuhaus, G. F., Roldan, L. W., Boulware-Gooden, R., & Swank, P. R. (2006). Parsimonious reading models: Identifying teachable subskills. *Reading Psychology, 27,* 37–58.

Nunes, T., Bryant, P., & Bindman, M. (1997). Morphological spelling strategies: Developmental stages and processes. *Developmental Psychology, 33,* 637–649.

Singson, M., Mahony, D., & Mann, V. (2000). The relation between reading ability and morphological skills: Evidence from derivational suffixes. *Reading and Writing: An Interdisciplinary Journal, 12,* 219–252.

White, T. G., Power, M. A., & White, S. (1989). Morphological analysis: Implications for teaching and understanding vocabulary growth. *Reading Research Quarterly, 24,* 283–304.

White, T. G., Sowell, J., & Yanagihara, A. (1989). Teaching elementary students to use word-part clues. *The Reading Teacher, 42,* 302–308.

Wysocki, K., & Jenkins, J. R. (1987). Deriving word meanings through morphological generalization. *Reading Research Quarterly, 22,* 66–81.

APPENDIX

Letter-Sound Patterns for the Teacher of Reading

CONSONANT PATTERNS

Single Consonants

Single consonant letters represent the sounds heard in the following words:

B,b	boat	buffalo	P,p	pig	popcorn
C,c	cat	city	Q,q	queen	quack
D,d	dog	donkey	R,r	ring	rabbit
F,f	fish	fox	S,s	sun	daisy
G,g	goat	gem	T,t	turtle	table
H,h	hat	hippopotamus	V,v	van	valentine
J,j	jet	jam	W,w	wagon	wave
K,k	kite	kangaroo	X,x	fox	exit
L,l	lion	lamp	Y,y	yo-yo	yellow
M,m	moon	monkey	Z,z	zipper	zoo
N,n	nut	nest			

- *W,w* and *Y,y* act as consonants when they are onsets, as in *wagon, wait, yellow,* and *barnyard.*
- Though *Y,y* represents the consonant sound heard in *yellow* when it is an onset, *Y,y* also acts as a vowel in many letter-sound patterns.
- *X,x* seldom represents the sound heard in *x-ray*, a favorite example in ABC books. Though *X,x* represents several sounds, the /ks/ in *fox* (particularly at the end of words) and the /gz/ in *exit* are most common.
- In addition to the letter *k*, the /k/ may be spelled with a *c* (*cat*), *ck* (*back*), and *ch* when combined with *r* to form *chr* (*chrome*).
- Consonants that represent more than one sound, such as *c, g,* and *s,* are explained later.

Silent Consonants

Silent consonants are usually a consequence of spelling changes over time in which (a) the consonant letters that are no longer pronounced remained in spelling or (b) words were borrowed from other languages in which the consonants are not pronounced in English. While nearly any letter can be silent at some time or another, the most common letters are

Silent b in mb	bomb	lamb	Silent b in bt	doubt	debt
Silent k in kn	knee	knead	Silent w in wr	write	wrong
Silent gh in ght	light	bought	Silent h in gh	ghost	ghetto
Silent gh	through	thigh	Silent n in mn	autumn	hymn
Silent l in lm	calm	film	Silent l in lk	chalk	folk
Silent t in tch	catch	witch			

- Generally speaking, the silent letters do not pose challenges for readers because we learn to ignore them when we read.
- The *b* is often silent when following *m* (*mb*) or *t* (*bt*).
- *K* is silent when followed by *n* at the beginning of a word.
- *L* may be silent when it precedes *m* (*lm*) or *k* (*lk*).
- The letter *t* may be silent when it precedes *ch* (*tch*)
- *Gh* is silent at the end a word or when it precedes *t* at the end of a word (*gh* and *ght*).
- *W* may be silent when it precedes *r* at the beginning of a word.
- *G* is silent when it precedes *h* at the beginning of a word.
- *N* is silent when it follows *m* at the end of a word.

Qu

When *Q,q* is present in spelling, it almost always precedes *U,u*.

Beginning qu /kw/ Sound		Middle qu /kw/ Sound		Final que /k/ Sound	
quack	quick	acquit	inquire	antique	physique
quarter	quiet	banquet	liquid	boutique	statuesque
queen	quit	elequent	request	critique	technique
question	quiz	frequent	require	oblique	Unique

- Words spelled with *que* are borrowed from French and reflect the influence of French on our spelling system.
- Occasionally the *u* in *qu* is silent and represents the /k/ heard in *mosquito, quay, croquette,* and *quiche*. This occurs so seldom in English words that it does not merit specific attention.
- *Q,q* occurs without *u* in a few words, as in *Iraq*, but this is so rare in English that it does not warrant special consideration, either.

Double Consonants

Formed whenever the same consonants are side by side, the sound represented is usually that of a single consonant, as in *rabbit* and *cotton*.

- When there is a double consonant in a word, the consonant sound most often goes with the preceding vowel to form a pattern, as in *rabbit* (/rab/) and *mitten* (/mit/). The exception occurs when words are joined together to make compounds, in which case both sounds may be heard, as in *headdress* and *bookkeeper*. For the purpose of dividing words into syllables, the syllable division is between the double consonants (*rab-bit*, *mit-ten*), and the first syllable is most often the syllable that is accented.
- In some words spelled with a double *c*, the first *c* represents the sound of /k/ in *kite* and the second the /s/ in *save*, as in *accent*, *accept*, and *accident*.
- When suffixes are added to some words, such as *slam* and *wrap*, consonants are doubled, as in *slamming* and *wrapped*. Whereas it is relatively easy to infer the pronunciation of double consonants, it is much more challenging for children to learn when (and when not) to double consonants in writing suffixes.

Consonant Blends (or Clusters)

The sounds represented by letters in a consonant blend are joined together during pronunciation. Some teachers' manuals refer to this pattern as a consonant cluster. The blends can be organized into those that include the letter *l*, the letter *r*, the letter *s*, and the letter *w*.

Two-Letter Blends

L Blends

bl	black	blank	bleach	block
cl	class	clean	clock	clown
fl	flag	flew	flower	fly
gl	flass	globe	glow	glue
pl	place	plant	plow	plus
sl	sled	sleep	slide	slip

R Blends

br	bread	brick	bride	brook
cr	cream	creek	crop	cry
dr	draw	dress	drive	dry
fr	free	fresh	friend	fruit
gr	grass	green	grew	grow
pr	pretty	price	print	proud
tr	train	tree	trick	true

S Blends

sc	scan	scare	scoop	score
sk	skate	skill	skip	sky
sm	small	smell	smoke	smooth
sn	snap	sneeze	snip	snow
sp	space	speak	speed	spoon
st	stand	star	step	stop
sw	swat	sweat	swift	swing

W Blends

dw	dwarf	dwell	dwelt	dwindle
tw	twelve	twenty	twice	twin

- The two-letter blends *sk*, *sm*, *sp*, and *st* occur at the beginning and the end of words, as in *mask*, *prism*, *clasp*, and *last*. All the other two-letter blends occur at the beginning of words, not the end.
- The letters *wr* do not form a blend. The *w* is silent, as in *wrap*, *write*, and *wreck*.
- Some letter combinations, such as *nd*, *mp*, *ld*, *nt*, *lk*, and *nk*, form a cluster at the end of words, as in *stand*, *jump*, *held*, *sent*, *talk*, and *sink*. Try teaching consonant blends at the end of words as part of rimes.

Three-Letter Blends

scr	scratch	screen	scribble	scrub
spl	splash	splatter	splendid	split
spr	sprain	spray	spread	sprung
squ	squad	square	squeeze	squirrel
str	straight	streak	strike	string

The following letters in these three-letter blends represent only two sounds:

chr	Christmas	chrome	chronic	chronicle
sch	schedule	schema	scholar	school
thr	thread	three	throat	throne

- Except for *Christmas*, *school*, and *schedule*, *chr* and *sch* are not often present in the words younger children are likely to read and spell.
- This is not the case for *thr*, which is part of many words.
- Teach the three-letter blends after readers know common two-letter blends.

Consonant Digraphs

The letters in a consonant digraph represent one sound that is different from the sounds the letters represent individually.

ch	chair	charge	cheese	chip
ph	phase	phone	photo	physical
sh	shape	she	sheep	show
th (voiceless)	thank	thick	think	third
th (voiced)	than	the	their	this
wh	what	wheel	while	white
tch	ditch	latch	match	watch
dg /j/	bridge	edge	fudge	wedge

- Other sounds that the *ch* digraph represent are the /sh/ heard in *chivalry* and the /k/ heard in *choir*. The sound in *chirp* is the most frequent sound. Advise readers to try this sound first.
- The digraph *ph* commonly represents the /f/ heard in *phone*. Every now and then *ph* represents the sound of /p/, and sometimes *ph* is silent.
- The digraphs *ch, ph, sh,* and *th* occur at the beginning of words, in the middle of words—such as *franchise, dolphin, bishop,* and *heathen*—and at the end of words, such as *perch, graph, fish,* and *teeth*.
- The letters *th* represent two sounds—the sound heard in *thank* (called voiceless) and that heard in *than* (called voiced). Advise readers to first try the voiceless /th/ in *thank*.
- When *wh* precedes *o*, it represents the /h/ in *who*. The /hw/ sound in *white* is much more common. Encourage readers to try this sound first. In some Americans' speech, the /h/ is not pronounced in a word such as *white*; just the /w/ is pronounced. This reflects readers' normal pronunciation and hence should not interfere with word identification.
- When the letter *e* follows the digraph *th* at the end of a word, such as in *bathe*, the *th* represents the voiced sound heard in *that*. This explains the difference in pronunciation between *cloth* and *clothe*, and *teeth* and *teethe*.
- The digraph *tch* occurs at the end of words, as in *catch, itch, match,* and *stretch*. Whereas readers should have no trouble inferring that the *t* in *tch* is silent, they must remember to include the *t* in spelling.
- The *dg* represents /j/ heard in *judge* and *pidgin*.
- The *ng* digraph always follows a vowel, for example, the *ang* in *sang, ing* in *ring, ong* in *song*, and *ung* is *rung*. The letter *n* may also represent /ng/ when it is followed by the letter *g* (*finger*–/fing-ger/) or the letter *k* (*pink*–/pingk/). Your dictionary may use the η to represent /ng/.
- The *ck* (which represents the /k/ at the end of words such as *back*) and the *ng* are not included here because they are quicker to learn as part of the rimes *ack, eck, ick, ock,* and *uck*, or the rimes *ang, ing, ong,* and *ung*.
- As an onset, the digraph *gh* represents /g/, though few English words begin with *gh*. When *gh* is not an onset, there are two options: the *gh* is silent, as in *thigh*, or it represents /f/ as in *laugh*. When words include the sequence *ght*, the *gh* is silent, as in *bought* and *night*.

S,s

As an onset *S,s* represents the /s/ in *sack*, never /z/. Only two alternatives, /s/ or /z/, are possible when *s* is a middle or the last letter in a syllable.

/s/ Onset	salt	seed	sell	sun
/s/ Final Sound	bus	dress	house	us
/z/ Sound	as	is	was	nose

- The words *sure* and *sugar* are exceptions; the *s* in the beginning of these words represents the sound of /sh/.
- If *i* or *u* follows *s* in the middle of a word, the *s* may represent the sound heard in *mansion* or in *pleasure*.
- When *-es* is a suffix as in *dishes* or *washes*, the *-es* represents /z/.

Ca, co, cu

When *c* precedes *a*, *o*, and *u* (*ca, co, cu*), the *c* usually represents the /k/ heard in *kite* (called a hard sound).

ca	cab	call	can	cat
co	coat	cold	come	cow
cu	cub	cube	curl	cut

Ce, ci, cy

In the *ce*, *ci*, and *cy* patterns, the *c* usually represents the sound associated with the /s/ in *soap* (called a soft sound).

ce	cement	cent	cereal	certain
ci	cider	circle	circus	city
cy	cycle	cylinder	cymbal	cypress

- As an onset, the *c* in *ci* represents /s/, but in the middle of words, *ci* usually represents the /sh/ sound, as in *social*.

Ga, go, gu

When *g* precedes *a*, *o*, and *u* (*ga, go, gu*), the *g* usually represents the sound associated with the /g/ in *gate* (called the hard sound).

ga	game	gap	gas	gay
go	goat	gold	got	gown
gu	guard	guest	gum	guy

Ge, gi, gy

In the *ge*, *gi*, and *gy* patterns, the *g* usually represents the sound associated with the /j/ in *jelly* (called the soft sound).

ge	gem	gentle	gerbil	gesture
gi	ginger	giraffe	magic	margin
gy	gym	gypsy	biology	energy

- The combinations *ge* and *gi* are not as dependable as the others. Support readers as they learn to first try the sound of /j/ in *jelly* for *ge* and *gi* and, if that fails, try the sound of /g/ in *goat*.

VOWEL PATTERNS

Short-Vowel Sounds and Short-Vowel Patterns

a   in *apple*

e   in *edge*

i   in *igloo*

o   in *octopus*

u   in *umbrella*

VC Short-Vowel Pattern

The VC pattern usually represents a short sound. This pattern consists of one vowel followed by one or more consonants in a one-syllable word or in a single syllable. Short vowel sounds are often indicated by a breve (căt), a single vowel preceding one or more consonants, as in VC-*at*; CVC-*cat*; CCVC-*chat* or *slat*; CCVCC-*black*; CCVCCC-*thatch*; CCCVC-*scrap*; CCCVCCC-*splotch*. The number of consonants following the vowel in this pattern does not affect the short-vowel sound, although, of course, there are exceptions.

VC	at		in		up
CVC	sat	bed	fin	hot	pup
CCVC	chat	shed	clip	drop	plug
CCVCC	clasp	fresh	crisp	frost	plump
CVCCC	catch	fetch	ditch	notch	bunch

- Sometimes the vowel in a VC pattern represents a long sound, as in *cold* (*old*), *colt* (*olt*), *find* (*ind*), *night* (*ight*), and *child* (*ild*). Considered within the context of rimes, combinations like these are quite predictable and, hence, best learned as rimes in word family words. Advise readers to try the short vowel first and, if that does not produce a meaningful word, to try a long sound.

VCCe Short-Vowel Pattern

In the VCCe pattern, the vowel generally represents a short sound and the *e* is silent. A consonant pattern before the vowel forms a CVCCe (*dance*) or CCVCCe (*chance*) sequence; it does not affect the sound the vowel in the VCCe pattern represents.

| CVCCe | dance | ledge | rinse | dodge | judge |
| CCVCCe | chance | pledge | fringe | sconce | twinge |

- The pattern *dge* usually represents /j/ and the final *e* is silent. Never an onset, *dge* is included in the spelling of many different words, and hence readers have ample opportunities to learn this pattern through reading and writing.
- Some of the words in the preceding list end with *ge* or *ce*. In spellings, the final *e* signals readers that the sound of the *c* is /s/ and the sound of *g* is /j/, consistent with the *ce* and *ge* patterns. Without the final *e*, readers might pronounce the final *c* as /k/ (*epic*) and the final *g* as /g/ (*chug*). In this way, the final *e* in these VCCe patterns makes our writing system a more predictable and dependable representation of sound.
- The VCCe short-vowel pattern is challenging to spellers because the *e* may be dropped when suffixes are added, as in *lodging* and *dancing*.
- If the short-vowel sound does not result in a meaningful word with a VCCe pattern, advise readers to try the long sound.

Long-Vowel Sounds and Long-Vowel Patterns

Long Vowel Sounds

a	in *apron*
e	in *eraser*
i	in *ice*
o	in *overalls*
u	in *unicorn*

VCe Long-Vowel Pattern

In the VCe pattern, the *e* is silent and the preceding vowel usually has a long sound, which is often indicated by a macron (ˉ). A consonant pattern before the vowel forms a CVCe (*sāve*) or a CCVCE (*shāve*) sequence and does not affect the sound that the vowel in the VCe long-vowel pattern represents.

aCe	bake	came	shape	trade
eCe	gene	scene	recede	theme
iCe	bike	drive	hide	side
oCe	hole	home	note	rope
uCe	cube	cute	fume	use

- There are some marked exceptions to the VCe long-vowel pattern, as we see in *have* and *love*.
- Words spelled with *r* usually conform to the r-controlled (Vr) pattern (*more*).
- When the last syllable is *ate* or *ite*, and when the syllable is not stressed in pronunciation, the *a* and the *i* do not represent a long sound (*climate* and *granite*).
- Some borrowed words from French (*café*) are exceptions and are pronounced accordingly.

CV Long-Vowel Pattern

In the CV pattern, the vowel usually represents a long sound. The CV is an open syllable (see Chapter 6).

Ca	flavor	later	paper	table
Ce	be	he	legal	zebra
Ci	giant	minus	pilot	spider
Co	,moment	no	program	total
Cu	bugle	future	human	music

- There are many exceptions to the CV long-vowel pattern, particularly if this pattern occurs in a syllable that is not accented—for example, the first syllable in *develop*.

The Letter Y,y as the Final Letter

The letter *y* at the end of a word acts as a vowel. When *y* forms a separate final syllable, it generally represents the sound associated with long *e*, as in *bunny* and *silly*. Y,y at the end of a word with *no other vowels* represents the sound associated with long *i*, as in *by* and *try*.

Final Syllable (long e)	any	baby	city	tiny
Only Vowel (long i)	by	fly	my	try

- Tell readers to try the sound of long *i* in short words and the sound of long *e* in longer words. If one sound does not work, the other one has a good chance of being correct.
- When the *-ly* is a suffix as in *deeply* and *cheaply*, it represents long *e*. Advise readers to try long *e* if they think the *-ly* is a suffix and long *i* if they think it is part of the base word. If one sound does not work, the other probably will.

VV Vowel Teams Long-Vowel Pattern

Vowel teams are two adjacent vowels (VV) that represent one vowel sound when they are in the same syllable. In the vowel teams of *ai, oa, ay, ee, ey,* and *ea,* the first vowel usually represents a long sound and the second is silent.

ai Team	main	paint	sail	train
ay Team	day	may	stay	way
ea Team	leaf	meat	sea	treat
ee Team	feel	green	keep	meet
ey Team	honey	key	money	turkey
oa Team	boat	coast	oak	road

- Sometimes two adjacent vowels in the VV vowel team pattern are referred to as a vowel digraph because two letters represent one sound.
- *Y,y* is a vowel when it follows *a* and *e*, thereby creating the vowel team patterns of *ay* and *ey*.
- Most of the time, *ai* represents long *a*, but occasionally it represents the sound heard in *said* (seldom the sound in *plaid*). Tell readers to first try the long *a* sound and, should that fail to create a meaningful word, to try the sound heard in *said*.
- The *ey* represents the sound in *key* and *they*. Advise readers to first try the sound of long *e* and, if that fails to produce a meaningful word, to try the sound of long *a*, as in *obey* and *they*.
- The *ea* sometimes represents the short *e* heard in *head*. Infrequently, *ea* represents a long *a* as in *great*. Advise readers to first try long *e* and, if that does not form a contextually meaningful word, to try short *e*.
- When two adjacent vowels are in different syllables, then both vowels represent a separate sound, as in *create*.
- Both *oe* and *ei* are taught as vowel teams in some phonics programs. The *oe* occurs in relatively few words. The *ei* occurs in more words, though these words are not often present in the material read by first- through third-graders. Additionally, the *ei* may represent the long *a* in *eight* and *neighbor*; the long *i* in *height*; in combination with *r* the sounds in *weird* and *their*. Rather than single out the *oe* and *ei* to teach as vowel teams, teach words with these patterns through spelling, and reading and writing experiences.

Other Vowel Patterns
Double oo
The double *oo* usually represents the sound heard in *school* or the sound heard in *book*.

oo in school	cool	moon	room	spoon
oo in book	foot	good	shook	wood

- Advise readers to try one sound and, if that does not result in a sensible word, to try the other sound.

Vowel Diphthongs

Ow, ou, oi, and *oy* often represent the following sounds in pronunciation: *ow* in *cow; oi* in *oil; ou* in *out; oy* in *boy.*

ow Diphthong	brown	cow	down	town
ou Diphthong	cloud	flour	ouch	shout
oi Diphthong	choice	coin	point	spoil
oy Diphthong	boy	enjoy	royal	toy

- The *ow* also represents the long-vowel sound /crow/, so readers have two sounds from which to choose: the /ow/ in /cow/ and the /o/ (long *o*) in /crow/. If one sound does not work, the other will.
- The *oi* may be part of the multiletter groups *oise* (as in *noise*) and *oice* (as in *voice*). Encourage readers to draw these conclusions during the normal course of reading and writing.
- Though *ou* frequently represents the sounds heard in *out* and *cloud*, these two letters represent several other sounds in words, for example, *soul, tour, group, shoulder, encourage, could,* and *double. Your, pour,* and *four* are examples of other exceptions to the *ou* pattern. However, authors use words like *your, four, should, would,* and *could* so frequently that children learn to read them through normal reading and writing experiences.

Vr or r-Controlled Pattern

The *r* affects pronunciation so that vowels cannot be classified as short or long.

ar R-control	car	farm	park	star
er R-control	after	enter	ever	her
ir R-control	bird	fir	shirt	third
or R-control	corn	for	sort	store
ur R-Control	burn	fur	hurt	turn

- The letters *ar* after *w* represent the sounds heard in *war* and *warm*, not the sound heard in *car*. This, however, is not overly difficult for observant readers to discover.
- The /or/ may be represented by *oor* in *door*, *ore* in *more*, *our* in *four*, and *oar* in *oar*.
- The /er/ is represented by five different spelling: the *er* in *her*, *ir* in *sir*, *ur* in *turn*, *or* in *work*, and the *ear* in *learn*.

The au and aw Patterns

The *au* generally represents the sound in *fault*. The *aw* represents the sound in *straw*.

au Pattern	author	cause	haul	pause
aw Pattern	claw	draw	lawn	saw

- The *au* and *aw* patterns are fairly reliable. The *au* does not occur at the end of words. The *aw* is used as an onset (*awe*), in the middle of words (*dawn*), and at the end of words (*draw*).

The ew and ue Patterns

The *ew* and *ue* patterns usually represent the sound in *blew* and *blue*.

ew Pattern	blew	drew	knew	threw
ue Pattern	blue	clue	glue	true

- The *ue* pattern cannot be counted on to represent the sound in *blue* when the *ue* follows a *q* or a *g* in spelling, as in *antique* and *guess*. When children have lots of experience reading and writing words spelled with these sequences, they learn the sounds these letters represent.

Key Vocabulary

Accented syllables   The stress given to syllables. Accent affects the way we pronounce the vowels in long words. The vowels in accented syllables, also called primary accents, tend to follow the pronunciation we would expect from their placement in letter-sound patterns.

Adding sounds   Attaching a sound to a word, such as adding /p/ to /an/ to form /pan/ or /bee/ to /t/ to pronounce /beet/.

Affixes   The prefixes and suffixes attached to the beginning or end of words.

Alphabetic principle   The principle that, in writing, letters represent sounds and, therefore, readers can pronounce any word that is spelled the way it is pronounced.

Alphabetic word learners   Children who are capable of reading new words by analyzing all the letter and sound patterns and then using this information to pronounce the new words they see in text.

Analogy-based phonics   A phonics teaching approach in which children learn to use the parts of words they know to identify new words that share the same patterns. Analogy-based phonics groups words with the same patterns into word families (the *it* family, for example, consists of *sit*, *fit*, and *lit*), and teaches children how to pronounce and spell families.

Analytic (implicit) phonics   Whole-to-part-to-whole phonics instruction in which children first learn a group of basic sight words with certain phonics patterns and then learn how the letter patterns in known words represent sound.

Automatic word recognition   Children who instantly recognize all the words in everyday text.

Base words   The smallest real English words to which prefixes and suffixes are added (*play* or *elephant*, for example).

Blending   The ability to combine sounds into words. Children might combine onsets and rimes (/sh/ + /ip/ = /ship/) or individual phonemes (/p/ + /a/ + /n/ = /pan/).

Cognates   Words that share a common origin in two languages. Some cognates are spelled the same in two languages, other cognates have similar spellings.

Compound words   Words that are formed when two words—for example, *finger* and *print*—are glued together to create a third word—in this case, *fingerprint*.

Configuration cues   Configuration consists of a word's word shape, word length, or unique letters. Some beginning readers use configuration cues to identify new words.

Consolidated word learner   Children who read new words by identifying and pronouncing meaningful and nonmeaningful multi-letter chunks in words.

Consonant blends   Two or more consonants that appear together, represent the same sounds as the individual consonants and are pronounced by sliding the sounds together (*bl*, *tr*, *sm*, *scr*).

Consonants   All the letters other than *a*, *e*, *i*, *o*, *u*, and *y* when *y* comes in the middle or at the end of a syllable.

Contractions   Words formed when one or more letters (and sounds) are deleted from other words, with the deleted letter(s) replaced by an apostrophe—a visual clue telling readers that a word is abbreviated, as in *hasn't*, *he's*, *she'll*, and *let's*.

Cross-checking   Making sure that corrections for misidentified words make sense in the reading context.

Decodable books   Books that have an unusually high number of words that sound like they are spelled. Often these books consist of many words that represent a certain letter-sound pattern.

Deleting sounds   Removing a sound or sounds from a word or syllable, such as taking the /b/ from /bit/ to pronounce /it/ or the /m/ from /seem/ to form /see/.

Derivational suffixes   Word endings that change the part of speech, as in changing *read* (a verb) into *readable* (an adjective).

Digraphs   Two letters that represent a sound that is different from the sounds the letters represent individually, such as *sh* (*ship*), *th* (*thud*), and *ch* (*child*).

Diphthongs   The vowel-like sounds represented by *oy* and *oi* as heard in /boy/ and /oil/, and by *ou* and *ow* as heard in /out/ and /cow/.

Embedded phonics   An approach to teaching phonics where children learn only the phonics letter patterns they need to decode words in the books they are currently reading.

Emergent spellers   Spellers who do not understand the alphabetic principle and, therefore, do not use letters to represent the sounds in the words they spell.

Environmental cues   Environmental cues consist of print in an everyday environment such as signs, logos, and package labels. Beginning readers associate meaning with these cues.

Greek and Latin roots   Word parts we borrowed from these two languages such at the *port* (from Latin meaning "to carry") in *portable*.

Inflectional suffixes   Word endings that clarify word meaning or make meaning more specific, as the *-s* added to *cats* or the *-ed* added to *played*.

Invented spelling   A problem-solving stance in which words are spelled like they sound, such as *comin* for *common*.

Isolating sounds   Pronouncing the beginning, ending, or middle sound in a word, such as saying that /man/ begins with /m/ or that /sun/ ends with /n/.

Letter name-alphabetic spellers   Spellers at the beginning of this stage use consonant letter-sound associations to spell. Later spellers use beginning and ending letters to spell and, finally, correctly spell words with short vowels.

Letter-sound patterns   Letters that routinely represent one or more sounds in words, such as the *ee* in *feet*, and *sh* and *or* in *short*.

Letter-sound phonics   The systematic relationship among letters and sounds which is the principle that underpins all alphabetic languages and an approach for teaching these relationships. Children use the letter-sound phonics when they associate sounds with letters to pronounce words they do not recognize.

Manipulating sounds   The act of deliberately changing the sounds in one word so as to pronounce a different word. Children might add a sound (/r/ + /at/ = /rat/), delete a sound (/rat/ − /r/ = /at/), or substitute one sound for another (change the /t/ in /rat/ to /n/ to pronounce /ran/).

Meaning (semantic) cues   Meaningful relationships among words in phrases, sentences, and paragraphs. Readers use these cues to determine whether an author's message is logical and represents real-world events and relationships.

Metacognitive awareness   The self-awareness of what we know, how we know it, and how and when to use information. As it pertains to word identification, readers with metacognitive awareness monitor their own reading, cross-check for meaning, and correct their own miscues.

Morphemic analysis Identifying the meaningful parts in words, most particularly the free and bound morphemes.

Onset The consonant(s) that comes before the vowel in a syllable or one-syllable word (the *s* in *sat* or the *ch* in *chat*).

Partial alphabet cues A portion of the letter-sound relationships in a word's spelling, such as beginning or ending letter sounds.

Partial alphabetic word learners These children use part of the alphabetic cues in spelling to identify words, such as associating the sound /m/ with *monkey*. As a consequence, children are apt to confuse *mouse*, *mother*, or *made* for the word *monkey*.

Phonemes The smallest sounds that differentiate one word from another. The /b/ in /bat/ is one phoneme, while the /h/ in /hat/ is another phoneme, as each sound differentiates one word (/bat/) from another (/hat/).

Phonemic awareness The ability to think analytically about the sounds in words, and the ability to act on the basis of this analysis to separate words into sounds and to blend sounds into words.

Phonetically regular words Words that can be pronounced by associating sounds with letters.

Phonogram The vowel and the consonants that come after it, such as the *an* in *man* and *can* or the *at* in *cat* and *mat*. Phonograms and rimes refer to the same letter groups inside short, one-syllable words or syllables.

Phonological awareness A broad term that refers to the awareness of and the ability to manipulate words, syllables, rhymes, and sounds.

Picture cues Suggestions about meaning that readers infer from the illustrations in storybooks.

Prealphabetic word learners Children who use environmental print, pictures, and word configuration when reading. These children lack phonemic awareness, do not know letter names (or know the names of only a few letters), and do not understand how letters represent sounds.

Prefix A separate syllable attached to the beginning of words that either changes the meaning of the root word completely or makes meaning more specific.

Rhyme awareness The ability to identify words that rhyme (/bad/ and /mad/), do not rhyme (/bad/ and /dog/), and think of rhyming words (/bad/-/sad/-/had/).

Rime The vowel and everything that follows it in a syllable or one-syllable word (the *at* in *sat* and *chat*).

Segmenting sounds Pronouncing each phoneme in the same order in which it occurs in a word, such as indicating that /mad/ consists of /m/-/a/-/d/.

Self-correcting The process of rereading for accuracy so as to fix a previous miscue.

Self-monitoring The ability to self-regulate one's own reading to be sure that it makes sense.

Sentence structure (syntactic) cues Cues readers use to decide whether an author's word order is consistent with English grammar. Readers use these grammar-based cues to predict words in phrases and sentences.

Sound boxes Connected boxes where each box represents a sound in a word.

Sound stretching Elongating sounds while pronouncing words, as in /fffiiinnn/. *Rubber banding* is another term for the same way of pronouncing words.

Spelling-based phonics An approach to teaching phonics where children learn through writing, sorting, comparing words spelled with the same and different patterns of letter sounds, and comparing words children do not know with words children already know how to read and spell.

Structural analysis Analyzing the structure of words into large multiletter chunks, including compound words, contractions, prefixes, suffixes, syllables, and Greek and Latin roots.

Substituting sounds Deleting a sound from a word and then adding another in its place to make a different word. Examples include substituting the /n/ in /man/ for a /t/ to pronounce /mat/ or substituting the /sh/ in /ship/ for a /ch/ to pronounce /chip/.

Suffix   Usually a separate syllable attached to the end of words that changes grammatical function, makes meaning clearer, or adds information.

Syllable   The basic unit of pronunciation. Each syllable has one vowel sound and, perhaps, one or more consonant sounds (/o/ + /pen/ = /open/). The number of syllables in a word equals the number of vowels heard.

Syllables and affixes spellers   Children spell words of more than one syllable and words with affixes.

Synthetic (explicit) phonics   Part-to-whole instruction in which children associate sounds with letters to read, or "sound out," new words.

Unaccented syllables   Syllables that are not prominent in stress. Most vowels in unaccented syllables have a soft, or short, sound.

Vowels   The letters *a, e, i, o,* and *u,* and *y* when it comes in the middle (*cycle*) or at the end of a syllable or short word (*try*).

Within word pattern spellers   Children learn and use long vowels, r-controlled vowels, and other vowels when spelling. By the end of this stage, children use a variety of letter-sound patterns when spelling.

Word family   A word group that shares the same rime or phonogram (*cat, rat, fat, sat, bat*).

Index